TEACHING RAPE IN THE MEDIEVAL
LITERATURE CLASSROOM

TEACHING THE MIDDLE AGES

Teaching the Middle Ages aims to reflect the best and most innovative in medieval pedagogies, providing resources for instructors, students, and administrators wishing to understand the current and future place of medieval studies in the modern academy. Books in Teaching the Middle Ages respond to current trends and debates reshaping modern classrooms and curricula, including issues of identity, race, gender, sexuality, religion, violence, disability, environment, technology, and how medievalists teach these topics in our classrooms. These projects are grounded in the scholarship of teaching and learning and/or data-driven pedagogical research methods.

Acquisitions Editor

Ilse Schweitzer VanDonkelaar

TEACHING RAPE IN THE MEDIEVAL LITERATURE CLASSROOM: APPROACHES TO DIFFICULT TEXTS

Edited by
ALISON GULLEY

British Library Cataloguing in Publication Data

A catalogue record for this book is available from the British Library

© 2018, Arc Humanities Press, Leeds

ISBN: 9781641890328
e-ISBN: 9781580443166

https://arc-humanities.org
Printed and bound by CPI Group (UK) Ltd, Croydon, CR0 4YY

CONTENTS

ACKNOWLEDGEMENTS

Many people have been helpful in producing this volume. First, of course, I'd like to thank the contributing authors who have collectively embraced the themes and goals of this collection, even though some of us have never met in person. Thanks to the Department of English and the College of Arts and Sciences at Appalachian State University for their financial support for parts of this volume. In addition, my department chair, Carl Eby, has provided both intellectual and emotional support. Many departments give lip service to the scholar–teacher model, but Carl and my fellow faculty really mean it. At the risk of missing some important individuals, I'd like to single out a few: on my hallway, Holly Martin and Jennifer Wilson, for helping me with teaching dilemmas, sometimes just as one of us is about to enter the classroom; Jill Ehnenn, David Orvis, Elaine O'Quinn, and Susan Staub for their friendship and advice as I brought this project to fruition. Additionally, Jill has organized many productive gatherings for faculty to discuss the joys and frustrations of teaching and brainstorm ways to improve our courses, as well as events that allow students and faculty to interact socially and intellectually outside of the classroom, where some of our most important conversations with students happen. I'm thankful, too, for my students who have been willing to take on the issues raised in the difficult texts we tackle together.

As the sole medievalist in my department, I rely heavily on support from outsiders, including fellow medievalists Mary Valante and Alexandra Sterling-Hellenbrand here at ASU. I'm also grateful to members of the Southeastern Medieval Association who have provided me with a friendly and helpful community of medieval studies scholars and teachers. Many of the ideas in this book resulted from conversations at conferences and through social media and email.

And finally, I'd like to thank several generations of UNC-Chapel Hill alumni for their ongoing friendship and mentoring. In particular, I want to acknowledge Alan Baragona, Debra Best, Kristen Carella, Elizabeth Harper, Jo Koster, Britt Mize, Elizabeth Rambo, William Smith, and Trish Ward. You'll note that several on this list are also contributors here. This is not coincidental in that not only do we share an educational pedigree, but over the years we have supported each other in our personal and professional endeavours, both long distance and in person as we gather each year at Kalamazoo for *gebeorscipe*.

Chapter 1

INTRODUCTION: TEACHING RAPE AND MEETING THE CHALLENGES OF THE TWENTY-FIRST-CENTURY CLASSROOM

ALISON GULLEY

This volume was conceived and written at a time of unprecedented attention in the United States to rape and rape prevention on college campuses and more specifically grows out of a panel that I organized for the May 2014 International Congress on Medieval Studies at Kalamazoo, in which I and two other presenters explored the problem of how to approach medieval texts that feature sexual violence, in ways that are both academically sound and ethically appropriate for our students. The panel itself resulted from an interaction with a student in a sophomore-level British Literature class. During a discussion of Geoffrey Chaucer's "The Wife of Bath's Tale," a student, referring to the rape that precipitates the knight's quest for the thing that women most desire, piped up: "How do we know she was really raped?" I was caught off guard, first, because the rape is unambiguously stated ("By verray force, he rafte hire maydenhed" [III. 886–9])[1] and, second, because the August 2012 rape of a Steubenville, Ohio teenager by her classmates—and the controversial response to it by both the community and the media—was very much in the news that week as the case went to trial. To me, and to much of the rest of the class, if the ensuing discussion is any indication, the question reflected the many disjointed and often contradictory attitudes toward women, sexuality, and violence. Despite having taught the tale many times and to hundreds of students over the years, I came away from the class feeling that I had not anticipated the kinds of questions and assumptions students bring to such a text and thus had not adequately prepared myself to teach the work in a such a specific modern context. Judging by the lively discussion that followed the presentations at Kalamazoo, I was not alone. Many teachers, it seems, are eager to develop pedagogical strategies for addressing sensitive topics in the classroom. To that end, this collection includes articles that contextualize scenes of rape, attempted rape, and false accusations in a variety of literary works within the politically charged environment that our students, and ourselves as teachers, study and learn.

---

1 Geoffrey Chaucer, "The Wife of Bath's Tale," in *The Riverside Chaucer*, ed. Larry Benson et al. 3rd ed. (New York: Oxford University Press, 1986), 105–22.

The difficulties created by such texts are manifold. Not only can the subject matter itself make us and our students squirm, but our students must also contend with a different language (or a translation, which raises its own issues) and a historical and cultural context far removed from our own. Evelyn Birge Vitz has criticized feminist studies of medieval rape for "being plagued by a tendency toward naive, anachronistic, and inappropriate readings of literary works, high levels of indignation and self-pity, and a pervasive hostility to men," suggesting that readers who focus on actual rape as they're reading about literary representations of it are at best simply uninformed and childish, or, at worst, fulfilling negative stereotypes of feminists and feminism. But Carolyn Dinshaw reminds us that reading fiction is far more complex than such a generalization acknowledges. For example, in discussing the well-known and ambiguous charge of rape against Chaucer, she notes that the existence of records showing that he is somehow involved in *raptus* reminds us that "there are not only fictional rapes—the rape of Philomela, the rape of Helen, the rape of the maiden in 'The Wife of Bath's Tale'—but there are real rapes as well."[2] Reflecting on Dinshaw's words here, in "Reading Chaucer, Reading Rape," Christine M. Rose describes a "profitable" reading of rape as one that necessitates readers simultaneously holding both kinds of rape—"*figurative* and *real* rape"—in their heads.[3] Lynn A. Higgins and Brenda R. Silver argue for a conscious rereading of rape in those instances where the act has been "deflected," that is, "where it has been turned into a metaphor or a symbol or represented rhetorically as titillation, persuasion, ravishment, seduction, or desire." Such a reading can "reclaim the physical, material bodies of women from their status as 'figures' and reveal the ways in which violence marks the female subject both physically and psychologically."[4] Far from being unrealistic or inappropriate, as Vitz would have it, such readings are *careful* readings in that they ask us to consider both the text's historical milieu and that of readers and critics.

In addition to the difficulties of crossing time and place, and perhaps even more vexing, is the problem of understanding the nature of rape itself, which even in the twenty-first century continues to be fraught with uncertainty. The question of what constitutes "real rape" is, of course, a thorny one, in that the term—and the act—are polysemous. The word "rape" comes from the Latin *raptus*, which literally means "theft" or "seizure." Before the late thirteenth century in England, in legal records the word usually denoted sexual assault, while *abductione* (or its verb form *abduxit*) and a variety of other terms (such as *cepit et imprisonauit*, "capture and imprison") were commonly used for those crimes classified as abduction.[5] The Westminster

---

2 Carolyn Dinshaw, *Chaucer's Sexual Poetics* (Madison: University of Wisconsin Press, 1989), 11.

3 Christine M. Rose, "Reading Chaucer, Reading Rape," in *Representing Rape in Medieval and Early Modern Literature*, ed. Elizabeth Robertson and Christine M. Rose, The New Middle Ages (New York: Palgrave, 2001), 31.

4 Lynn A. Higgins and Brenda R. Silvers, eds., *Rape and Representation* (New York: Columbia Press, 1991), 4.

5 Caroline Dunn, *Stolen Women in Medieval England: Rape, Abduction, and Adultery, 1100–1500* (New York: Cambridge University Press, 2013), 26–8.

Statutes of 1275 and 1285 paired rape with abduction and employed *raptus* in reference to both, but, to further complicate matters, also frequently combined it with *abduxit/abductione*, which almost always meant a woman's seizure and not sexual assault.[6] Despite these recognized patterns of use, the ambiguity continued through the fourteenth and fifteenth centuries, albeit to a lesser extent. Kathryn Gravdal notes a similar lack of linguistic clarity surrounding the act of rape in Old French: "there is no word that corresponds to the modern French *viol* to designate rape. Medieval culture does not search to find one term to denote forced coitus. The Old French language favors periphrasis, metaphor, and slippery lexematic exchanges as opposed to a clear and unambiguous signifier of sexual assault."[7] Thus we find euphemisms such as *faire sa volanté* (to do one's will) and *faire son plaisir* (to take one's pleasure) or the word *esforcer* (derived from the Latin *fortis*, "force") used within the same text to mean both "to strive" and "to rape."[8]

To complicate matters, not just the language of rape but the act itself is difficult to pin down. In some cases, the concept of rape is embedded in practices that blur the line between consensual and nonconsensual sex. Early medieval Germanic law recognized as legitimate *Raubehe,* or marriage contracted through abduction and ravishment, a practice which continued after Christian conversion and which may have influenced another form of legal marriage, *Friedelehe*, in essence, elopement, which is seen throughout the medieval period.[9] Christopher Cannon, in his study of the already referenced and much-debated release of the charge of *raptus* against Chaucer by Cecily Chaumpaigne, notes other obstacles to understanding, asking,

> What definition will we use for rape … when we ask what *raptus* means? What does the Chaumpaigne release really say if the *raptus* it refers to is an act that, according to the vigorously defended affective states of both those involved in it, is at *once* rape and not rape? What does the Chaumpaigne release teach us if that act is one that we would now call 'rape' (because, say, Chaumpaigne felt it was but Chaucer did not) but that fourteenth-century law was entirely happy to throw into a category it understood as 'abduction?'[10]

He points to an even bigger predicament: "a legal document in the fourteenth century as well as now is necessarily an instrument at some remove from 'what happened' and, second, because sexual violence is itself a crime where 'what happened,' the very act that might constitute the crime, can be variously defined even by those who have

---

6 Ibid., 37.

7 Kathryn Gravdal, *Ravishing Maidens: Writing Rape in Medieval French Literature and Law* (Philadelphia: University of Pennsylvania Press, 1991), 2.

8 Ibid., 3.

9 James A. Brundage, *Law, Sex, and Christian Society in Medieval Europe* (Chicago: University of Chicago Press, 1987), 129. For a discussion of elopement in the later Middle Ages, see Dunn, 98–119.

10 Christopher Cannon, "Chaucer and Rape: Uncertainties' Certainties," in Robertson and Rose, 257.

identical 'facts' in hand."[11] None of this, however, is to suggest that we can't try to make sense of the word and act, both as teachers and scholars.

Rape as a subject of literary study is a fairly new phenomenon, dating back to the rise of feminist theory and scholarship in the 1960s, '70s, and '80s. In medieval studies, the focus is even more recent, despite the fact that, as Elizabeth Robertson and Christine M. Rose note in their important collection *Representing Rape in Medieval and Early Modern Literature*, the "omnipresence of images of rape in Western literature illustrates how the rapable body has been woven into the very foundations of Western poetics."[12] One of the first books to focus on literary rape was Higgins and Silver's 1991 collection *Rape and Representation*, which spans several centuries and genres, including literature and film, beginning with Ovid's story of Philomela. In reexamining such texts, they argue that discourse about rape is a rhetorical device that, instead of simply denoting rape, symbolizes "other social, political, and economic concerns and conflicts."[13] For example, an American rape narrative such as the so-called Central Park Jogger case of 1989 reflects the crime of rape not just as an act of sexual violence but, through the sensationalized press coverage which referred to the suspects as a "wolf pack," as "a conflict between two parties clearly distinguished by race, ethnicity and class."[14] The year 1991 also saw the publication of Gravdal's influential monograph *Ravishing Maidens: Writing Rape in Medieval French Literature*, which addressed violence against women in medieval law and a variety of French literary texts of multiple genres. Her argument is that, particularly in the romance, rape is not only normalized to the extent that we expect to encounter it, but also that it is even romanticized. That is, when we see a beautiful maiden, we expect a forceful knight to ravish her. At the same time, paradoxically the romance teaches that "rape is wrong," a contradiction that remains unresolved.[15] Although in many ways literature of the medieval period can be seen as silent on the question of rape, in that, paradoxically, it is so pervasive as to be unworthy of comment, Gravdal notes that instead it is rather the silence of literary scholars on the subject that is noteworthy. Ultimately, her study reveals rape in actions that previously had been glossed over by readers. Two influential books appeared in 2001, joining the relatively short list of books on the topic. Rose and Robertson's collection began with the premise that because rape is systemic, the very act of analysis is problematic because our methodology and tools are themselves implicit in the act of rape. The essays in their book explore the ways in which rape, in addition to being an act of violence, also reflects a society's linguistic, social, and institutional practices. Corinne Saunders, in *Rape and Ravishment in the Literature of Medieval England*,

---

11 Ibid., 256.

12 Robertson and Rose, "Introduction," 2.

13 Lynn A. Higgins and Brenda R. Silvers, eds., *Rape and Representation* (New York: Columbia Press, 1991), 2.

14 Ibid., 1. The convictions were later overturned due do a confession and corroborating evidence from another man. For a full accounting of the case, see Benjamin Weiser, "5 Exonerated in Central Park Jogger Case Agree to Settle Suit for $40 Million," *New York Times*, June 19, 2014, www.newyorktimes.com, accessed October 11, 2016.

15 Gravdal, *Ravishing Maidens*, 67.

tackles the legal and religious dimensions of rape, the question of why rape is so present in the literature of the early period, and its function in the power relationship between the sexes. She stresses the problematic nature of applying modern notions to a study of medieval discourse and notes that contrary to modern assumptions that rape was trivialized and treated dismissively in the Middle Ages, it "was rather the subject of a lively, often politicized, dialogue, which could be acutely sympathetic to women as well as misogynistic." She points to such things as the complexity of law regarding rape and abduction, the Church's concern for the loss of virginity, and of the rhetorical and emotional effect of rape on medieval writing, "precisely because," she writes, "there was a marked consciousness of individual and social, public and private trauma caused by rape and ravishment."[16]

Building on these earlier studies, one goal of this volume is to address the important question of how we as medieval scholars and teachers can provide the appropriate historical, cultural, and literary milieu in which a text is produced. Just as important, however, is how we do so in a way that recognizes that we don't teach in a vacuum—our students bring a variety of experiences to the classroom that necessarily colour their reception and understanding of what they read, in both positive and negative ways. This reality challenges us, in Tison Pugh's words, to "create a classroom environment sensitive to ethical issues, to model for ... students a pedagogical ethos that demonstrates our own difficulties with [a] complex issue, and to encourage our students to explore their own relationships to the past through an analysis of ethics, ethos, and literature."[17]

The contributors to this volume meet these challenges within the broader context of what many perceive as a crisis in higher education, made manifest by political and popular demand for a "relevant" college education, understood generally as one that will get students a job, and by the increasing need to show the connections between what we do in the classroom and life outside the academy. For the humanities, these calls are particularly vexing because of widely held, and frequently inaccurate, views about the relevance of a liberal arts education. I use the word "show" deliberately, for those of us in the humanities in general and in medieval studies specifically know that what we do *is* relevant and connected, even as others, sometimes even within higher education, don't understand our role. At an institution where I taught earlier in my career, the dean of students drew the ire of my colleagues when he "explained" that *our* responsibility was to provide academic instruction in the classroom, while *his* responsibility was to teach students about life. Students and teachers of literature know, however, that we're not dealing just with a bunch of words on a page, or even just a bunch of beautiful and entertaining words on a page. On the contrary, good literature (or bad literature for that matter) is about life and can open a whole new world of places, ideas, experiences, and lessons for readers.

---

16 Corinne Saunders, *Rape and Ravishment in the Literature of Medieval England* (Cambridge: Brewer, 2001), 14.

17 Tison Pugh, "Chaucer's Rape, Southern Racism, and the Pedagogical Ethics of Authorial Malfeasance," *College English* 67 (2005): 571.

Of course, not all literature is accessible, particularly when, as medievalists do, we are dealing with writings from a distant time, place, and, not least, world view. The task becomes that much harder given widely held but inaccurate notions about the Middle Ages. Students come to us bearing a pop culture understanding of the era, thanks in part to the popularity of television shows like *Game of Thrones* or *The Vikings*, but are also influenced by the pejorative use of the word "medieval" to describe the atrocities of terrorist groups such as ISIS or the mindset of school boards challenging the inclusion of certain texts in public school curricula. On the opposite end of the spectrum are those who believe that rather than being some barbaric, superstitious Other, far removed from the modern and enlightened Western mind and experience, medieval people are just like us, or at least not that different. Even as we strive to eradicate those persistent myths about the Middle Ages, we are faced with showing our students that there are some real, quantifiable differences between the medieval and modern world views. The readiness with which students accept the "reality" of *jus primae noctis* (thanks to *Braveheart*) or its cousin "the rule of thumb," which supposedly allowed men to beat their wives with impunity as long as the stick they used was no larger than their thumb, illustrates that medieval women are of particular interest. In one common narrative, medieval women were almost universally and continuously ill-treated, with the exception of courtly ladies, who were placed on a pedestal and treated with courtesy and reverence.

The teacher of medieval literature, then, must navigate a large temporal, perceptual, and linguistic gulf between the Middle Ages and the twenty-first-century student. Each fall since 1998 the Mindset List from Beloit College in Wisconsin provides insight into the lives of entering college freshmen. Describing students who have been born since the turn of the century, among such entertaining facts as "wire-rim glasses are associated with Harry Potter, not John Lennon" and "[s]tudents have always been able to dance at Baylor," we find more sobering information about the world that our students have grown up in. For example, their memories include seeing "endlessly repeated images of planes blasting into the World Trade Center,"[18] so that the fear of terrorism colours their existence much as the Cold War overshadowed the lives of previous generations of young people. Our students also bring a different set of concerns and preoccupations specific to their college experience. They come to us less academically prepared than their predecessors;[19] they are more likely to seek psychological

---

18 "The Mindset List," beloit.edu, accessed April 26, 2015, www.beloit.edu/mindset/2018/.
19 The numbers on student preparedness from the U.S. Department of Education's National Assessment of Educational Progress are misleading, in that a higher percentage of Americans, from a cross-section of society, attend college. For example, the percentage of eighteen to twenty-four year olds enrolled in college increased from 35.5 per cent in 2000 to 41 per cent in 2012 (National Center for Education Statistics, http://nces.ed.gov/fastfacts/, accessed April 26, 2015). The percentage of students deemed "proficient" in reading and mathematics has remained relatively stable during that time. (Math proficiency has slightly increased, while reading proficiency fell from 1992 to 2009, from 40 per cent to 38 per cent, where it has remained.) www.nationsreportcard.gov/reading_math_g12_2013/#/what-knowledge, accessed April 26, 2015.

counselling from student health services;[20] and they will graduate with more debt than their predecessors even as the job market has become less secure for recent college graduates.

Within this increasingly volatile environment, educators are called upon to do more and be more for our students. While the stereotypical professor—old, aloof, slightly dishevelled, pipe-smoking, and of course white and male—has not been around for quite some time (if he ever really was) except on the large and small screen, or, perhaps, in the uppermost reaches of academia, the real professor—still mostly white, but now also female, and frequently contingent—is expected not only to teach, but also to nurture students and engage in crisis management. Of particular concern for the contributors in this volume are demands that colleges and universities find ways to effectively address the problem of sexual violence on college campuses. Several high-profile cases in which students charged that their institutions did not respond appropriately to rape allegations led the U.S. Department of Education to issue reminders, in the form of a letter called colloquially the "Dear Colleague Letter," that the Title IX portion of the 1972 Education Amendments (usually known simply as Title IX)—which bans sexual discrimination, harassment, and violence in institutions that receive federal aid—also applies to instances of sexual violence.[21] Then, in April 2014, the Obama administration released the findings and recommendations of the White House Task Force to Protect Students from Sexual Assault, followed in September of that year with the launch of its own campaign against sexual violence on college campuses, "It's On Us." As President Obama explained, "This is on all of us, every one of us, to fight campus sexual assault … [We] are going to organize campus by campus, city by city, state by state."[22]

While sexual assault is not new among college students, or even more prevalent than in earlier years, because of efforts like these, American society has become more cognizant of it. Although the exact numbers of victims and perpetrators of sexual violence continue to excite debate, a frequently cited statistic is that by the time they graduate from high school, more than one in ten girls will have been physically forced to have sexual intercourse. In college, nearly one in five women, and about six out of one hundred men, will be the victims of attempted or actual sexual assault.[23] We care about these numbers not only because of the academic problems

---

20 A 2013 survey found an increase in the number of students with severe psychological problems and that the conditions most likely to drive a student to seek help continued to be anxiety, depression, and relationship issues. Libby Sander, "Campus Counseling Centers 'Are as Busy as They Ever Have Been,'" *The Chronicle of Higher Education*, April 15, 2013, http://chronicle.com, accessed April 15, 2013.

21 The letter, dated April 4, 2011 and signed by Russlyn Ali, Assistant Secretary for Civil Rights in the Department of Education, can be found at www.whitehouse.gov/sites/default/files/dear_colleague_sexual_violence.pdf, accessed May 19, 2015.

22 Juliet Eilperin, "Seeking to End Rape on Campus, White House Launches 'It's on Us,'" *The Washington Post*, September 19, 2014, accessed May 19, 2015, www.washingtonpost.com/blogs/post-politics/wp/2014/09/19/seeking-to-end-rape-on-campus-wh-launches-its-on-us/. The task force report can be accessed at www.notalone.gov/assets/report.pdf.

23 "Dear Colleague Letter: Sexual Violence Background, Summary, and Fast Facts," April 4, 2011, www2.ed.gov/about/offices/list/ocr/docs/dcl-factsheet-201104.html, accessed May

that sexual assaults cause—including difficulty concentrating, poor grades, absenteeism, and a lower likelihood of graduating with a degree[24]—but also because as teachers we care about more than our students' academic achievement; while we might not all subscribe to the philosophy of *in loco parentis*, anyone charged with cultivating the minds of students is necessarily engaged in the cultivation and care of the whole person. We are looked to as authority figures, particularly by traditional college students, and within our disciplinary spheres are generally regarded as expert. Thus, when academic and extra-curricular collide in the classroom, as they increasingly seem to, we have the opportunity, and some would argue, the responsibility, to help our students navigate between the two.

Arguably, nowhere is this tension more noticeable than when reading and discussing texts about sexual violence. All the essays in this volume address this point in some form, but Suzanne M. Edwards tackles the issue head on by showing how teaching hagiographical texts can open a dialogue between medieval and modern representations of rape. From there, Christina di Gangi and Wendy Perkins apply principles from victimology to illuminate the nature of sexual assault itself, the characterization of victims, and the function in texts of bystanders. Elizabeth Hubble further focuses on the bystander, in this case proposing a model for actively engaging students in such a way that reading becomes an overtly political act. While most college teachers have been confronted with inappropriate comments during class discussions, sometimes to the point that students become uncomfortable or in extreme cases can feel harassed or victimized, Hubble asks pointedly about commonly assigned classical, patristic, and medieval writings involving women, "what if those inappropriate comments and attitudes don't come from the people in the classroom, but from the texts assigned and the analyses brought to them?" Alexandra Sterling-Hellenbrand similarly uses the concept of bystander awareness to frame her teaching of an episode in the *Nibelungenlied* in which a humorous scene of thwarted wedding night sex becomes offset by a subsequent scene that can be clearly identified as rape.

Several of the essays in this volume address the works of Chaucer, who continues to figure prominently in the medieval literature curriculum. Emily Houlik-Ritchey shares a two-day lesson plan that helps students distinguish between legal and ethical culpability in Chaucer's "The Reeve's Tale"; my own essay recommends using a modern retelling of "The Wife of Bath's Tale" to wrestle with the sexual violence of the Prologue and tale; and Tison Pugh shows how having students examine gender stereotypes, particularly those involving speech and silence, illuminates the various ways that literary depictions of rape both reinforce and undermine medieval constructions of gender in several of Chaucer's works.

19, 2015. Sexual violence is not confined to college campuses, of course, and in fact, according to the Bureau of Justice Statistics, and as reported in the "Dear Colleague Letter," the rate of rape and sexual assault was 1.2 times higher for nonstudents (7.6 per 1,000) than for students (6.1 per 1,000).

24 West Virginia Foundation for Rape Information and Services, 1998–2014, www.fris.org/CampusSexualViolence/CampusSexViolence.html, accessed May 19, 2015.

The remaining essays cover the broad and varied genre of romance. Marie de France is the subject of both Elizabeth Harper's essay, which looks at an instance of false rape accusation in *Lanval*, and Misty Urban's, which discusses approaches to the *Lais* for general education and upper division major courses. Although most of the works discussed in this collection involve female victims and male perpetrators, David Grubbs draws our attention to male victims in chivalric romance, specifically in *Amadis De Gaulle* and Malory's *Morte d'Arthur*. He approaches these texts with reference to the "positive consent model," which holds that yes-means-yes should replace no-means-no as the standard for sexual consent.[25] Daniel O'Sullivan continues the conversation about the difficult problem of consent, this time by asking students to deconstruct notions of consent and seduction in troubadour lyrics. Alan Baragona's contribution also focuses on men, here as readers of the romances of Chrétien de Troyes, with a peculiarly modern take on the role of chivalry wrought by the values of a public military college, which changed from male-only to co-ed during Baragona's tenure there. Finally, William Smith's essay on *Sir Gowther* takes up the nature of identity in the medieval world, with reference to Gowther's parentage (he is conceived when his mother has intercourse with a demon in the guise of her husband), his sins (which include raping a community of nuns and destroying their convent), and his ultimate repentance.

The reader will find in this collection suggestions for specific classroom activities and student-friendly editions, as well as insight into the needs and concerns of a variety of students attending many different types of institutions. While the included topics might be of special interest to scholars in feminist and gender studies, anyone teaching within the context of current educational and political trends, or with the desire to integrate curricular and co-curricular activities, will find useful suggestions and resources. The essays in this volume also reflect the experiences of teachers at various stages of their career, from those relatively new to the profession as well as those in mid- or later career, and thus also serve to model the method and value of a responsive and reflective pedagogy. The contributors, many of them award-winning teachers, bring their experience from across the higher education spectrum, including two-year community colleges, private four-year church-affiliated institutions, regional comprehensive universities, doctorate-granting universities, and a public military college. In each essay, the writers strive to make connections between the unique needs of students in their particular programs and the needs of college students more broadly. To that end, the collection includes a range of pedagogical strategies appropriate for the general education classroom, upper-division courses for majors, and specialized graduate seminars.

When my co-authors and I began this collection, we spoke of the urgency of the project, given the attention being paid to rape in the media. The words "rape culture"

---

25 For a discussion of the unintended consequences of such a model, see Janet Halley, "The Move to Affirmative Consent," *Signs: Journal of Women in Culture and Society* 42 (2016): 257–79. Halley argues that while this kind of policy is appealing to many feminists, it reinforces traditional, conservative ideas of female passivity and male dominance.

were being used in a way that seemed if not new in and of themselves, at least representative of a new kind of awareness. And yet I look back at the words of Higgins and Silver, in 1991, when I was just beginning my training as a medievalist. "The urgency of this project," they wrote, "derives from the fact that rape and the threat of rape are a major force in the subjugation of women. In 'rape cultures' such as the United States, the danger, the frequency, and the acceptance of sexual violence all contribute to shaping behavior and identity, in men and women alike."[26] In the early decades of the twenty-first century, it is unnerving that the same can be said. What I hope is different, however, is that the new awareness of and concentrated effort to address this rape culture will render such studies in the future, if not unnecessary, at least not as urgent. Our hope is that our essays, the literature they address, and the teachers who undertake to help students understand both the Middle Ages and their own culture, will be a step toward that day.

Although the impetus for this volume is the spate of calls to action at the institutional, state, and federal levels concerning sexual violence on campus, there's nothing new in the fact that most educators are driven to provide their students with the best possible education. What I hope the readers of this book will find is not only practical advice for improving or augmenting their current approaches to the many literary texts discussed here, but also a path to the holistic teaching method so eloquently described by bell hooks. Approaching difficult texts in the college classroom can be a deeply political act. Too frequently professors are characterized as either distant ivory-tower scholars out of touch with day-to-day concerns and intent on avoiding teaching and other student interaction or, conversely, provocateurs exploiting the teacher–student relationship to advance a radical agenda and destroy traditional values. To hooks, and to many of us in education, the true agenda is simple: good teaching seeks to provide an environment in which students and professors recognize each other "as 'whole' human beings, striving not just for knowledge in books, but knowledge about how to live in the world."[27]

Works Cited

Ali, Russlyn. "Dear Colleague Letter." www.whitehouse.gov/sites/default/files/ dear_colleague_sexual_violence.pdf (accessed May 19, 2015).

Beloit College. "The Mindset List." www.beloit.edu/mindset/2018/ (accessed April 26, 2015).

Brundage, James A. *Law, Sex, and Christian Society in Medieval Europe*. Chicago: University of Chicago Press, 1987.

Cannon, Christopher. "Chaucer and Rape: Uncertainties' Certainties." In *Representing Rape in Medieval and Early Modern Literature*, edited by Elizabeth Robertson and Christine M. Rose, 255–80. New York: Palgrave, 2001.

---

26 Higgins and Silver, *Rape and Representation*, 1–2.
27 bell hooks, *Teaching to Transgress: Education as the Practice of Freedom* (New York: Routledge, 1994), 14–15.

Chaucer, Geoffrey. "The Wife of Bath's Tale." In *The Riverside Chaucer*, edited by Larry Benson et al., 3rd ed., 105–22. New York: Oxford University Press, 1986.

"Dear Colleague Letter: Sexual Violence Background, Summary, and Fast Facts," April 4, 2011. www2.ed.gov/about/offices/list/ocr/docs/dcl-factsheet-201104.html (accessed May 19, 2015).

Dinshaw, Carolyn. *Chaucer's Sexual Poetics*. Madison: University of Wisconsin Press, 1989.

Dunn, Caroline. *Stolen Women in Medieval England: Rape, Abduction, and Adultery, 1100–1500*. New York: Cambridge University Press, 2013.

Eilperin, Juliet. "Seeking to End Rape on Campus, White House Launches 'It's on Us.'" *The Washington Post*, September 19, 2014. www.washingtonpost.com/blogs/post-politics/wp/2014/09/19/seeking-to-end-rape-on-campus-wh-launches-its-on-us/ (accessed May 19, 2015).

Gravdal, Kathryn. *Ravishing Maidens: Writing Rape in Medieval French Literature and Law*. Philadelphia: University of Pennsylvania Press, 1991.

Halley, Janet. "The Move to Affirmative Consent." *Signs: Journal of Women in Culture and Society* 42 (2016): 257–79.

Higgins, Lynn A., and Brenda R. Silvers, eds. *Rape and Representation*. New York: Columbia Press, 1991.

hooks, bell. *Teaching to Transgress: Education as the Practice of Freedom*. New York: Routledge, 1994.

National Center for Education Statistics. http://nces.ed.gov/fastfacts/ (accessed April 26, 2015).

Pugh, Tison. "Chaucer's Rape, Southern Racism, and the Pedagogical Ethics of Authorial Malfeasance." *College English* 67 (2005): 569–86.

Rose, Christine M. "Reading Chaucer, Reading Rape." In *Representing Rape in Medieval and Early Modern Literature*, edited by Elizabeth Robertson and Christine M. Rose, 21–60. New York: Palgrave, 2001.

Sander, Libby. "Campus Counseling Centers 'Are as Busy as They Ever Have Been.'" *The Chronicle of Higher Education*, April 15, 2013. http://chronicle.com (accessed April 15, 2013).

Saunders, Corinne. *Rape and Ravishment in the Literature of Medieval England*. Cambridge: Brewer, 2001.

The Nation's Report Card. www.nationsreportcard.gov/reading_math_g12_2013/#/what-knowledge (accessed April 26, 2015).

United States Department of Justice. "Protecting Students from Sexual Assault." www.notalone.gov/assets/report.pdf. Updated October 10, 2016.

Weiser, Benjamin. "5 Exonerated in Central Park Jogger Case Agree to Settle Suit for $40 Million." *New York Times*, June 19, 2014. www.newyorktimes.com (accessed October 11, 2016).

West Virginia Foundation for Rape Information and Services, 1998–2014. www.fris.org/CampusSexualViolence/CampusSexViolence.html (accessed May 19, 2015).

Chapter 2

MEDIEVAL SAINTS AND MISOGYNIST TIMES: TRANSHISTORICAL PERSPECTIVES ON SEXUAL VIOLENCE IN THE UNDERGRADUATE CLASSROOM

SUZANNE M. EDWARDS

Although most undergraduate students enter the college classroom with little or no experience reading medieval texts, they are avid consumers of popular culture—and they are confident that rape was more widespread and considered less serious in the Middle Ages than it is the contemporary United States. Because student perspectives on the long history of sexual violence are more likely to have their source in contemporary novels, movies, and television shows like the popular HBO series *Game of Thrones* than in medieval texts like the *Life of St. Agnes*, they tend to identify pervasive acts of sexual violence and callous, misogynist attitudes toward rape as signs of historical alterity. At the private university where I have taught English literature and gender studies for the last nine years, I design my courses to complicate this perspective.

The guiding premise of this essay is that medieval representations of rape can be a valuable tool in students' exploration of contemporary anti-rape politics and practices, and not only as one more example of misogyny in the long history of rape culture. Over the last twenty-five years, feminist scholars have rightly pointed out that teachers of medieval literature have too often sanitized medieval misogyny by passing over representations of sexual violence without comment or, worse, by glossing rape as seduction.[1] To correct this elision, instructors have increasingly foregrounded medieval representations of rape, such as those endured by Malyne and Symkyn's wife in Chaucer's "The Reeve's Tale."[2] Yet, an exclusive focus on moments that normalize sexual assault can confirm students' confidence that there was more rape in the Middle Ages than there is today and that women then

---

1 See, for example, Kathryn Gravdal, *Ravishing Maidens: Writing Rape in Medieval French Literature and Law* (Philadelphia: University of Pennsylvania Press, 1991).

2 See, for example, Rachel Moss, "Chaucer's Funny Rape: Addressing a Taboo in Medieval Studies," *Meny Snoweballes* (blog), September 11, 2014, https://menysnoweballes.wordpress. com, accessed October 20, 2016. For the argument that rape in "The Reeve's Tale" comprises part of Chaucer's critical investigation of gender, social status, desire, and domination in Fragment One of the *Canterbury Tales*, see Nicole Nolan Sidhu, " 'To Late for to Crie': Female Desire, Fabliau Politics, and Classical Legend in Chaucer's *Reeve's Tale*," *Exemplaria* 21 (2009): 3–23.

did not enjoy as much autonomy (sexual or otherwise) as women do now. While these views are correct to an extent, they miss the complexity of both medieval and modern attitudes toward rape, and they allow students' own comparatively progressive attitudes to escape critical examination. The Middle Ages can become an emblem of gender inequalities that contemporary culture—particularly on college campuses where much anti-rape activism has focused over the last few years—has transcended.

Complicating any straightforward sense of the moral and ethical superiority of the present moment helps students to think more deeply about the subtle operations of misogyny and patriarchy in both medieval and modern attitudes toward sexual violence. Making medieval rape visible is critical to raising consciousness about the history of gender oppression. At the same time, foregrounding misogynist medieval perspectives on rape can inadvertently shore up the belief, also fundamental to rape culture, that women's agency *can ever* be completely elided—that women were not, in fact, meaningful historical actors.[3] Attitudes toward rape in medieval England were in fact quite varied. As Corinne Saunders argues in her extensive study of rape and ravishment in literature, they could be "acutely sympathetic to women as well as misogynistic."[4] Moreover, when it came to sexual violence, medieval women could be resourceful and effective actors. Much of the most recent scholarship on sexual violence in medieval England—including Caroline Dunn's historical study of legal cases, Elizabeth Robertson's work on consent, Carissa Harris's article on pedagogies of rape prevention, and my own book on discourses of survival—focuses on women's agency under conditions of gendered inequality.[5] Much like medieval studies classrooms that ignore representations of sexual violence and coercion, a classroom that insists on it too much can reinscribe a patriarchal model of history that places

---

3 In her book on rape in contemporary literature and culture *Framing the Rape Victim: Gender and Agency Reconsidered* (New Brunswick: Rutgers University Press, 2014), Carine M. Mardorossian argues that accounts of sexual victimization as the opposite of fully self-possessed, autonomous agency ultimately shore up gendered models of post-Enlightenment subjectivity (1–23). By implicitly conflating agency with domination, even some feminist scholarship on rape has adopted a neoconservative, nationalist rhetoric that equates victimization with moral weakness (41–67).

4 Corinne Saunders, *Rape and Ravishment in the Literature of Medieval England* (Cambridge: Boydell, 2001), 14. For diverse perspectives on sexual violence in medieval art, see Diane Wolfthal, *Images of Rape: The 'Heroic' Tradition and Its Alternatives* (Cambridge: Cambridge University Press, 1999).

5 Caroline Dunn, *Stolen Women in Medieval England: Rape, Abduction, and Adultery, 1100–1500* (Cambridge: Cambridge University Press, 2012); Elizabeth Robertson, "Public Bodies and Psychic Domains: Rape, Consent, and Female Subjectivity," in *Representing Rape in Medieval and Early Modern Culture*, eds. Elizabeth Robertson and Christine Rose (New York: Palgrave Macmillan, 2001), 281–310, and "*Raptus* and Poetic Married Love in Chaucer's *Wife of Bath's Tale* and James I's *Kingis Quair*," in *Reading Medieval Culture*, eds. Robert M. Stein and Sandra Pierson Prior (Notre Dame: University of Notre Dame Press, 2005), 302–23; Suzanne M. Edwards, *The Afterlives of Rape in Medieval English Literature* (New York: Palgrave Macmillan, 2016); and Carissa Harris, "Rape Narratives, Courtly Critique, and the Pedagogy of Sexual Negotiation in the Middle English Pastourelle," *Journal of Medieval and Early Modern Studies* 46 (2016): 263–87.

raped women at the margins of history, even if it directs students' attention to the existence of those margins. It turns out that, in certain circumstances, even anti-rape rhetoric and politics can support misogyny.

In my classes, I have found hagiographic texts, particularly virgin martyr legends, to be especially effective in cultivating a transhistorical perspective on medieval and modern representations of rape for several reasons. First, saints' lives facilitate subtle comparisons in the undergraduate literature classroom, because they share easily recognizable narrative patterns and yet vary meaningfully in their details. Since the virgin martyr legends, which are widely available in annotated Middle English editions as well as in Modern English translations, are short, it is possible to discuss a rich group of texts over three or four class meetings. Second, a grouping of hagiographic texts can work well in different types of courses—from a survey course in medieval literature, to a course focused on Chaucer's *Canterbury Tales* (where they enrich discussions of "The Physician's Tale" or "The Second Nun's Tale"), to a course on sexual violence in contemporary culture (where they provide an often-overlooked historical context). Third, saints' lives explore the complex relationship between victimization and agency as a central theme, exploring the fraught epistemological territory between enduring suffering at someone else's hands and exercising autonomous choice. Finally, virgin martyr legends that are set in late antiquity but translated, revised, and circulated widely among late medieval readers explicitly raise the relationship between the past and the present as an interpretive issue.[6] Consequently, saints' lives lend themselves organically to consideration of the links and divergences between medieval and modern attitudes toward rape.

Following a structure that I often use in my courses, this essay moves from an examination of diverse perspectives on sexual violence in medieval hagiography to the contemporary political uses of transhistorical comparison. In the first half of the essay, I identify some of the hagiographic texts that I have used successfully with undergraduates, along with practical suggestions for facilitating discussions about them. In the second half, I share strategies for pairing medieval texts with modern representations of rape as "medieval" in class discussions.

Sexual Violence and Saints' Lives

I have found two different types of virgin martyr narratives to be particularly useful in undergraduate discussions about sexual violence: lives in which the saint steadfastly refuses a tyrannical ruler's efforts to marry or seduce her and lives in which the saint faces the threat of being sent to a brothel. In the first category, St. Katherine of Alexandria and St. Margaret of Antioch work well. Both were widely read in the medieval Europe, and several Middle English versions of the narrative are available

---

6 This claim draws on Catherine Sanok's argument that female saints' lives in Middle English literary culture prompt readers to reflect on the historicity of gender and devotional practice. *Her Life Historical: Exemplarity and Female Saints' Lives in Late Medieval England* (Philadelphia: University of Pennsylvania Press, 2007).

in the TEAMS Middle English Text series.[7] I often use the texts from the Katherine Group, which is readily available in translation, because it is explicitly addressed to a female audience and thus raises questions about how female audiences read these narratives.[8] In the second category, the lives of St. Lucy, St. Agnes, and the unnamed Virgin of Antioch (all of which appear in Jacobus de Voragine's extremely popular *Golden Legend*) make for productive comparisons.[9] In this section of the essay, I outline strategies for building up to nuanced comparisons, starting with exploration of students' presumptions about medieval attitudes to sexual violence, then exploring how and why different hagiographic narratives represent the threat of rape, and finally turning to questions about gendered agency and consent in these texts.

To make students' preconceptions an explicit part of the discussion from the start and to define key terms, I begin by asking them to make lists comparing sexual violence in the Middle Ages and today. They typically describe rape in the Middle Ages as widespread and routine, suggest that feminine consent (rather than non-consent) was the presumption, and assert that medieval legal systems rarely credited victims' testimony or injuries. In contrast, they tend see "modern" discussions about rape as more discerning about consent and attentive to survivors' voices. These claims about the Middle Ages, I point out, are accurate in many ways. Affirmative consent, the idea

---

7 All of the TEAMS texts are available online as well as in affordable paperbacks. Reames includes three different versions of the lives of Katherine and Margaret, from the *Speculum Sacerdotale*, Mirk's sermons, and a stanzaic form. Sherry L. Reames, ed., *Middle English Legends of Women Saints* (Kalamazoo: Medieval Institute Publications, 2003). Capgrave's *Life of Saint Katherine* is in Karen A. Winstead, ed., *The Life of Saint Katherine*, TEAMS Middle English Texts (Kalamazoo: Medieval Institute Publications, 2000). There are several editions of the Katherine Group lives suitable for the undergraduate classroom: Emily Rebekah Huber and Elizabeth Robertson, eds., *The Katherine Group (MS Bodley 34)*, TEAMS Middle English Texts (Kalmazoo: Medieval Institute Publications, 2016) includes both lives, with facing-page translations. Anne Savage and Nicholas Watson, eds. and trans., *Anchoritic Spirituality: Ancrene Wisse and Associated Works* (New York: Paulist Press, 1991) includes translations of Margaret's and Katherine's lives from the Katherine Group; and Bella Millett and Jocelyn Wogan-Browne, eds. and trans., *Medieval English Prose for Women: Selections from the Katherine Group and Ancrene Wisse* (Oxford: Clarendon Press, 1992) contains a facing-page translation of Margaret's life.

8 On the subject of the female audience for the saints' lives in the Katherine Group, see Bella Millett, "The Audience of the Saints' Lives of the Katherine Group," *Reading Medieval Studies* 16 (1990): 127–56."

9 A translation of Jacobus de Voragine's *Legenda Aurea* that makes these texts accessible in the undergraduate classroom is Jacobus de Voragine, *The Golden Legend*, trans. William Granger Ryan, 2 vols. (Princeton: Princeton University Press, 1993). Ambrose's accounts of the Virgin of Antioch and Agnes stories in *De virginibus* can be an interesting comparison, although this text is much older, and the narratives, set into his arguments about virginity, are less straightforward. In advanced undergraduate and graduate courses, it is interesting to compare Jacobus's Virgin of Antioch to Goscelin of St. Bertin's rendering of the same story in his *Liber confortatorius* addressed to Eve of Wilton, which is available in two recent Modern English translations: *Goscelin of St. Bertin: The Book of Encouragement and Consolation*, ed. and trans. Monika Otter (Woodbridge: Brewer, 2004); and *Liber Confortatorius*, in *Writing the Wilton Women: Goscelin's Legend of Edith and Liber Confortatorius*, ed. and trans. Stephanie Hollis with W. R. Barnes, Rebecca Hayward, Kathleen Loncar, and Michael Wright (Turnhout: Brepols, 2004), 99–207.

that the absence of "no" does not automatically mean "yes," was not the standard governing rape in medieval ecclesiastical or civil law. But, nor is it—except on some college and university campuses—the standard in contemporary U.S. law. Although English legal records between the twelfth and fifteenth centuries do not document a large number of rape claims, we know from our own historical circumstances that legal cases do not accurately reflect the prevalence of sexual violence in any given culture.[10] It is a reasonable assumption that, just as it does today, rape in the Middle Ages happened more often than historical documents record it. Further, patriarchal social structures, like *coverture*, and misogynist beliefs about women's carnality shaped cultural attitudes toward feminine autonomy and, concomitantly, sexual assault. Yet, even though women have full independent status in contemporary U.S. law, anti-rape rhetoric often frames women's value in terms of their relationships to men. For example, the "1 is 2 Many" anti-rape video PSA from the White House urges masculine responsibility to prevent sexual assault by saying, "It's happening to our sisters, and our daughters, our wives, and our friends."[11] This exercise and the mini-lectures on what we do and do not know about medieval legal procedures concerning rape are opportunities to affirm much of what students believe about the Middle Ages, with reference to historical scholarship. They are also opportunities to raise questions about a straightforward contrast between the past and the present, for much of what students assume about the past derives, in part, from what we know about the present.

With these historical details and framing questions in place, students read virgin martyr narratives with an eye toward the conventions of the genre and, more specifically, the representation of gendered violence. Our discussion the next day begins with a consideration of the features the texts share in common: a virgin saint, pagan tormentors, spectacular torture scenes, the saint's pronouncements on Christian doctrine and her faith, the conversion of witnesses to the saint's suffering, the saint's impassivity, associated miracles, and the fact that rape does not come to pass in any of these texts (nor in any other virgin martyr's life). In each of these narratives, a tyrannical ruler wants to expose the saint's faith as misguided and weak by getting her to renounce her religious commitments through promises of earthly rewards and threats of physical violence. Likewise, in all five saints' lives, a tyrannical ruler's earthly power pales next to God's supernatural governance, manifested in the saint's holy martyrdom. The fact that rape never happens confirms God's omnipotence as well as the saint's merit.

When I ask my students to consider whether individual narratives represent rape as a threat and, if so, as *a harm to what* and *according to whom*, subtle distinctions among the representations of sex, force, and consent come in to view.

---

10 On the number of rape claims in medieval England and social factors determining the likelihood of their prosecution, see Dunn, *Stolen Women*, 53–81. The 2007 Campus Sexual Assault Study reports that 2 per cent of women assaulted by an acquaintance on campus report the crime. Christopher P. Krebs et al., *The Campus Sexual Assault Study*. National Institute of Justice, Document Number 221153. Washington, DC: U. S. Department of Justice, 2007.

11 The PSA can be viewed at www.whitehouse.gov/1is2many.

To help focus students' attention on textual details, I use a range of strategies. In lower-level courses, I excerpt quotations from the saints' lives in a handout; this helps to pinpoint comparisons by eliminating the need to shuffle between texts. In more advanced classes, I often ask students to work in small groups to identify key passages to anchor discussion of several key questions: What, precisely, is the threat? Who makes it? How does the saint respond? What logic drives her response? What intervenes, if anything, to avert the threat? In courses where students need practice engaging criticism, I have found it effective to raise these questions by highlighting the critical debate in feminist scholarship about whether the lives of St. Katherine and St. Margaret represent sexual violence and asking students to evaluate the textual evidence.[12]

In the *Life of St. Katherine*, the tyrant Maxentius does not explicitly invoke sex at all, but Katherine does; she thereby exposes how political life in Alexandria depends structurally on gendered and sexual domination. For his part, Maxentius promises Katherine a powerful position in the court akin to the queen's advisory role, but apparently without the sexual obligations that attend marriage: "Go and salute our gods, whom you have enraged; and you will forever be second after the queen in court and in chamber, and I will order the business of my kingdom according to your judgment."[13] While Maxentius' offer perhaps implies that Katherine will effectively become his concubine, it is Katherine who explicitly understands it that way, as a betrayal of her heavenly marriage and defilement of her chastity:

> [N]either prosperity nor riches nor any worldly honor, nor any suffering or torture can turn me from the love of my lover in whom I believe. He has married my maidenhood with the ring of true faith, and I have committed myself to him truly. We are so fastened and tied as one, and the knot so knotted between us two, that no desire, or mere strength either, of any living man will loosen or undo it.[14]

Importantly, Katherine does not interpret Maxentius' coercion as a threatened rape. Rather, she reads it as an attempted seduction and stresses her own capacity to choose or refuse it.[15] As her reply makes clear, Katherine understands the proposed role, supportive of and subordinate to Maxentius' political power, as predicated on

---

12 For examples of feminist scholarship on sexual violence and saints' lives that read the violence of torture as "symbolic rape," see Gravdal, *Ravishing Maidens*, 21–41 and Catherine Innes-Parker, "Sexual Violence and the Female Reader: Symbolic 'Rape' in the Saints' Lives of the Katherine Group," *Women's Studies* 24 (1995): 205–17. Robert Mills considers the parallels between virgin martyrs' suffering and pornography from a different angle, attending to viewership and gendered identification in *Suspended Animation: Pain, Pleasure, and Punishment in Medieval Culture* (London: Reaktion, 2005), 59–82. For feminist critics who caution against collapsing torture with sexualized violence, see Sara Salih, *Versions of Virginity in Late Medieval England* (Woodbridge: Brewer, 2001) and Jocelyn Wogan-Browne, "The Virgin's Tale," in *Feminist Readings in Middle English Literature: The Wife of Bath and All her Sect*, eds. Ruth Evans and Lesley Johnson (London: Routledge, 1994), 165–94.

13 Savage, *Anchoritic Spirituality*, 274–75.

14 Ibid., 275.

15 Salih, *Versions of Virginity*, 51–65 and Wogan-Browne, *Saints' Lives*, 92–105.

her sexual availability, even if *he* elides that implication. By rebutting Maxentius with an appeal to her divine marriage, Katherine redeploys the logic of masculine prerogative in order to subvert it. Her obligations to a heavenly spouse depend on a gendered hierarchy between husband and wife, between deity and human being, but they also authorize her escape from the gendered violence, both symbolic and physical, of Maxentius' Alexandria. Katherine does not use the contemporary term "rape culture," but her strategic use of the rhetoric of masculine supremacy and feminine subordination nonetheless resonates with it.

In contrast to the Katherine narrative, the *Life of St. Margaret* describes the tormentor's motives as transparently erotic, as he proposes marriage and attempts to coerce the saint's consent to it. When Olibrius, the sheriff of Antioch, spies Margaret tending sheep in a field, he orders his men to kidnap her. He says, "If she's a free woman, I'll have her and keep her as a wife; if she's a slave, I choose her for a concubine, and will free her with treasure and with gold, and she'll be lucky with everything I have because of her pretty face."[16] Olibrius never threatens Margaret with rape. Instead, he aims to elicit her consent to a sexual relationship first with the promise of material rewards and then with threats of torture. Margaret's willing abdication of her chastity—and not the forcible seizure of her physical virginity— is Olibrius' primary objective.[17] Coerced consent amounts to rape in modern legal definitions, but students are often surprised to learn that medieval ecclesiastical law likewise vacates consent to marriage obtained through force or the threat of force.[18] When asked why and how this distinction between forced consent and forced sex without consent might be significant in the *vitae*, students notice that the former foregrounds the efficacy and autonomy of the saint's will and that the latter focuses on the tyrant's power, his capacity to wound the saint's body whatever she wills. Like other hagiographic narratives, the *Life of St. Margaret* never suggests that forced consent to marriage or sex would be anything other than sexual violence; it only suggests that a *saint's* consent cannot be coerced.

The lives in which a tyrant threatens to force a saint into prostitution pose rape as an explicit danger. St. Agnes, for example, faces a coerced "choice" between making a sacrifice to idols and being "thrown into a house of harlots and handled as they are handled."[19] A forced choice between these two options pits the saint's worship of a Christian god against her chastity, a mainstay of that faith. Even faced with two bad options, Agnes's decision is easy to make, because she has divine assurance that no one in the brothel will be able to touch her: "[N]o one can sully my virtue because I have with me a guardian of my body, an angel of the Lord."[20] As evidence of this protection, Agnes's hair miraculously grows to keep her body hidden from lustful

---

16 Savage and Watson, *Anchoritic Spirituality*, 289.
17 See Salih, *Versions of Virginity*, 51–65.
18 Richard Helmholz, *Marriage Litigation in Medieval England* (Cambridge: Cambridge University Press, 1974), 90–94. This claim about the law elides the significant difficulties of proving that consent had been coerced in medieval ecclesiastical courts.
19 Jacobus, *Golden Legend*, 101.
20 Ibid., 103.

gazes, and the angel transforms the house of prostitution into a house of prayer. The saint's foreknowledge of her divine protection undercuts the coercive potential of the tyrant's threat, for she is confident that no one can touch her without her consent.[21] Without assurance of material protection, St. Lucy's resistance to forced prostitution rests on her conviction that rape will have no material effect on her chastity. St. Lucy rebuts Paschasius' threat to send her to a brothel by saying that "the body is not defiled ... unless the mind consents. If you have me ravished against my will, my chastity will be doubled and the crown will be mine."[22] Lucy's insistence that her *body* will remain undefiled, so long as she does not consent, often surprises students given modern legal proceedings that prioritize physical signs of forcible sex as evidence of rape. Yet, they also recognize that all of the hagiographic narratives feature saints who endure unthinkable tortures and, miraculously, do not manifest the expected wounds on their bodies. In this sense, Lucy's claims assimilate the threatened violence of rape to the violence of torture.

Yet, threatened rape is not so easily framed as torture in the Virgin of Antioch narrative's variation on the trope of forced prostitution. Like St. Agnes, the Virgin of Antioch faces a forced choice between worshipping idols and entering a house of prostitution. Like St. Lucy, the Virgin of Antioch rehearses the belief that physical violence, including rape, cannot harm her chastity: "It is more meritorious to keep the mind virginal than the flesh. Both are good if possible, but if not possible, let us at least be chaste in God's sight if not in men's."[23] At the same time, the Virgin of Antioch's circumstances appear more dire; she doesn't have Agnes's certain knowledge of divine protection, and even though she knows the theological argument, she doesn't appear to share Lucy's confidence about the immateriality of rape. It seems that the Virgin of Antioch must "choose" prostitution in order to refuse worshipping idols, a choice that would look uncomfortably like a willing renunciation of her chastity. The test thus foregrounds the difference between the torture a saint can fervently desire as a form of redemptive suffering and the rape she cannot.[24] As in the *Life of St. Margaret*, the threat is not simply that the Virgin of Antioch will suffer rape, but that she may be tricked into thinking that, in these extreme circumstances, consent to sex is the best course of action. The Virgin of Antioch is not fooled, of course. Instead, she says nothing at all, worried her words might be taken as a sign of her willingness to enter the house of prostitution.[25] The narrator argues that the saint's savvy management of this attempt to coerce her consent means that, even if she were to suffer rape, she would nonetheless remain chaste in body and mind: "Judge whether she, who would not commit adultery even by the

---

21 For a detailed argument along these lines, see Saunders, *Rape and Ravishment*, 131–33.

22 Jacobus, *Golden Legend*, 28. For this reading of the Lucy legend in its various forms, see Saunders, *Rape and Ravishment*, 127–30.

23 Jacobus, *Golden Legend*, 251.

24 On rape, martyrdom, and chastity in the Virgin of Antioch narrative, see Edwards, *Afterlives of Rape*, 21–52 and Maud Burnett McInerney, *Eloquent Virgins from Thecla to Joan of Arc* (New York: Palgrave Macmillan, 2003), 67–83.

25 Jacobus, *Golden Legend*, 251.

sound of her voice, could commit it with her body."[26] With the narrator's address to the reader, the Virgin of Antioch narrative highlights competing perspectives on the kind of threat that rape poses. The tyrant believes that rape will coerce the saint into renouncing her chastity and her faith, and the saint fears that it might. But, the narrator claims that any good reader will realize that it could not. This distinction between the tyrant's understanding of power and freedom in corporeal terms and the reader's implied commitment to the unknowable will as the true seat of agency makes an implicit argument about historical progress. The narrator urges the medieval reader of the *Golden Legend* to recognize the late antique tormenter's view as morally, ethically, and spiritually backward—as well as historically distant.

With the basic elements of these medieval representations of sexual violence and sanctity on the table, the classroom conversation can shift to a consideration of how these texts match up with students' expectations about sexual violence in the Middle Ages. Students notice that rape is not ubiquitous in these saints' lives and that women's consent is a focus of the narratives. Women in these texts resist coercive practices from marriage to forced prostitution and claim a sense of self-determination, grounded in their faith and their spiritual marriages to Christ. Further, they point out that the texts neither represent rape as trivial nor disregard the potential of women's suffering. On the contrary, the lives represent sexual violence as a more disabling threat than torture, in part because they are interested in the possibility of consent under conditions of inequality and coercion.

As this conversation unfolds in the classroom, I point out that several of these issues resonate with twentieth- and twenty-first-century feminists' questions about sexual violence: Is rape sex or is rape violence? What is the relationship between representations of sexual violence and material acts of rape? Is women's consent to heterosexual erotic activity ever free from coercion if women do not have access to the social and economic power that men enjoy? The differences between torture and rape in the saints' lives help students to think through the implications of viewing rape as sex, violence, or a distinctive combination of the two. The relationship between representations of threatened rape and women's material experiences of violence proves a particularly rich area of conversation, since this topic ovelaps with conversations about trigger warnings in college classrooms: how would medieval women, who might have been or have known rape survivors, have experienced these hagiographic narratives? Returning to the texts in search of evidence, students identify a range of possibilities. Some argue that medieval survivors could have seen the saints' miraculous escape from rape as a source of shame. They read the texts as examples of victim-blaming, narratives primarily focused on the victim's culpability or innocence rather than on the perpetrator's responsibility. In identifying escape from sexual violence with feminine virtue, the lives may give credence to the misogynist notion that women who do suffer rape have "asked for it" through their own moral failings.[27] Other students argue that medieval women could have

---

26 Ibid.
27 For more on rape as a narrative impossibility in hagiographic texts, consult Kelly, *Performing Virginity*, 40–62; McInerney, *Eloquent Virgins*, 47–84; and Salih, *Versions of Virginity*, 87–90.

read saints as inspiring heroes who model strategies for fighting against rape and sexual coercion with rhetorical eloquence, with silence, and with enduring faith in the transformative power of their own choices. As Jocelyn Wogan-Browne puts it, the virgin martyr legend might have been a resource for women who endured rape without the glories of sanctity: "It articulates a position where 'no' means 'no,' even if that 'no' cannot by itself prevent rape."[28]

On the subject of consent, the saints' lives prove particularly sophisticated and, from students' perspectives, surprisingly modern. The *Life of St. Katherine* hints that, under the conditions of masculine tyranny, coercion always compromises feminine consent; serving as a political adviser amounts to sexualized exploitation, even if the latter might look or feel like relative autonomy.[29] By valorizing a saint who will not say "yes" to the brothel, the Virgin of Antioch narrative anticipates affirmative consent, the idea that enthusiastic agreement to erotic activity ("yes means yes") is a better ethical standard than the absence of non-consent ("no means no"). And the idea that physical experiences do not fully determine either bodily or mental states, as expressed in Lucy's assertion that rape will not change the physical fact of her virginity, calls to mind rape survivors' efforts to define their identities in the aftermath of rape. In one essay from the important collection of Third-Wave feminist perspectives on rape, *Yes Means Yes*, this resonance is explicit. Hanne Blank's "Process-Oriented Virgin" begins with Augustine's claim that a raped Christian woman would remain a virgin, so long as she had not consented in her mind:

> Two thousand years before the trend toward conscious, feminist theory-based reclamation of sexuality by survivors of sexual violence promoted a similar understanding, Augustine articulated a profound truth about the sexual body as distinct from the self. What *happened* to you sexually was not necessarily what you *were* as a person.[30]

Of course, not all of Augustine's views about rape can be as easily reconciled to contemporary feminist thought. But, the point remains that the legacies of medieval thought about sexual violence are neither monolithic nor straightforward, much like the unsettled answers to questions about consent, autonomy, and responsibility to others that continue to surface in contemporary conversations about rape.

These transhistorical connections extend to the representation of potential perpetrators as well. The tendency in contemporary popular culture to portray

---

28 Wogan-Browne, *Saints' Lives*, 150.

29 Together, the saints' lives outline the continuum between marriage and rape Catharine A. MacKinnon argues is characteristic of sexuality defined by the eroticization of gendered domination, in "Feminism, Marxism, Method, and the State: Toward Feminist Jurisprudence," *Signs* 8 (1983): 635–58. More recent feminist work has criticized this "collapsed continuum" for foreclosing possibilities for women's agency under conditions of inequality. For an excellent explication of MacKinnon's position and criticisms of it, see Ann J. Cahill, *Rethinking Rape* (Ithaca: Cornell University Press, 2001), 36–47.

30 Hanne Blank, "The Process Oriented Virgin," in *Yes Means Yes! Visions of Female Sexual Power and a World without Rape*, eds. Jaclyn Friedman and Jessica Valenti (Berkeley: Seal Press, 2008), 289, emphasis in original.

callous attitudes toward rape as medieval has a parallel in the saints' lives, which associate potential perpetrators of sexual violence and coercion with a historically distant culture, marked by its religious difference from Christianity. Identifying religious, racialized, and historical others as potential rapists has a long history, both in the Middle Ages and today. As historian Anne Curry points out, medieval sources denigrate political enemies as rapists, particularly when that enemy is not Christian.[31] In the United States, as Krystal Feimster and Estelle Freedman have shown, rhetoric about rape has historically legitimated the power of white men by framing victims as chaste white women and perpetrators as black men.[32] This rhetorical trope finds a clear analogue in contemporary politics with Donald Trump's claims that migrants from Mexico to the United States are likely to be "rapists."[33] This connection opens into a more explicit consideration of what interests are served today by portraying widespread rape or callous attitudes toward women's sexual suffering as artifacts of a distant past.

Back to the Future: Rereading Contemporary Perspectives on Rape as "Medieval"[34]

Returning to their original assumptions that rape was more pervasive in the Middle Ages than it is today, students' reading of the hagiographic narratives inspire a fresh look at contemporary representations of medieval rape. In this section of the essay, I suggest some strategies for facilitating reflection on the relationship between the past and the past-in-the-present. As examples of this comparative method, I discuss two texts that have worked well for me over the last few years, the popular HBO series *Game of Thrones* and critical responses to a political candidate's 2012 claims that "legitimate rape" never ends in pregnancy. Instructors adapting strategies from this essay for their own courses will want to use whatever texts loom large in students' perceptions about attitudes toward sexual violence in the distant past. Contemporary representations of rape as a reality for medieval women make visible a history that has too often been ignored, but they also trade on the twin convictions that women today have it pretty good and that the contemporary representations in no way trade in the misogynist violence that they situate in the distant past.

---

31 Anne Curry, "The Theory and Practice of Female Immunity in the Medieval West," in *Sexual Violence in Conflict Zones from the Ancient World to the Era of Human Rights*, ed. Elizabeth D. Heineman (Philadelphia: University of Pennsylvania Press, 2011), 187.
32 Krystal Feimster, *Southern Horrors: Women and the Politics of Rape and Lynching* (Cambridge, MA: Harvard University Press, 2011); and Estelle B. Freedman, *Redefining Rape: Sexual Violence in the Era of Suffrage and Segregation* (Cambridge, MA: Harvard University Press, 2015).
33 Michelle Ye Hee Lee, "Donald Trump's False Comments connecting Mexican Immigrants and Crime," *Washington Post*, July 8, 2015, online.
34 I refer to the 1985 Robert Zemeckis film *Back to the Future*, in which the protagonist's intervention in the attempted rape of his mother helps to reshape her past and their shared future.

I begin by asking students to bring in a contemporary representation of rape in the Middle Ages along with an interpretive question about it based in their knowledge of medieval hagiographic narratives. In recent semesters, *Game of Thrones*—a television series based on fantasy novels by George R. R. Martin—has dominated students' examples. The series, which loosely alludes to historical details like Hadrian's Wall and the Wars of the Roses, includes repeated scenes of sexual violence as part of its "medieval" setting. When faced with criticism about the novels' representations of rape, Martin explained the pervasive sexual violence in *Game of Thrones* in terms of historical accuracy and cultural change: "In a medieval society, there was no such thing as marital rape ... I am glad we have evolved to the point that we have, but I am not writing about 21st-century America."[35]

One broad topic in students' questions concerned the ways in which representations of sexual violence shape relationships between a historical world and a contemporary audience. Several students, drawing on our conversations about how medieval rape survivors might have interpreted virgin martyr narratives, wondered about the relationship between graphic, on-screen representations of rape in *Game of Thrones* and forestalled representations of sexual violence in hagiographic narratives. As one student put it, how do we compare a literary genre that represents rape as always avoided by "good women" to one that emphasizes the visceral "realism" of sexual violence? Hagiographic narratives suggest that virtue is the best protection against rape, but they also insist explicitly that rape is a moral wrong and highlight women's resistance. In *Game of Thrones*, in contrast, the explicit and often unremarked scenes of sexualized violence as entertainment make rape into a site of viewers' enjoyment.

Women's agency or its absence as a sign of historical accuracy emerged as another theme in students' questions. The "realism" in *Game of Thrones* that stresses medieval women's vulnerability to rape contrasts sharply with medieval hagiographic narratives that stress women's rhetorical engagements with their would-be rapists. Students began to see George R. R. Martin's invocation of "historical realism" as a refusal of responsibility for his own representations of gender—and race as well, since one of the earliest representations of sexual violence and coerced consent in the series turns on a marriage between a white woman from a royal family and a darker-skinned man from a tribal, nomadic culture. "After all," one student pointed out, "there were no dragons in the Middle Ages, so the series uses artistic license throughout: why is women's status as rape victims a historical truth that the author can't change?" Martin claims that representing rape is a critical part of his books' ethical perspective: "To omit them [rape and sexual violence] from a narrative centered on war and power would have been fundamentally false and dishonest."[36] Yet, Martin's contemporary

---

35 Quoted in Katherine Don, "Dimwits and the Dark Ages," *In These Times*, May 6, 2014. For mass media responses to representations of rape in *Game of Thrones*, see David Itzkoff, "For 'Game of Thrones,' Rising Unease over Rape's Recurring Role," *New York Times*, May 2, 2014, online, and Sonia Saraiya, "Rape of *Thrones*," *A.V. Club* (blog), April 20, 2014, www.avclub.com/article/rape-thrones-203499, accessed January 15, 2015.
36 Quoted in Alison Flood, "George RR Martin Defends Game of Thrones' Sexual Violence," *The Guardian*, May 6, 2014, online.

representations of "medieval" women as rape victims is as much a fiction as medieval representations of would-be rape survivors as holy martyrs. Both hagiographic texts and *Game of Thrones* promote selective blindness about rape, its survivors, and its perpetrators, albeit in very different ways. This resonance attunes students to the uneven ideological and cultural work these representations do in their own historical moments. The idea, in *Game of Thrones*, that women's vulnerability to rape is a marker of historical authenticity promotes contemporary viewers' sense of themselves as ethically superior, foreclosing critical consideration of the misogyny and racism that haunt Martin's fantasy.

As students continue to practise this comparative method, branching out to other generic examples provides students with a chance to broaden their knowledge about medieval discourses. To conclude our discussion of sexual violence in hagiography, I typically bring in brief examples of other representations of sexual violence from other medieval genres, like legal cases, romances, or theological *summae*. In one recent course, we examined a medieval medical text in relation to the brouhaha surrounding a U.S. politician's claims about "legitimate rape." In 2012, Representative Todd Akin, the Republican Senate nominee from Missouri, absurdly claimed that pregnancies resulting from rape were rare, and several news outlets characterized his remarks as a *medieval* theory of conception.[37] Todd Akin said, "It seems to me, from what I understand from doctors, [pregnancy from rape is] really rare. If it's a legitimate rape, the female body has ways to try to shut that whole thing down."[38] I asked my students to compare Akin's comments with the views of twelfth-century scholastic writer William of Conches, which more than one editorial cites as evidence for the would-be senator's "medieval" sensibilities. In his dialogue, the *Dragmaticon Philosophiae*, William writes, "Although raped women dislike the act in the beginning, in the end, however, from the weakness of the flesh, they like it. Furthermore, there are two wills in humans, the rational and the natural, which we often feel are warring with us: for often what pleases the flesh displeases the reason. Although, therefore, a raped woman does not assent with her rational will, she does have carnal pleasure."[39]

Akin's comments bear a superficial similarity to William's, but there are significant differences as well. Both strive to defend a deeply held belief against a strong challenge that the circumstances of rape pose to it. For Akin, pregnancy as a result of rape tests the limits of an anti-choice perspective that equates women's

---

37 See Vanessa Heggie, "'Legitimate Rape'—A Medieval Medical Concept," *The Guardian*, August 20, 2012, online, and Jennifer Tucker, "The Medieval Roots of Todd Akin's Theories," *New York Times*, August 23, 2012, online. These pieces both oversimplify medieval views on the mechanics of conception to make their points. For more information, see Joan Cadden's critique of Thomas Laqueur's one-sex model and discussion of sexual violence (*Meanings of Sex*, 96–98).

38 John Eligon and Michael Schwirtz, "Senate Candidate Provokes Ire with 'Legitimate Rape' Comment," *New York Times*, August 19, 2012, online.

39 William of Conches, *Dragmaticon Philosophiae*, trans. Matthew Curr and Italo Ronca (Notre Dame: University of Notre Dame Press, 1997), 209–10.

responsibility for their sexual activities with carrying any pregnancy to term. For William of Conches, pregnancy following from rape poses a counterexample to a Galenic theory of conception that requires the emission of seed, attendant upon orgasm, from both partners.[40] Both Todd Akin and William of Conches struggle to reconcile medical and theological beliefs. Akin invokes medical science as an empirical basis for opposition to reproductive rights that is grounded in religious convictions about the "sanctity of human life." William of Conches turns to a theological understanding of a will divided into rational and fleshly components to shore up a scientific theory of conception. When asked to compare attitudes toward consent in these two views, students notice that Akin's theory holds the feminine will and body to work in utter unison. In contrast, William views a rational will as often at war with a fleshly will. The hagiographic texts dramatize the saint's capacity to feel pain or pleasure without changing the disposition of her rational will or even physical body. In other words, to use William's idiom, the virgin martyrs' lives are stories about what happens when what would please the flesh displeases reason. Students notice, moreover, that the virtuous woman Akin's narrative imagines looks a lot like a medieval saint; rape cannot change her bodily state. The medieval lives are no more likely to represent a raped saint than Todd Akin is to tell the story of a raped pregnant woman. For both, that would mean reckoning with a divine plan that looks like horrific injustice and coming to terms with the social, spiritual, and ethical implications of gender inequality. Identifying Akin's twenty-first-century perspective on "legitimate rape" with medieval theories of conception disguises the extent to which his misogyny is modern, and not medieval.

Classroom discussions like these unsettle students' confidence in a narrative of progress in cultural attitudes toward rape. Medieval accounts of sexual violence, like William's and the hagiographic narratives, and modern representations, like Todd Akin's or George R. R. Martin's, both leave much to be desired when it comes to feminist politics. Comparative practice helps students to reflect on what it means when any text identifies a problematic attitude toward sexual violence with the distant past. To call today's misogynist or callous representations of rape "medieval" intertwines ethical superiority with a narrative of historical progress and sidesteps enduringly difficult questions about political power, autonomy, social responsibility, and belief (whether in God or science or justice). For these reasons, teaching rape and its representations in the Middle Ages can help students to think more deeply about their own views and—one hopes— ultimately to foster more substantive and nuanced political conversations about rape today.

---

40 Hiram Kümper makes this often-overlooked point about the rhetorical context for William's comments in "Learned Men and Skillful Matrons: Medical Expertise and the Forensics of Rape in the Middle Ages," in *Medicine and the Law in the Middle Ages*, eds. Wendy J. Turner and Sara M. Butler (Leiden: Brill, 2014), 88–108.

Works Cited

Ambrose of Milan. *De virginibus*. In *Ambrose*, translated by Boniface Ramsey, 71–116. New York: Routledge, 1997.

Blank, Hanne. "The Process Oriented Virgin." In *Yes Means Yes! Visions of Female Sexual Power and a World without Rape*, edited by Jaclyn Friedman and Jessica Valenti, 287–98. Berkeley: Seal Press, 2008.

Cadden, Joan. *Meanings of Sex Difference in the Middle Ages: Medicine, Science, and Culture*. Cambridge: Cambridge University Press, 1995.

Cahill, Ann J. *Rethinking Rape*. Ithaca: Cornell University Press, 2001.

Capgrave, John. *The Life of Saint Katherine*. Edited by Karen A. Winstead. Kalamazoo: Medieval Institute Publications, 1999.

Curry, Anne. "The Theory and Practice of Female Immunity in the Medieval West." In *Sexual Violence in Conflict Zones from the Ancient World to the Era of Human Rights*, edited by Elizabeth D. Heineman, 173–88. Philadelphia: University of Pennsylvania Press, 2011.

Don, Katherine. "Dimwits and the Dark Ages." *In These Times*, May 6, 2014.

Dunn, Caroline. *Stolen Women in Medieval England: Rape, Abduction, and Adultery, 1100–1500*. Cambridge: Cambridge University Press, 2012.

Edwards, Suzanne M. *The Afterlives of Rape in Medieval English Literature*. New York: Palgrave Macmillan, 2016.

Feimster, Krystal. *Southern Horrors: Women and the Politics of Rape and Lynching*. Cambridge, MA: Harvard University Press, 2011.

Freedman, Estelle B. *Redefining Rape: Sexual Violence in the Era of Suffrage and Segregation*. Cambridge, MA: Harvard University Press, 2015.

Goscelin of St. Bertin. *Liber confortatorius*. In *Goscelin of St. Bertin: The Book of Encouragement and Consolation*, edited and translated by Monika Otter. Woodbridge: D. S. Brewer, 2004.

——. *Liber confortatorius*. In *Writing the Wilton Women*: *Goscelin's Legend of Edith and Liber Confortatorius*, edited and translated by Stephanie Hollis with W. R. Barnes, Rebecca Hayward, Kathleen Loncar, and Michael Wright, 99–207. Turnhout: Brepols, 2004.

Gravdal, Kathryn. *Ravishing Maidens: Writing Rape in Medieval French Literature and Law*. Philadelphia: University of Pennsylvania Press, 1991.

Harris, Carissa. "Rape Narratives, Courtly Critique, and the Pedagogy of Sexual Negotiation in the Middle English Pastourelle." *Journal of Medieval and Early Modern Studies* 46 (2016): 263–87.

Helmholz, Richard H. *Marriage Litigation in Medieval England*. Cambridge: Cambridge University Press, 1974.

Huber, Emily Rebekah, and Elizabeth Robertson, eds. *The Katherine Group (MS Bodley 34)*. Kalmazoo: Medieval Institute Publications, 2016.

Innes-Parker, Catherine. "Sexual Violence and the Female Reader: Symbolic 'Rape' in the Saints' Lives of the Katherine Group." *Women's Studies* 24 (1995): 205–17.

Jacobus de Voragine. *The Golden Legend*. Translated by William Granger Ryan. 2 vols. Princeton: Princeton University Press, 1993.

Kelly, Kathleen Coyne. *Performing Virginity and Testing Chastity in the Middle Ages*. London: Routledge, 2000.

Krebs, Christopher P., et al. *The Campus Sexual Assault Study*. National Institute of Justice, Document Number 221153. Washington, DC: U.S. Department of Justice, 2007.

Kümper, Hiram. "Learned Men and Skillful Matrons: Medical Expertise and the Forensics of Rape in the Middle Ages." In *Medicine and the Law in the Middle Ages*, edited by Wendy J. Turner and Sara M. Butler, 88–108. Leiden: Brill, 2014.

MacKinnon, Catharine A. "Feminism, Marxism, Method, and the State: Toward Feminist Jurisprudence." *Signs* 8 (1983): 635–58.

Mardorossian, Carine. *Framing the Rape Victim: Gender and Agency Reconsidered*. New Brunswick: Rutgers University Press, 2014.

McInerney, Maud Burnett. *Eloquent Virgins from Thecla to Joan of Arc*. New York: Palgrave Macmillan, 2003.

Millett, Bella. "The Audience of the Saints' Lives of the Katherine Group." *Reading Medieval Studies* 16 (1990): 127–56.

Millett, Bella, and Jocelyn Wogan-Browne, eds. and translated by *Medieval English Prose for Women: Selections from the Katherine Group and Ancrene Wisse*. Oxford: Clarendon Press, 1992.

Mills, Robert. *Suspended Animation: Pain, Pleasure, and Punishment in Medieval Culture*. London: Reaktion, 2005.

Reames, Sherry L., ed. *Middle English Legends of Women Saints*. Kalamazoo: Medieval Institute Publications, 2003.

Robertson, Elizabeth. "Public Bodies and Psychic Domains: Rape, Consent, and Female Subjectivity." In *Representing Rape in Medieval and Early Modern Culture*, edited by Elizabeth Robertson and Christine Rose, 281–310. New York: Palgrave Macmillan, 2001.

———. "*Raptus* and Poetic Married Love in Chaucer's *Wife of Bath's Tale* and James I's *Kingis Quair*." In *Reading Medieval Culture*, edited by Robert M. Stein and Sandra Pierson Prior, 302–23. Notre Dame: University of Notre Dame Press, 2005.

Salih, Sarah. *Versions of Virginity in Late Medieval England*. Woodbridge: Brewer, 2001.

Sanok, Catherine. *Her Life Historical: Exemplarity and Female Saints' Lives in Late Medieval England*. Philadelphia: University of Pennsylvania Press, 2007.

Saunders, Corinne. *Rape and Ravishment in the Literature of Medieval England*. Cambridge: Boydell, 2001.

Savage, Anne, and Nicholas Watson, eds. and translated by *Anchoritic Spirituality: Ancrene Wisse and Associated Works*. New York: Paulist Press, 1991.

Sidhu Nicole Nolan. " 'To Late for to Crie': Female Desire, Fabliau Politics, and Classical Legend in Chaucer's *Reeve's Tale*." *Exemplaria* 21 (2009): 3–23.

William of Conches. *Dragmaticon Philosophiae*. Translated by Matthew Curr and Italo Ronca. Notre Dame: University of Notre Dame Press, 1997.

Wogan-Browne, Jocelyn. *Saints' Lives and Women's Literary Culture, 1150–1300: Virginity and Its Authorizations*. Oxford: Oxford University Press, 2001.

———"The Virgin's Tale." In *Feminist Readings in Middle English Literature: The Wife of Bath and All her Sect*, edited by Ruth Evans and Lesley Johnson, 165–94. London: Routledge, 1994.

Wolfthal, Diane. *Images of Rape: The 'Heroic' Tradition and Its Alternatives*. Cambridge: Cambridge University Press, 1999.

Chapter 3

TEACHING MEDIEVAL RAPE CULTURE ACROSS GENRE: INSIGHTS FROM VICTIMOLOGY

WENDY PERKINS AND CHRISTINA DI GANGI

For advanced undergraduates as for their instructors, medieval literary texts depicting victims and victimization present special interpretive challenges. Medieval texts stereotype and/or typologize both victims and victimizers in terms of highly symbolic categories, beginning with categories of sex and class. Crimes against women in particular bear the hallmarks of medieval misogynistic discourse; moreover, when these crimes are sex crimes, medieval authors often depict both victimization and resistance to victimization (as in female saints' lives) as ambiguously and aesthetically pleasing. In teaching undergraduates, there is a strong argument to be made that appreciating textual ambiguity is a skill to be fostered. At the same time, given the pressures already inherent in teaching required early-period literature classes—beginning with the pressure on students to assimilate complex material—texts like those we draw on here may strike a given instructor as being simply more trouble than they are worth.

Yet, as is implicit in what we argue below, it is precisely their characteristic difficulties that may invest certain medieval texts involving rape with concrete utility to the undergraduate literature classroom.[1] Kathryn Gravdal wrote of the pastourelle genre in 1991 that "[i]n two centuries of literary criticism, the sanguine representation of sexual violence in these songs has eluded analysis."[2] With the rise of internet culture, late twentieth- and early twenty-first-century students have often encountered

---

[1] The discussion of rape in the classroom may be uncomfortable and contentious as students come to terms with their own views about the topic. In addition, some students may have been a victim of or been accused of rape or some other form of sexual assault. It is at the discretion of the professor to issue a "trigger warning" to students prior to raising the issue so they can be emotionally prepared for the discussion. At various times, we have adopted syllabus statements and in-class warnings when discussing certain contentious materials. Even if no trigger warning is issued, we do highly advise professors to provide students with information about how to get counselling for rape trauma and how to report incidents of rape. Professors may obtain this information from campus support services or a local rape crisis centre.

[2] Kathryn Gravdal, *Ravishing Maidens: Writing Rape in Medieval French Literature and Law* (Philadelphia: University of Philadelphia Press, 1991), 105 and *passim*.

qualities similar to those Gravdal outlines for the pastourelle in pop culture, peer culture, and/or social media. To cite but one example, knowyourmeme.com credits Chicago hip hop artist Twista's 2004 single "So Sexy" dedicated to women "that want to keep the D up inside of 'em," with originating the "D meme," going on to trace the expression "She Wants The D" through porn sites to social media like the "She Wants The D" twitter feeds now popular with undergraduates.[3] Here in a nutshell we have a literary ancestor of Robin Thicke's allegedly "rapey" summer pop hit "Blurred Lines" (2013) whose iterations of "I know you want it, I know you want it" remind us at least faintly of the thirteenth-century pastourelles which Gravdal studied and categorized in terms of their depictions of rape, many involving stereotyped analogies between riding and sexual behaviour (*chevauchant*), jaunty trimeter, insistent monorhymes— all in the service of showing sexual victimization:

> Et quant il en ot fait
> Et quant il en ot fait
> s'en torne, s'en vait,
> et elle crie et brait.[4]

Pastourelles tell certain events—courting, consensual sex, rape even—over and over again in different ways. They may thus also furnish a useful flashpoint for students wishing critically to examine the relationships among retelling, crime, and social media. Early twenty-first-century discourse came to call such repetitive, perhaps compulsive, telling and retelling of contemporary crimes, some involving young adults and social media, "going viral"—but there may also be a parallel to be drawn with the medieval penchant for repetitive, perhaps compulsive, reworking of sources. Why retell and reinterpret narratives, investing some, like the rape of the Roman matron Lucretia, with deep literary authority? When is such retelling

---

3 "The D," Cheezburger Group, accessed January 15, 2015, http://knowyourmeme.com/memes/the-d. Infinite examples of this meme from popular and internet culture include "If it's her birthday, she wants the d," "We just made eye contact ... she wants the d," "Moment of silence for all the guys who thought they were getting laid on finals week. She wants the A way more than she wants the d." See, e.g., "She Wants The D Quotes," SearchQuotes, accessed February 12, 2015, www.searchquotes.com/search/She_Wants_The_D/1/. Kenneth W. Horne's "A Constructivist Grounded Theory of Social Media Literacy and Identity Influence: Traditional-Age Undergraduate Students and Their Experiences" (M.Ed. diss., University of Chicago, 2013, p. 45) quotes one anonymous male subject in the context of fraternity life:

> Dude we even have our own hashtag. It's like a secret code for us. We'll be at a party or somethin' and if a girl slips us the look we tweet hashtag she wants the d. We all know what that means.
>
> (@Fratlife69, Transcription)

4 "And when he'd done it [finished], and when he'd done it, he turned and left, and she shouted and sang out." Text from Karl Bartsch, *Romances et pastourelles des XIIe et XIIIe siècle* (Leipzig: Vogel, 1870), II 12, 120. All unattributed translations are authorial. From a teaching standpoint, it is suggested that instructors use translations in an English-language literature class but that they also include some focus on translation or original language, given that factors such as rhyme scheme, rhythm, and language choice may indicate some of the concepts from victimology presented in what follows.

ethical? Is retelling ethical if its intent is to elicit shock? To "teach and delight"? To reinforce fear of rape and remind women of their place as subservient to men?

All of these questions and more may come to the fore if these problematic texts come to be assigned to undergraduates. In general, however, we are arguing from experience that giving undergraduates the ability to draw connections between medieval texts and recent media phenomena is desirable in a classroom context, as long as they are tied to clear interpretive outcomes. Accordingly, in what follows, we propose a set of principles from teaching victimology to undergraduates which may in turn be applied in the undergraduate literature classroom. First emerging as a primary field of study in the 1940s, victimology is, simply stated, the study of criminal victimization; victimologists are especially concerned with examining the characteristics of people who experience crime, the effect of crime on victims, and the criminal justice and societal response to crime victims.[5]

As applied to the teaching of medieval rape narratives in advanced undergraduate literature courses, principles from teaching victimology, potentially team-taught with a victimologist, illuminate three key issues in medieval texts: the nature of sexual assault itself, the characterization of victims, and the function in texts of bystanders. In what follows, then, we apply principles from teaching victimology to texts from two broad generic subsets: moralizing tales where the victim possesses name, fame, and symbolism on the one hand (in particular, we refer to tragedies of Lucretia); and Old French and Middle English pastourelles on the other, short dialogues where female victims possess neither name nor social standing. Ostensibly disparate, both text sets reveal aspects of an across-the-board medieval rape culture, both highly conventional and highly stylized, with which students may engage.

Clearly Defining Rape

In each of the three sections which follow, we will outline key problems associated with teaching medieval rape narrative, going on in each instance to discuss how the application of principles from teaching victimology can sharpen and enrich classroom discussion. One of the first difficulties the instructor will face when introducing these texts to undergraduates, of course, is that, by the 2000s, definitions of rape had evolved beyond medieval norms. In the first place, whereas a concept of consent is integral to present-day definitions of rape, the importance of mental and bodily consent is in flux in legal thinking throughout the Middle Ages.[6] Also, as Ruth

---

5 Victimology first emerged as a primary field of study in the 1940s with the publication of research by Hans von Hentig, Benjamin Mendelsohn, and Marvin Wolfgang (Leah Daigle, *Victimology: The Essentials* (Los Angeles: Sage, 2013), 2–6). Directly related to the crime of rape, in 1948 Menachem Amir published a study examining factors that precipitate rape. For an overview of the victimology field, see Daigle, *Victimology*, 1.

6 We have drawn in particular on Gravdal, *Ravishing Maidens*; James A. Brundage, *Law, Sex, and Christianity in Medieval Europe* (Chicago: University of Chicago Press, 1987); and Ruth M. Karras, *Sexuality in Medieval Europe: Doing unto Others* (New York: Routledge, 2005). Of particular interest is here the notion that the concept of consent gained in importance directly before the Renaissance.

M. Karras has stated, "Many depictions of rape do not so much make women complicit as make women's consent irrelevant."[7] In pastourelles, in point of fact, rape *in spite of* refusal often works as the structural and stylistic backbone of a given love lyric: "Lors l'embrachai. Ele dist: 'Fui de moi!' Més onc pour ce ne laissai."[8] Or consider how the shepherdess's responses in the following passage, throughout which she actively *denies* consent, work merely in the service of the comedy of her potential to be raped:

> Franc chevalier, lessiez mester,
> je n'ai cure de vo gaber;
> vez ci la nuit oscure.
> lessiez moi mes aigniax garder,
> de vostre gieu n'ai cure.[9]

Elsewhere, denial of consent shapes form, with the motion from resistance through assault to acceptance mirrored in stanzaic ordering. We cite this in full to depict the motion involved:

> Quant par ma proiere n'i poi avenir,
> par les flans l'ai prinse, si la fis chaïr.
> Levai la pelice,
> La blanche chemise;
> A molt bele guise
> mon jeu li apris.
> Va de la doudie,
> ele print a rire
> quant je m'an parti.[10]

Teaching about consent in medieval rape narratives is also problematized in that many medieval interpretations of rape follow Augustine's oft-cited chapters on the rape of of Lucretia from his *City of God* in dualizing bodily and mental consent.

---

7 Karras, *Sexuality in Medieval Europe*, 113.

8 "I embraced her, she told me, 'Go away!'"—but I didn't stop just because of that." *Chansonnier de Montpellier* Pièce no. CII, Jean Claude Rivière, *Pastourelles: Texte des chansonniers de la Bibliothèque nationale (suite) et de la Bibliothèque vaticane, motets anonymes des chansonniers de Montpellier et de Bamberg, avec notes* (Geneva: Droz, 1974), 74.

9 "Noble knight, let me be. I care nothing for your joking. Here comes the dark night. Let me watch my lambs." Bartsch, *Romances et pastourelles,* II 28, 146.

10 Since I couldn't succeed by asking
I took her by the sides and made her fall.
    I lifted up her fur-lined coat,
    Her white shirt;
    In the very nicest way
    I taught her my game.
    Va de la doudie.
  She began to laugh
    When I took my leave.

Text and translation from William D. Paden, ed. and trans., *The Medieval Pastourelle* (New York: Garland, 1987), 118.

Augustine's Lucretia acquiesced in body but resisted in mind (I.18–19). Take, for instance, John Lydgate's highly conventional account of Lucretia's rape by Sextus Tarquinius, narrated by Lydgate's Lucretia in Books II and III of the encyclopedic *Fall of Princes* (1431–1439).[11] Whether or not he follows his Continental sources, Boccaccio and Laurent de Premierfait, in his translation of Lucretia, Lydgate deliberately places this Augustinian emphasis in Lucretia's own words: "Mi bodi corupt, my sperit aboode cleene";[12] after all, Lucretia's body here is still "corupt," problematizing in terms of more recent understanding of rape her status qua rape victim.[13]

Medieval love poetry thus often blurs the lines between resistance and acquiescence in the service of formal and stylistic pleasure, arguably creating a textual analogue to the rape act itself. Inseparable, then, from the problem of how to present and discuss the issue of consent in medieval rape narratives is the problem of how to broach and use in a classroom context medieval definitions of sexual assault. It is obviously necessary when introducing medieval literary texts involving rape to undergraduates concurrently to introduce standard, albeit evolving, medieval accounts of *raptus*, derived from Gratian. Whether we attempt to historicize medieval rape narratives through theological definitions or legal texts, meanwhile, the outcome will still be gendered, with female voices or figures framed by male retellings.

Medieval authors thus most frequently depict famous rape narratives as conflicts among elements in a male-dominated structure: as expressed in the legal concept of *raptus*, a named female's violation or resistance to violation is the product of conflict among the men to whom she most closely relates.[14] On the one hand, Lydgate's accounts of Lucretia envelop a literarily ornate retelling of the crime from her perspective:

> Firste be his fals[e] subtil compassying
> He gan espie thestris off the place;

---

[11] All citations from Lydgate's *Fall of Princes* are from the standard edition by Henry Bergen: John Lydgate, *Fall of Princes*, ed. by Henry Bergen, 4 vols., EETS ES, 121, 122, 123, 124 (London: Oxford University Press, 1924–1927). We refer to book and line numbers within these volumes.

[12] Lydgate, *Fall of Princes*, III.1107–8.

[13] This is from the second account of the rape of Lucretia found in Lydgate's *Fall of Princes*. In the first account, in Book II, the language used expresses a body–soul duality even more directly: "Thouh off force thi bodi corrupt be, / Thi soule inward and thyn entencioun / Fraunchised been from al corupcioun (Lydate, *Fall of Princes*, II.1152–53). The speaker is Lucretia's husband, reinforcing our sense that eclipse of the female voice is a characteristic feature of medieval rape narrative. Students might find comparing Augustine's interpretation of Lucretia to the multiple vernacular accounts of the fourteenth and fifteenth centuries to be a useful exercise for throwing light on questions of voice, perspective, gendered characterization, and male versus female narration.

[14] It will readily be seen that, while interpretations of female subjectivity (for instance, Irigaray's and Kristeva's) are not the primary focus of the present study, our comments on male transactions and female victimhood in this context may furnish a useful jumping off point to considering this aspect of literary criticism in the advanced literature classroom—also, we would argue, a useful counterpoise or concretion mechanism to this particular choice of emphasis.

> And whan a-bedde alone I lay slepying,
> Lik a leoun, ful sterne of look and face,
> With his lefft hand my throte he dede enbrace,
> And in his other heeld ageyn al lawe
> Me for to oppresse a naked suerd idrawe.[15]

Yet, if we move to consider Lydgate's reiterated philosophic interpretation of the rape, we find that Sextus' crime may be depicted as less horrifying in terms of its violent physicality than in terms of its violent undoing of Lucretia's "wifli trouthe" (II.974), of her "chast and wiffli innocence" (II.1196)—properties of significance to her father and husband. This is very clearly intended to be a woman's account of her own rape, and classroom space should be given to discuss it as such, yet Lydgate, generally a voice for his own culture's social and religious norms, gives permeation of the inner recesses of Lucretia's husband's property ("thestris off the place") every bit as much space as he gives Lucretia's suffering. Lucretia herself has objected earlier that her violation occurred "[i]n a castell which is called Collace, / *Off which my lord heer hath the gouernaunce*" (1051–52; emphasis added). Her rapist, Lucretia says, acts "ageyn al lawe" and, later, "[a]geyn [his] knyhthod" (1101). What he damages in damaging her body—by her own interpretation, beyond repair—is Lucretia's wifehood, her powerful relation to a male-mandated order, "lawe ciuyle and natural also" (III.1091):

> ... I am nat worthi that men sholde me call,
> Or haue the name in no maner wise,
> For thoffence, which ye han herd deuise,
> To be callid, in this wrecchid liff,
> Of Collatyn from hen[nes]foorth the wiff.[16]

Actually, what is most germane about Lucretia's story to Lydgate's larger political project in the *Fall of Princes* is its precipitation of Sextus' disruption of the Roman state.

In one sense, the conventionality of Lydgate's rendering of the Lucretia narrative is a boon to a group of students who with their instructor are intent on tracing women's status and depiction in medieval texts. At the same time, as seen above, the fact that this is a rape narrative centred on a female figure may become eclipsed in line-by-line classroom discussion by a necessary attention to the female figure's male context; the drive to historicize and situate may abet this imbalance. The instances above are instances where the victim's rape is presented as fact. In preparing still other literary genres for the classroom—taking as our examples here a great proportion of thirteenth-century pastourelles—teaching strategy may be complicated by the realization that, for the medieval author, rape does not occur even where force does:

---

15 Lydgate, *Fall of Princes*, III.1093–99.
16 Lydgate, *Fall of Princes*, III.1114–20.

desor l'erbe la getai
ne s'en pout deffendre
lou jeu d'amors sens atendre
li fix per delit,
et elle a chanteir se prist
de jolit cuer amerous ...[17]

As we have said, we are by extension implying the utility of studying lines like these in tandem with "named" or famous texts like the Lucretia narratives, for the sake of contrast within a more broad concept of medieval rape culture. In contrast to the passages from Lydgate, where stylistically and morally focused circumlocution fills lines and lines, here, the use of sexual force fills just over two: "ne s'en pout deffendre / lou jeu d'amors sens atendre / li fix." Formal elements—in particular the riding rhythm set by "m'alai chevalchant" earlier in the same poem, together with its rhyme scheme and singsong refrain—frame the transition between assault ("You know you want it") and acceptance ("She wanted it"), in the name of art or entertainment. Here as elsewhere, the reader is to assume that the female victim in the pastourelle experiences pleasure: implicitly, given an original context of sung entertainment, who would not?[18] All of this, of course, is potential classroom dynamite. We would be remiss if we did not put forward the debate around the number of French pastourelles which actually do contain rape as constituting a highly useful set of contextual readings for undergraduates;[19] however, it cannot be denied that ongoing classroom speculation about whether a rape has occurred must be very carefully framed.

It is precisely in the context of the teaching difficulties outlined above that principles from victimology can intervene, focusing attention back on the crime and victim, as depicted in a given text. First, victimology's stress on consent, as iterated in legal definitions of rape, redirects interpretive energy to the victim's self-expression, even as this is created or rendered by a male author.[20] In many pastourelles, we can point out to fellow readers that the male narrator's demand *for* consent is of far greater rhetorical weight than the female subject's acquiescence: as seems characteristic for more developed thirteenth-century renditions of the genre, the motion

---

17 "I threw her on the grass—she couldn't defend herself—I did the game of love to her—she started singing with a joyful heart." Bartsch, *Romances et pastourelles*, II 8, p. 112.

18 On performative qualities of pastourelles, for instance, in the Montpellier texts, see Sylvia Huot, *Allegorical Play in the Old French Motet* (Stanford: Stanford University Press, 1997).

19 See inter al. the following exchange of views on rape in the pastourelle genre: Kathryn Gravdal, "Camouflaging Rape: The Rhetoric of Sexual Violence in the Medieval Pastourelle," *Romanic Review* 76 (1984), 361–73; William Paden, "Rape in the Pastourelle," *Romanic Review* 80 (1989), 331–49; Gravdal, *Ravishing Maidens*, 105 and *passim*.

20 Of course, rape laws vary among states and countries. In line with our interdisciplinary approach here, we recommend—dependent on classroom context—giving students the opportunity to research rape laws germane to them, perhaps in the context of a daily journal assignment or of study questions. In the United States, these laws might be researched through a nonprofit website such as RAINN's "The Laws In Your State," Rape, Abuse, and National Incest Network, accessed January 15, 2015, www.rainn.org/public-policy/laws-in-your-state.

from resistance through rape to the female character's expression of pleasure will often span two or more stanzas. The outcome (which we argue should always be a pedagogical focus in texts like the one under discussion) will often run as follows:

> Quant l'ai despucelee,
> si s'est en piez levee;
> en haut s'est escri
> "Bien vos suis eschapee!"
> Treize anz a que fui nee,
> par mien escient;
> onques més n'oi matinee
> que j'amasse tant!"[21]

There are many aspects of this lyric which might prove difficult to discuss with undergraduates: the highly non-euphemistic report of taking of virginity (or does he, based on the closing lines?), the ironic reaction of the thirteen-year-old victim ("Bien vos suis eschapee!"). We are not suggesting that this reading assignment would work well with every group of students. Still, within skilfully crafted language, students can readily locate her denial of consent—"ele s'escrie et jure / que de mon geu n'a cure"—and subsequent cries of pain: "tant m'est asprete et dure." A focus on locating textual elements which show consent may give certain students a deeper understanding of ethically involved *explication de texte*.

At the same time as it allows its research subjects to identify their experiences as rape or not rape, victimology applies a legal definition to the physical events of rape: in most American states, penetration of the vagina, mouth, or anus by a penis, fingers, or objects as the result of force or being unable to give consent or resist due to a mental or physical impairment caused by an illness or by some form of intoxication. In the literature classroom, invoking clear legal definitions works to refocus interpretation on physicality and literalness of a given depiction of rape. This countervails a necessary focus on symbol to produce a balanced reading, given that medieval literature almost always deploys symbol. In Lydgate's Lucretia narratives, for example, rape's presence is deflected via simile and quasi symbolism:

> Lik a leoun, ful sterne of look and face,
> With his lefft hand my throte he dede enbrace,
> And in his other heeld ageyn al lawe
> Me for to oppresse a naked suerd idrawe.[22]

---

21 "When I had taken her virginity,
    She got up on her feet;
    She cried aloud,
    I got away from you!
    It's thirteen years since I was born,
    As I well know;
    I've never spent a morning
    That I've enjoyed so much!"

Text and translation from Paden, *The Medieval Pastourelle*, 67.
22 Lydgate, *Fall of Princes*, III.1093–99.

Secular love lyric, meanwhile, is one with Lydgate's stylized love tragedy in its use of physical elements in the service of sexual innuendo. If stylized deployment of symbol in the foregoing examples is seen as divesting the rape acts depicted of their physicality, this may create confusion during a period of study, the undergraduate literature major, when students are just learning to decode complex symbolism. Introducing legal definitions of rape to classroom discourse—a teaching principle borrowed from victimology—by contrast both resituates physicality and encourages active interpretation of physicality in narratives of rape containing complex literary elements. For instance, using a current legal definition, Piece LXXXXV in the Chansonnier de Montpellier could not be more direct in its poetic rendering of rape:

> "An Diex! an! que ferai?
> Tu me bleches trop de ton ne sai quoi,
> n'onques a tel jeu certes ne jouai
>
> ...
>
> Pour Diu, espargne moi
> fei toi, lieve toi!"[23]

Metre and rhyme are clearly intended formal features of this selection; ostensibly, the dialogue intends humour. In a physical and legal context, however, what is happening is clearly rape. Passages like this clearly suggest to us that including a *current* legal definition of rape is a *sine qua non* when teaching such texts. The teaching challenge here may differ from the poem cited above: the issue is not so much to extrapolate consent and the action of rape from literary innuendo as it is to interrogate the meaning of a more readily identifiable physicality. Such physicality might be also be resituated via study in "grander" medieval texts—tragedies allegedly based in history, as Lydgate's and Gower's Canacee, Virginia, Lucretia, and so on, some of which have the Augustinian biases in terms of female sexuality discussed above—using the same definitions used by law and victimology in tandem with more explicit accounts of rape such as those in the pastourelle cited above. Pairing or grouping texts of different stylistic levels in this way reveals rape culture as a functional aspect of medieval literary discourse.

As a concluding note to this section, here or elsewhere there is an argument to be made for students' attempting their own translations of Old French or Middle English texts; even where there is little or no pre-existing study of either language, dictionary assignments focusing on individual words (what does *geu* mean here? *despucelee*?) work well in early-period literature classes. We are also operating from the assumption that texts like these were known to Chaucer and other Middle English authors and can provide yet another useful context for them. In instances like those cited here, again, such assignments give the students enhanced understanding of the physicality of a given poem—something which in-class discussion of symbol or

---

23 "Oh God! oh! what shall I do? You are hurting me too much with your don't-know-what. I have surely never played this game ... Dear God, spare me! Stop! Get off me!" Rivière, *Pastourelles*, 55.

metaphor will sometimes obscure—as does a deliberate emphasis on tone. This is by extension an argument for helping students to ground interpretive speculation in concrete elements, mainline or marginal, of the texts involved.

The Victim Herself: Characterological Judgments, Victim-Blaming, Precipitating Factors

Victimology, once again, is the study proper of being a victim. In terms of literature classes which cover the Middle Ages, this makes victimology's concept of victimhood a useful counterpoise to classroom discussion of medieval anti-feminism, which on the one hand serves to historicize many or most later medieval texts about women but which on the other hand tends both to mute the voices and to negate the physical presences of female figures or characters depicted as suffering sexual violence. Medieval texts' constructions of victimhood, like their constructions of the rape act, constitute specific teaching problems. For instructors wishing to teach such texts, awkward moments in teaching spring from texts' stereotyping of female behaviours and characteristics, as well as from their symbolic misogynies: as Rachel Warburton has remarked, in medieval literature, "[n]otions of femininity, particularly the evaluative 'good woman,' are intimately linked to concepts of 'rapability.' "[24] Students will be analyzing these linked concepts with all the difficulty that that entails. First, to put it bluntly, women are stereotyped in medieval romantic texts in terms of their physical qualities. For instance, many pastourelles imply that a female character has participated in her own assault simply because her physical qualities have incited the male narrator to lust:

> moult se gamente forment
> maix ceu m'alume et esprant,
> ke je vix par la viselle
> la char desous la mamelle
> plus blanche ke nul airgent.[25]

Together with the shepherdess's solitary state, here as throughout the genre ("Seule sanz compaignon estoit"), her exposed skin and beauty become the narrator's cue to rape her. All of this in some sense goes back to traditional medieval anti-feminism, and excerpts from an anthology of anti-feminist texts (Blamires's *Woman Defamed and Woman Defended* springs to mind) may well assist the instructor in providing context. As we have seen, meanwhile, the "flip side" of the women stereotyped in the pastourelles as approachable, as "rapable" "loose women," even, is the idealization of unattainable chastity such as that delineated by Isidore in his *Sentences*: "Amanda

---

24 Rachel Warburton, "Reading Rape in Chaucer; Or, Are Cecily, Lucretia, and Philomela Good Women?," in *Diversifying the Discourse: The Florence Howe Award for Feminist Scholarship, 1990–2004*, eds. Roseanne Default and Mihoko Suzuki (New York: MLA, 2006), 270–87.
25 "She lamented loudly, but this only turned me on as I saw the skin under her breasts, whiter than any silver." Bartsch, *Romances et pastourelles*, II 2, 107.

est pulchritudo castitatis, cuius degustata delectatio dulcior invenitur quam carnis. Castitas enim fructus suavitatis est, et pulchritudo inviolata sanctorum. Castitas securitas mentis, sanitas corporis."[26] Yet, tragedies of chaste women are one with the pastourelles' figuration of women in their simultaneous reduction of victim and victimization to and complexification of victim and victimization *via* symbolhood. Female figures in these tragedies of "good women" come to stand in for abstract virtues at the expense of their human qualities. This, in fact, is what Lydgate's tragedy of Lucretia, with its noun-dense poetic, most suggests.

We might, for instance, pair the depersonalizations of women we have seen in the pastourelle with the rendering as allegory of an ostensibly literal female constituted by the following passage, one of Lydgate's accounts of Lucretia's reaction to her own rape (told through a male narrator). Both reveal a "rape culture" of some kind. In the *Fall of Princes*, Lucretia's husband tells her that during her rape

> ... thou [Lucrece] were off herte ay oon,
> To all fals lustis contraire in gouernaunce
> Mor like an ymage korue out off a ston,
> Than lik a woman flesshli of plesaunce ...[27]

It will be seen that this passage, while it lauds Lucretia's conduct, nonetheless renders her more as an object ("like an ymage") rather than as a human entity; even in a passage that draws on the Augustinian mind–body duality cited above, the only way for her to have resisted rape is to have become object-like. Thus this passage objectifies a female rape victim, hence representing rape culture, as surely as do any of the pastourelles we have discussed above.

In the contemporary literary classroom, whose students are generally the products of a culture that is intensely visual in nature, there may well be a tendency to take this visual cum moral stereotyping of women's characters on trust. This makes it easy to forget or, under time constraints, to gloss over a cultivated understanding that, while these poems are popular entertainments, they are also the product of a society that used the physical as a cipher for the moral: precisely the cipher that justifies depiction of rape within a given text.

While textual moments like those described above may lead the instructor very readily to draw analogies between the pastourelle and other medieval genres and contemporary humour or satire like the "D" meme we mentioned above, this may prove to be a double-edged sword. Students are not always comfortable with such analogies, which may facilitate discussion with one group of students even as they close it down for another. What is clear, in any case, is that none of the interpretive issues outlined above—texts' stereotyping of women, body and soul, texts' reliance on the broader tradition of medieval anti-feminism—should preclude interpretation of female figures

---

26 "The beauty of chastity is to be loved, whose delight once tasted is found to be sweeter than that of the flesh. Indeed, chastity is the fruit of sweetness and the inviolate beauty of the saints. Chastity is security of the mind and health of the body." Isidore of Seville, *Sententiarum libri tres*, II.40.5 (PL 83.643–4).
27 Lydgate, *Fall of Princes*, II.1177–80.

in these texts qua victims. Absent consent, physical encounters like those outlined above should be read as rape; nor, by victimological standards, does a given female character's isolation or state of dress mean that we should automatically read her fate in a given text as punishment *or* reward (another pitfall of time-constrained classroom discussion. None of these texts is precisely a moralizing fable).

Given the problems inherent in these texts for beginning students of medieval literature, then, victimology's research-based characterizations of the victim will prove as pertinent as victimology's definitions of rape itself. First, victimology addresses notions of "characterological judgment." Victimology would express the stereotyping inherent in medieval constructs of gender as "characterological judgment," whether it be a judgment on the victim ("She's a bad person, so she deserves it." "She was pretty, so she deserves it") or on the victimizer ("He's too nice to be a rapist"). Victimology likewise emphasizes that neither trait relates to the physicality or legality of rape.[28] With this in mind, we can turn back to medieval texts with renewed awareness that anti-feminist stereotypes *are* characterological judgments. On the one hand, in passages like those cited above, the rapist/narrator's account of the shepherdess/victim's isolation and exposed dress, those elements which lead him to rape her, may be described as "characterological" evaluations.

On the other hand, the framing of this rape narrative in courtly love poetry quite arguably demands of the reader a parallel judgment that teller and tale are benign ("He is a noble lover." "His poetic sensibilities are too fine for him to be committing harm"); indeed, it might be argued that courtly poetry in general contains an element of pleading to be so judged. In a classroom context, this gives literature students in particular great power over reading materials: reading a given narrator's statements as characterological judgments strikes a middle place between trying and failing to read authorial intent on the one hand and trying and half-succeeding to read love lyrics simply as historical or sociological documents on the other.

A second concept from victimology of utility in the medieval literature classroom meanwhile, intimately connected to victimology's discussion of characterology, is that of victim-blaming. In victimology terms, blaming rape victims for what has happened to them is an unfortunate but common occurrence, and from the victimologist's perspective, this concept is an important one to explain to undergraduates.[29] Student

---

28 Barrie Bondurant, "University Women's Acknowledgement of Rape: Individual, Situational, and Social Factors," *Violence Against Women* 104 (2001): 300–1.

29 Studies show that college students of both genders encounter interpretive issues associated with victim-blaming. In particular, male college students who endorse myths about rape tend to blame victims more so than women and believe that if a woman really wanted to do so, she could prevent rape, thus supporting the male point of view presented in the literature. At the same time, women college students also blame rape victims under certain conditions believed to have contributed to the assault. College women blame rape victims whose behaviour was "inappropriate"—drinking too much, dressing in too little, and going to parties with strangers. Because drinking is a part of the college experience on some campuses, this becomes an important point of discussion in the classroom. See, e.g., Katherine P. Luke, "Drunk Girls Are Easy: Engagement with the 'Slutty' Discourse and its Implications for Sexual Violence," paper presented at the meeting of the American Sociological Association, Montreal, Canada, August 2006.

understanding of rape myths may thus impact reading by both genders of medieval texts involving rape, and we may also situate victim-blaming within the text itself. In many pastourelles, for example, the narrator may view his intended "conquest" as independently ready for intimacy, perhaps even as pleasuring herself: "resgardai la tousete / ke se desduisoit."[30] Pastourelles in particular will often draw an analogy between a female figure's outward and inward appearance, emphasizing in particular the traditional, textually reinforced assumption that women are fickle: "[F]emme fait bien ceu k'elle doit," Robin, the raped woman's stock swain, remarks in the first lyric we cited.[31] That is, she does what she "should." She does what is in her "nature." Some poems show the woman transferring her affections from Robin to the narrator once raped; still others have her berating her erstwhile swain for leaving her even as she and the narrator are engaged in intercourse.

All of this may be categorized as victim-blaming by the narrator or author ("She brought the situation on herself through her open behaviour." "As a woman, incitement was only to be expected of her")—and discussed as such in class. The concept of "victim-blaming" may thus serve to problematize instructors' and students' tendencies to draw simple dichotomies between literal and symbolic aspects of a literary scenario. In other words, instead of simply drawing a distinction between literal and figurative aspects of the victim as portrayed in a literary depiction of rape (many of which use symbolic anti-feminism) we can also ask our students and ourselves to interrogate whether or not a male figure or male narrator practises victim-blaming. The result will be to reascribe attitudes and utterances *to* these male figures, reinforcing to students the value of concrete, text-based readings.

A final aspect of victimology which can foster ethical and innovative readings in the medieval literature classroom is victimology's conceptualization of precipitating factors. Victimology currently emphasizes examining contributing factors to rape without assigning characterological blame. While, during the field's emergence, research largely focused on identifying characteristics of people that make them more likely to experience a criminal victimization, this approach has been criticized for contributing to judging victims for their experiences; however, by contrast, one aspect of modern victimology focuses on identifying the precipitating factors to rape without passing judgment on the victim, including those which can be misinterpreted by perpetrators as an invitation to engage in sexual activity.[32]

This concept of precipitating factors is an especially useful one to raise when teaching about medieval crime, about texts which depict rape in particular: as we have seen, such texts convert precipitating factors to objects of literary symbolism.

---

30 "I beheld the girl, amusing herself." Bartsch, *Romances et pastourelles*, II 8, p. 112.

31 The sense is "woman does what is expected of her" or "woman does what is in her nature to do." Bartsch, *Romances et pastourelles*, II 12, p. 120.

32 Examples of precipitating factors include drinking by either person, the victim's reputation, or the going inside one of their houses. The concept of precipitating factors originates in part in Menachem Amir, "Victim Precipitated Forcible Rape," *Journal of Criminal Law, Criminology & Police Science* 493 (1967), 493–502.

Participants in classroom discussion might refocus and regenerate interpretations by using the concept from victimology of precipitating factors to explore setting in pastourelle narratives. Distant kin to the classic *locus amoenus*, or else to the garden of youth in Guillaume de Lorris's *Roman de la Rose*, wooded spaces in the pastourelle genre carve out a "play space" where rape may occur.[33]

Equally, pastourelle may be viewed as an allegory of class, one where the knight (narrator, rapist) asserts his rights over a peasant victim: as Geri L. Smith remarks, "Rape is the scenario in which status and gender collide most explosively."[34] When this is recognized in a classroom context by focusing on precipitating factors, it breaks the discussion wide open: instead of stereotyping "knights," "ladies," and "love stories," we can situate the text in a wider conversation about how injustice of circumstance leads to rape, both in the literal meaning of the poem and in the wider context of class allegories.

In literary study, it is even possible, as in the case of the retellings of the Lucretia tragedy, to carry the idea of precipitating factors out to interpret the senses in which a rape victim becomes the victim of a broader context, historical or literary. Per Lydgate, Tarquin the Elder's descendants "longe in Rome hadde dominacioun / Till his kynrede and generacioun, / For thoffence doon onto Lucrece, / Caused off kynges the name [for] to cese."[35] While Sextus Tarquinius' rape of Lucretia is what led to the line's downfall, this may be read as a sort of victim-blaming all the same. At the same time, the *Fall of Princes* (like the text of which it purports to be a translation, Boccaccio's *De casibus virorum illustrium*) is an encyclopedic history of, in part, the workings of Fortune in the universe. Lucretia may well be a victim of cosmic or allegorical "precipitating factors," one accordingly who suffers commensurate or appropriate violence.[36]

Bystander Theory

A final area where principles from victimology can provide both support and innovation in the undergraduate classroom is in terms of their interacting with medieval concepts of a bystander or bystanders. The term "bystander" in victimology differs radically from notions of the bystander inherent in medieval texts. Whereas victimology acknowledges that very few rapes happen in the presence of witnesses, literary depictions of crime in the late Middle Ages are *notable* for being framed through bystanders, right down to affective lyric portrayals of, say, Mary's suffering at the

---

33 Corinne Saunders notes the close kinship between the *fin'amors* and violence presented both in the *Roman de la rose* and in the pastourelle itself. Corinne Saunders, *Rape and Ravishment in the Literature of Medieval England* (Cambridge: Boydell, 2001), 191.
34 Geri L. Smith, *The Medieval French Pastourelle Tradition: Poetic Motivations and Generic Transformations* (Gainsville: University Press of Florida, 2009), 31.
35 Lydgate, *Fall of Princes*, III.936–8.
36 One of the most provocative treatments of Lucretia qua political allegory, also of potential utility to classroom explorations such as those outlined here, is Stephanie Jed, *Chaste Thinking: The Rape of Lucretia and the Birth of Humanism* (Bloomington: University of Indiana Press, 1989).

Crucifixion: indeed, samples of affective lyrics might present a useful teaching analogue to concepts of the bystander in victimology as applied to medieval literature, as might manuscript images of Lucretia's suicide, in which she is characteristically surrounded by males of specific family and social ranks. Late medieval renderings of these tragedies parallel their depictions, deflecting women's sufferings on to those of her male relatives and other bystanders. Classroom discussion predictably focuses on such deflections; however, at the same time, paradoxically enough, devoting classroom time to them can perpetuate an emphasis on the male figures, rather than refocusing attention to what traces of the victim and her victimhood remain in a text that works in this fashion.

In pastourelles, meanwhile—once again, we are suggesting that these texts exist on a broad continuum with texts like the Virginia and Lucretia narratives— the female victim's perspective is wholly subsumed to that of her male rapist. We might begin by making the perhaps basic point that pastourelles depicting rape are almost exclusively first-person narratives by rapists! At the same time, bystanders in pastourelles (notably the woman's swain, sometimes named Robin) often prove ineffective when the female character or speaker is assaulted.

Even in those texts where a Robin prevails, either in loving his lady or in fighting off her assailant, a male narrator continues to control the scene qua voyeur, as do narrators in related forms (romance, romantic love lyric). In one lyric from the Montpellier texts we even have a remarkable example of this phenomenon where the rapist coopts not just the body of the woman whom he encounters but her very thought processes: "truis pastoure / samblant fait de plourer / Je li requis."[37]

The approaches outlined above mandate a focus on text: one where individual words and expressions, both from victimology and from the source texts, should be given classroom space in the service of generating classroom-driven interpretations. Time will be of the essence, and the direction of discussion will vary from group to group. Consequently, instructors may feel that they are re-enacting or re-implementing a text's voyeuristic framework through retelling, rather than interpreting it as misogynistic voyeurism. Bystander theory from victimology can step in here, giving undergraduates new reading tools to apply to these literary models. From a victimological perspective, the term "bystanders" refers to people who may witness events leading up to a rape or communication that might encourage a rape, with special emphasis on the role of male peer presence: research suggests, that in some male-dominated groups, an atmosphere exists that encourages rape even if the woman will not consent to sex.

"Male peer presence"[38] in particular is a concept that can be carried out to classroom interpretations of the genres under discussion in this study. We might even

---

37 "I found a shepherdess pretending to cry. I asked her what her thoughts were." Rivière, 77.
38 For a discussion of male peer presence/support, see Martin D. Schwartz, Walter S. DeKeseredy, David Tait, and Shahid Alvi, "Male Peer Support and a Feminist Routine Activities Theory: Understanding Sexual Assault on the College Campus," *Justice Quarterly* 18 (2001): 623–49.

broach in classroom discussion the idea of romantic love poetry of the thirteenth century written by males as being entries in literary competition, rather than as being written for a female audience, or else the male-dominated discourse of Lydgate's fifteenth-century patronage model, both of which arguably create a "male peer presence" context for rape narratives. Yet equally, in victimology, when people fail to intervene at primary points preceding rape, they become bystanders to the circumstances that set up a rape event, perhaps even to a rape itself, essentially contributing to the commission of a crime. As we saw above, the rape tragedies like Lucretia are framed by male narration but also the offence is dislocated on to male bystanders. It is possible to identify these bystanders as non-interveners contributing to commission as described.

Ultimately, it is hoped, introducing victimology's theorization of bystander roles may serve to counterbalance medieval literature's frequent assertions that rape, especially of noble women, is a crime against a larger social group, even against society as a whole, rather than first and foremost a crime against the woman herself. On the one hand, this is a highly useful historicizing lens through which to study texts like the medieval Lucretia and Virginia narratives. On the other hand, by contrast, reading these texts through victimology's construction of the bystander resituates attitudes and behaviours in male plots and characters, facilitating a more balanced classroom approach to texts with potent but antiquated symbolism. Given evidence of group involvement in rapes and rape culture on college campuses, it seems that bystander issues may be especially sensitive. Still it seems that being aware of these terms would give students of medieval literature tools for critical consideration of the literature while informing their lives as students on a college campus.

Conclusion

We feel that the approach to teaching we have outlined above has many advantages. In the first place, an emphasis on "outlier" texts like the ones we have described can facilitate readings of medieval texts that are (1) more mainstream (read: more likely to be included in undergraduate literature curricula) and (2) more subtly expressive of what might be described as rape culture, in whatever literary period. From seeing how interplay between literature and victimology concepts operates in the raw, undisciplined space which these lyrics inhabit, students and instructor alike may turn with fresh eyes to the more closely guarded spaces of romance and personification allegory. Apart from the advantages associated with a focus on context, teaching perspectives from victimology can, as we have seen, resituate texts in their physicality, paradoxically honing and rendering more sophisticated students' reading of symbol. Admittedly, we are arguing here for a focus on the literalness of rape in texts from a literary period, broadly conceived, where the concept of literature is almost inseparable *from* its symbolic dimensions. It may also be true that many beginning students of literature are attracted to medieval literature precisely because it embeds decoding mechanisms, just as some undergraduates are also attracted to gaming, fantasy literature, and other complex imaginative worlds and will thus find a focus on a text's concrete and material elements less immediately attractive. As small liberal arts college professors, however, we have come to believe that students of the early 2000s need sensitive and innovative strategies as they negotiate the complex interpretive demands of the world around them. Some of these they cultivate themselves: the #rapeculture hashtags on tumblr, twitter, and so on spring to mind.[39] At other points, as with the Steubenville rape case of 2012, young adults may simply find themselves in the middle of interpreting social and news media and the law itself. Concepts of readership appear to evolve and make new demands on incipient college-level readers. Sometimes a new concept is an old concept made new: a student who can scan a pastourelle for upbeat end rhymes and read them against his outline of a crime expressed in literature, or who can analogize a glossed Bible or manuscript image of Lucretia to concepts of the bystander from victimology, is a student who is more equipped than his or her peers to handle further interpretive challenges.

In all of this, we may enjoy the classroom *in se* as a space of play and open dialogue. Ultimately, however, what we have argued for here is a thoroughgoing interdisciplinary approach, one that fails to shy away from the interpretive complexity of these materials. We are not saying that students who can discern rape in a medieval text will be able to interpret rape as specialists; we are saying that principles from victimology can make students more savvy, more empathetic, and more ethical readers of literature, ultimately (we trust) of the world at large.

Works Cited

Amir, Menachem. "Victim Precipitated Forcible Rape." *Journal of Criminal Law, Criminology & Police Science* 58 (1967): 493–502.

Bartsch, Karl. *Romances et pastourelles des XIIe et XIIIe siècle.* Leipzig: Vogel, 1870.

Bondurant, Barrie. "University Women's Acknowledgement of Rape: Individual, Situational, and Social Factors." *Violence Against Women* 7 (2001): 294–335.

Brundage, James A. *Law, Sex, and Christianity in Medieval Europe.* Chicago: University of Chicago Press, 1987.

"The D." Cheezburger Group. http://knowyourmeme.com/memes/the-d (accessed January 15, 2015).

Daigle, Leah. *Victimology: The Essentials.* Los Angeles: Sage, 2013.

Gravdal, Kathryn. "Camouflaging Rape: The Rhetoric of Sexual Violence in the Medieval Pastourelle." *Romanic Review* 76 (1984): 361–73.

———. *Ravishing Maidens: Writing Rape in Medieval French Literature and Law.* Philadelphia: University of Philadelphia Press, 1991.

Horne, Kenneth W. "A Constructivist Grounded Theory of Social Media Literacy and Identity Influence: Traditional-Age Undergraduate Students and Their Experiences." M.Ed. thesis. University of Chicago, 2013.

---

[39] See, e.g., Carrie A. Rentschler, "Rape Culture and the Feminist Politics of Social Media," *Girlhood Studies* 7 (2014): 65–82.

Huot, Sylvia. *Allegorical Play in the Old French Motet.* Stanford: Stanford University Press, 1997.

Isidore of Seville. *Sententiarum libri tres.* Edited by J. P. Migne. Patrilogia Latina. Vol. 83. Paris, 1844–1855.

Jed, Stephanie. *Chaste Thinking: The Rape of Lucretia and the Birth of Humanism.* Bloomington: University of Indiana Press, 1989.

Karras, Ruth M. *Sexuality in Medieval Europe: Doing unto Others.* New York: Routledge, 2005.

"The Laws In Your State." Rape, Abuse, and National Incest Network (RAINN). www.rainn.org/public-policy/laws-in-your-state (accessed January 15, 2015).

Luke, Katherine P. "Drunk Girls Are Easy: Engagement with the 'Slutty' Discourse and its Implications for Sexual Violence." Paper presented at the meeting of the American Sociological Association. Montreal, Canada. August 2006.

Lydgate, John. *Fall of Princes*, edited by Henry Bergen. 4 vols., EETS ES, 121, 122, 123, 124. London: Oxford University Press, 1924–1927.

Paden, William D., ed. and translated by *The Medieval Pastourelle.* New York: Garland, 1987.

———. "Rape in the Pastourelle." *Romanic Review* 80 (1989): 331–49.

Rentschler, Carrie A. "Rape Culture and the Feminist Politics of Social Media." *Girlhood Studies* 7 (2014): 65–82.

Rivière, Jean Claude. *Pastourelles: Texte des chansonniers de la Bibliothèque nationale (suite) et de la Bibliothèque vaticane, motets anonymes des chansonniers de Montpellier et de Bamberg, avec notes.* Geneva: Droz, 1974.

Saunders, Corinne. *Rape and Ravishment in the Literature of Medieval England.* Cambridge: Boydell, 2001.

Schwartz, Martin D., Walter S. DeKeseredy, David Tait, and Shahid Alvi. "Male Peer Support and a Feminist Routine Activities Theory: Understanding Sexual Assault on the College Campus." *Justice Quarterly* 18 (2001): 623–49.

"She Wants the D Quotes." SearchQuotes. www.searchquotes.com/search/She_Wants_The_D/1/ (accessed February 12, 2015).

Smith, Geri L. *The Medieval French Pastourelle Tradition: Poetic Motivations and Generic Transformations.* Gainsville: University Press of Florida, 2009.

Warburton, Rachel. "Reading Rape in Chaucer; Or, Are Cecily, Lucretia, and Philomela Good Women?" In *Diversifying the Discourse: The Florence Howe Award for Feminist Scholarship, 1990–2004*, edited by Roseanne Default and Mihoko Suzuki, 270–87. New York: MLA, 2006.

Chapter 4

BRINGING THE BYSTANDER INTO THE HUMANITIES CLASSROOM: READING ANCIENT, PATRISTIC, AND MEDIEVAL TEXTS ON THE CONTINUUM OF VIOLENCE

ELIZABETH A. HUBBLE

Introduction

Every spring semester at The University of Montana-Missoula (UM), I teach a first-year Women's and Gender Studies course entitled WGSS 163L Historical and Literary Perspectives on Women with an average enrollment of thirty-five students.[1] The "L" in the title indicates that the course fulfils a general education requirement as a Literary Studies course, and thus it always attracts a fair number of students (50 per cent) who are not necessarily seeking a degree in Women's and Gender Studies, but who have at least a passing interest in women's history and literature. In general, the class demographics are fairly typical of Women's and Gender Studies classes—primarily traditional-aged women (over 75 per cent) and LGBTIQ-identified students majoring in the humanities and social sciences. This class serves as a feminist counterpart to UM's Great Books courses, LSH 151L Introduction to the Humanities I, and LSH 152L Introduction to the Humanities II.[2] These two Liberal Studies courses are exactly that—an overview of canonical texts in the Western tradition. WGSS 163L engages with the same time periods (ancient through medieval and early modern to present) but few of the same authors.[3]

In WGSS 163L, students read excerpts from the Bible, excerpts from the patristic theologians St. Jerome and Tertullian, and excerpts from the late fifteenth-century

---

1 In spring 2014, the course had the maximum enrollment of thirty-five students, only two of whom identified as male.

2 I do not in any way wish to imply that LSH 151L and LSH 152L cannot be feminist courses. I regularly teach both of those classes, and my approach is definitely feminist. However, those courses require the instructor or students to bring a feminist lens to the readings of canonical texts, as opposed to WGSS 163L where the objectives of the course are *a priori* feminist.

3 The only overlap in the way I teach the courses are excerpts from the Bible (Genesis, Ruth, Esther, Judith, The Song of Songs, and the Letters of Paul), Sappho, Euripides' *Medea*, Christine de Pizan, and Mary Wollstonecraft. In LSH 152L, brief excerpts of *The Book of the City of Ladies* and *A Vindication of the Rights of Women* are taught in some sections, including my own. Students read the complete books in WGSS 163L.

witch-hunter text *Malleus Maleficarum* by Heinrich Kramer and Jacob Sprenger as context for the world in which the ancient and medieval women authors I assign produced their works.[4] In the medieval period, students read both *The Selected Writings of Hildegard of Bingen* and Christine de Pizan's *Book of the City of Ladies*.[5] The learning outcomes for the course state:

1) Students will develop an understanding of the different ways Western societies and cultures have viewed and constructed gender, oppression, and privilege.

2) Students will learn to analyze social norms and institutions (including governments, educational systems, the church, and the family) as they relate to gender and other concepts such as sexuality, race, and class.

3) Students will develop an awareness of the role women authors have played throughout history and learn to evaluate texts authored by women within and against the context of the Western canonical tradition.

4) Students will develop critical thinking and communication skills through in-class discussions, exams, informal writing assignments, and online discussion forums.

5) Students will learn the basics of how Western historiographical and literary studies traditions have evaluated, included, and/or excluded women authors' texts and contributions.

I inform the students from the first day that they will be encouraged to connect the readings to contemporary issues, as outlined in Learning Outcomes 1 and 2. This approach has always allowed me to use the patristic and medieval texts to examine the ways that discourses of misogyny have shifted (or not) over time. More recently, building on Learning Outcome 4 and in response to UM's specific circumstances (see below), I have started utilizing these texts and the responses to them explicitly as teaching moments around the issue of rape culture on campuses and in our society today, using the bystander intervention trainings and techniques I discuss below as the theoretical lens.

Institutional Background

The University of Montana-Missoula is a midsize, liberal arts, state university located in western Montana and has an annual enrollment of around 13,500 students, both undergraduates and graduates. In Autumn 2011, UM received notification that the

---

4 "Jerome 347–419 AD," www.womenpriests.org/traditio/; "Tertullian 155–245 AD," www.womenpriests.org/traditio/; excerpts of the *Malleus Maleficarum* by Heinrich Kramer and Jacob Sprenger (1486) from Alan Charles Kors and Edward Peters, *Witchcraft in Europe, 400–1700: A Documentary History*, 2nd ed. (Philadelphia: University of Pennsylvania Press, 2001), 176–229. NB: It is widely accepted that Kramer is the primary author of the *Malleus*.
5 Hildegard of Bingen, *Selected Writings*, trans. Mark Atherton (New York: Penguin, 2001). Christine de Pizan, *Book of the City of Ladies*, trans. Rosalind Brown-Grant (New York: Penguin, 1999).

United States Department of Justice (DOJ), Department of Education, and the DOJ Office of Civil Rights were initiating a Title IX investigation in regards to the handling of sexual assaults on campus.[6] The investigation began, in part, because of two high-profile sexual assault cases involving UM students and athletes in late 2011 with allegations of mishandling on the part of university employees, but expanded to include cases dating back to 2008. The investigation and the outcomes received extensive local and national media coverage.[7]

Prior to the arrival of the DOJ investigators in Summer 2012, UM President Royce Engstrom, who had only been in the job for one year, engaged the service of former Montana Supreme Court Justice Diane Barz to conduct a separate investigation. The Barz Report made nine recommendations based on her findings that victim services were underfunded, that employees and students were undertrained, and that employee mandatory reporting requirements were vague and unclear.[8] UM put interim measures in place in response to the Barz Report, prior to the release of the DOJ findings and agreement in May 2013. In part, because of preemptive actions, the DOJ praised UM's cooperation throughout the investigation.[9]

The May 9, 2013, DOJ letter to UM President Engstrom states that UM's DOJ "[a]greement will serve as a blueprint for colleges and universities throughout the country to protect students from sexual harassment and assault."[10] In response to the Barz Report and the DOJ agreement and as a result of receiving a grant from the DOJ Office of Violence Against Women (OVW),[11] UM has instituted number of changes in place, including the creation of an online sexual assault prevention tutorial called PETSA (Personal Empowerment Through Self-Awareness), which I co-authored, and a reorganization and strengthening of the University Council on Student Assault (UCSA).

---

6 The DOJ also conducted investigations of the UM Campus Police, the Missoula Police Department, and the Missoula County Attorney's Office with separate agreements.

7 *The Montana Kaimin*, the UM student newspaper, provides a timeline of the investigation. See Ashley Nerbovig, "Sexual Assault Timeline," *Montana Kaimin*, last modified February 6, 2013, accessed January 21, 2015, www.montanakaimin.com/article_4d5c63c5-2ae4-53c6-a517-7a9e2914e731.html. The timeline references the national media coverage and Freedom of Information Act claims by the *Wall Street Journal* and the local newspaper, *The Missoulian*. Written for a general, non-academic audience, *Missoula* is the source of many non-Montanans' knowledge of the DOJ investigation. See Jon Krakauer, *Missoula: Rape and the Justice System in a College Town* (New York City: Doubleday, 2015).

8 Diane Barz, "Investigation Report," accessed January 20, 2015, www.umt.edu/president/docs/DBarzInvestigationReport.pdf.

9 Anurima Bhargava and Gary Jackson, Letter from U.S. Department of Justice and U.S. Department of Education to President Royce Engstrom and Lucy France, re: DOJ Case No. DJ 169-44-9, OCR Case No. 10126001, accessed January 20, 2015, www2.ed.gov/documents/press-releases/montana-missoula-letter.pdf.

10 Ibid.

11 Our campus grant is actually called a Cooperative Agreement, indicating a higher level of oversight from OVW as a result of our mandated agreement with the DOJ. The grant program is the OVW Grants to Reduce Sexual Assault, Domestic Violence, Dating Violence, and Stalking on Campus Program.

PETSA is mandatory for all UM students, and must be completed before students are allowed to register for their second semester of classes.[12] This requirement is enforced through an electronic registration hold on their student account. Thus, almost all the students in my spring WGSS 163L course have taken it. One of the many benefits of PETSA is that it includes a brief discussion of rape culture and bystander intervention, which means that my students have been presented, even if only briefly, with these concepts. In PETSA, it states:

> College campuses are a part of a larger U.S. culture and many scholars warn of a rape prone culture where prevalent attitudes, norms, and behaviors excuse, minimize, and even encourage sexual violence. This environment creates stereotypical beliefs about women, men, sexuality and power that can lead to a whole range of negative consequences. These stereotypes are reinforced through images, ideas and conversations we are exposed to every day. Without careful thought, we may simply accept them as a way of life.[13]

Moreover, one of the PETSA videos is called "Stand Up, Don't Stand By," and it offers the basics of bystander intervention, including techniques like distraction and separation, providing students with a brief introduction to this promising prevention model which the UCSA builds on in longer trainings.

UCSA, which I co-chair, is the coordinated campus response team to sexual violence and organizes violence prevention efforts on campus.[14] As a university, we recognize that a single, one-time student tutorial is only part of the solution, and many of UCSA's efforts are now focused on reaching students who will never be exposed to violence prevention outside of PETSA. UCSA works tirelessly on campus programming and outreach, including providing longer bystander intervention trainings and integrating violence prevention more broadly into academic curricula through initiatives such as the Student Advocacy Resource Center's (SARC) service "Don't Cancel That Class," a program for absent instructors across campus with workshops on bystander intervention, self-care, healthy relationships, and first responder training.[15]

---

12 As of January 2015, over 23,000 UM students have taken PETSA. UM has also instituted a more broad-based online tutorial covering all forms of sexual harassment and misconduct for employees called the Discrimination Prevention Tutorial. This tutorial is also mandatory.
13 Danielle Wozniak and Elizabeth Hubble, "University of Montana PETSA," 2013. The videos and all materials except for the quiz can be accessed at www.umt.edu/petsa/. PETSA only takes students about 20–25 minutes to complete, so all material in it is presented in a condensed fashion.
14 UCSA has existed since the early 1990s, but had become overly large and unorganized over the years. It has been significantly reorganized based on mandatory OVW technical assistance trainings as a result of UM's grant. Our student advocate centre (SARC) has also been active since the 1990s, but was chronically underfunded and suffered from a lack of campus awareness of their services, in part because of that lack of funding. It has also been reorganized and professionalized through the grant.
15 "Don't Cancel That Class" has proved quite popular, in particular with Psychology, Social Work, Economics, and WGSS professors and instructors. In its inaugural year, AY 2013–2014, over 600 students participated.

Even with the publicity around sexual assault on our campus and with the success of our initiatives, it will always prove difficult to integrate violence prevention into certain classrooms and with certain instructors and students. As many of us who work in this field know, the concept of rape culture is a contested one. To give a personal example, Danielle Wozniak, Christine Fiore, and I published a 2013 article in the journal *Montana Professor* entitled "Transforming a Rape-Prone Culture: Community Change in Cyber Space" about our work on PETSA.[16] At the public forum about the outcome of the UM's DOJ investigation in Spring 2013, a small group of UM faculty members protested this article and publically stated that they would not agree to any sanctions that required them to acknowledge the existence of rape culture, a concept they categorically rejected. Fortunately, while faculty in no way have to agree about the existence of rape culture, UM administration still allowed us to include a discussion of rape culture in our prevention education efforts.

In response to the situation at UM and as an activist and an academic, I have started to work on ways to integrate violence prevention more into my own classes where it was not necessarily an obvious fit (i.e. my first-year literature courses), and to make such curricular infusion part of what is offered at UM.[17] In Spring 2014, I found that using bystander intervention techniques as the theoretical framework to analyze the misogyny in certain literary and historical texts could be an effective way to engage students with little interest in ancient and medieval literature and history by providing a connection to their lived experiences.

Bringing the Bystander into Literary Analysis

As part of UM's multi-faceted efforts to address campus sexual and gender-based violence, we have implemented bystander intervention trainings for all interested parties with a particular focus on Residence Life (RAs), ROTC, Athletics, and student groups. As I stated above, PETSA includes a brief video on bystander intervention techniques, and we build on that introduction in our longer trainings. The trainings are not mandatory, so most of my students have not participated in them.[18] In our bystander-intervention training model (Bringing in the Bystander),[19] we demonstrate how low-risk, high-frequency behaviours such as stereotyping and sexist

---

16 Danielle Wozniak, Christine Fiore, and Elizabeth Hubble, "Transforming a Rape-Prone Culture: Community Change in Cyberspace," *The Montana Professor* 23 (2013), http://mtprof. msun.edu.

17 I also teach WGSS 263S Introduction to Women's and Gender Studies where an entire unit focuses on gender-based violence. Other courses in Social Work, Psychology, and Counsellor Education on our campus directly connect to violence prevention.

18 I offer extra credit to students who choose to participate in the trainings over the course of the semester.

19 R. P. Eckstein, M. M. Moynihan, V. L. Banyard, and E. G. Plante, "Bringing in the Bystander: A Prevention Workshop for Establishing a Community of Responsibility" (2013). "Bringing in the Bystander" is a nationally recognized, best-practice product of Prevention Innovations at the University of New Hampshire.

jokes contribute to rape culture and sexual/gender-based violence. In our trainings, we identify these low-risk, high-frequency behaviours as the best and safest place to intervene along the continuum of violence. We use scenarios such as "you're sitting on your residence hall steps with some friends who start cat-calling women who walk by" and then ask students to brainstorm intervention techniques. In the past, when I thought about how these bystander intervention techniques could be used in the classroom, I had always considered giving students the tools to intervene when someone in the classroom made similarly inappropriate comments. But what if those inappropriate comments and attitudes don't come from the people in the classroom, but from the texts and authors assigned? How can we effectively intervene in those situations and give students tools to read these texts in meaningful ways that acknowledge the issue of gender-based violence?

In my WGSS 163L course, students are required to participate in weekly online discussion forums. Each student is required to start a discussion thread with a comment or question about that week's assigned texts and then respond to two threads initiated by classmates. My classrooms are student-centred, and I often use the online discussion forums to guide classroom discussions. In the discussion forum about the *Malleus Maleficarum* in Spring 2014, one of my students noted:

> I noticed this [constant repetition of women's faults] as well ... It seems that many authors are constantly trying to reiterate the faults of women; but the constant repetition makes me question the point of view of the author. Why must women be portrayed by their faults? It becomes a challenge to read.[20]

As I thought about this comment, I came to realize that, by its very nature, patristic and medieval misogynistic discourse falls on the continuum of gender-based violence on numerous levels. The low-risk, high-frequency behaviours we analyze in our bystander intervention training are not just things that we experience on the streets and in our personal lives, but are also micro-aggressions that we experience in academic texts and discussions.

I started to wonder if the methods we use to intervene when we hear sexist, racist, or homophobic jokes today could also be used to read and understand texts such as Tertullian's. For example, in *De cultu feminarum*, Tertullian states, "You (woman) destroyed so easily God's image, man,"[21] a sentiment that fits into the Pyramid of Hate at the bias/prejudice level. In the rest of this article, I will draw parallels between discussions of St. Jerome, Tertullian, and the *Malleus Maleficarum* and bystander intervention training insights and techniques. In particular, I will look at how statements and attitudes we analyze in bystander intervention trainings—in

---

20 All students' names have been removed and permission was received from all students whose comments appear in this article. I have not edited their comments for grammar or spelling. All comments are from WGSS 163L Students, Online Discussion Forum on the Bible and Church Fathers, and Online Discussion Forum on *The Malleus Maleficarum*, 2014.

21 Tertullian, *De cultu feminarum*, bk 1, chap. 1, accessed January 21, 2015, www.womenpriests.org/traditio/tertul.asp.

particular: 1) Boys Will Be Boys and 2) #NotAllMen—have parallels with what students encounter in assigned texts and classroom discussions around ancient, patristic, and medieval belief systems.

Boys Will Be Boys: The Inevitability/Naturalness of Patriarchy

As my student above noted, misogyny is incredibly repetitive, both within and across texts. The common occurrence of such comments across numerous authors and texts from the ancient, patristic, and medieval world calls to mind Christine de Pizan's statement at the beginning of *The Book of the City of Ladies* that "It is all manner of philosophers, poets and orators too numerous to mention, who all seem to speak with one voice and are unanimous in their view that female nature is wholly given up to vice."[22] In his book *Medieval Misogyny and the Invention of Western Romantic Love*, R. Howard Bloch quotes this passage and cites numerous scholars who have pointed out the same thing—that discourses of misogyny are surprisingly uniform across numerous ancient, patristic, medieval, and later authors.[23] As I do with my students, Bloch looks at Tertullian, Jerome, and other early church fathers to make this point.[24] The threat, from Bloch's point of view, is that "the uniformity of the discourse"[25] leads to arguments for its inevitability—in other words "boys will be boys" because that's just the way things are, i.e. patriarchy is natural, and women are meant to be inferior. In this line of reasoning, women are going against nature by opposing patriarchy. Thus, for the medieval inquisitors who wrote the *Malleus*, the reason that "boys will be boys" was simple—it was because of women's inherent evil, more specifically the work of witches who were behaving "unnaturally."

In the section of the *Malleus* entitled "Why Superstition is chiefly found in Women," Kramer writes:

> What else is woman but a foe to friendship, an unescapable [sic] punishment, a necessary evil, a natural temptation, a desirable calamity, a domestic danger, a delectable detriment, an evil of nature, painted with fair colours![26]

He builds on this description to state:

> Others again have propounded other reasons why there are more supersti-tious women found than men. And the first is, that they are more credulous ... The second reason is, that women are naturally more impressionable ... The third reason is that they have slippery tongues ...[27]

---

22 Pizan, *Book of the City of Ladies*, 6.
23 R. Howard Bloch, *Medieval Misogyny and the Invention of Western Romantic Love* (Chicago: University of Chicago Press, 1991), 2–3.
24 See, in particular, Bloch, *Medieval Misogyny*, chap. 2, "Early Christianity and the Estheticization of Gender."
25 Ibid., 3.
26 Kors and Peters, *Witchcraft in Europe*, 183.
27 Ibid.

In response to these statements about what women are "naturally" like, one of my students pointed out the problem of such essentialism in the discussion forum on the *Malleus*:

> Also, years and years of misogynistic writing probably made it seem easy, even *natural*, to assume that the evil, vile, sinful creatures known as women had to be the sole reason for so much suffering.

I really appreciated her placing of the word "natural" in italics, which demonstrated her awareness that women's evil is not natural but made to "seem" that way. Such comments open up discussions of how gender differences are made to *seem* natural so that gender hierarchies (and rape culture) can be upheld.[28]

One risk of looking at the "uniformity of the discourse" is leaving students feeling disempowered and disheartened at the millennia of misogyny, however "unnatural" it may be. The question for me becomes: How do I both acknowledge the millennia of misogyny while arguing against its inevitability? In the face of such pervasive misogyny, how do I argue that "boys will NOT be boys" and show my students that the processes by which boys become boys are social constructions that can be changed? In response to the student comment above about the repetitiveness of these texts, we discussed how if patriarchy were inevitable or natural, the discourse supporting it wouldn't need to be so repetitive (and it wouldn't constantly be failing to keep women and men in line), and it wouldn't need to be coercive or punitive. In fact, the repetitiveness doesn't point to its inevitability, but to its failure. If female inferiority were natural, women wouldn't have to be continually punished for straying from the "traditional" constructions of femininity, and men wouldn't be punished for "acting like girls."

I ask the students where they see repetitive, coercive, gender policing today. Examples that we come up with include beauty standards (shaving, make-up, dieting), the abstinence movement, and calling men and boys "pussies" and "fags." We further talk about what it means to be a man in patristic theology compared to what it means to be a man today, and discuss how those gender constructions have shifted in some ways while still maintaining patriarchy and male privilege. To provide contrast to the patristic and medieval constructions of masculinity, I show them a painting of King Louis XIV of France (1638–1715) and ask them to compare it to a photo of *People Magazine*'s Sexiest Man of the Year (in 2014, the singer Adam Levine). We brainstorm about what it meant to be a man in patristic and medieval times versus seventeenth-century France versus the United States today. Students note that for the earlier authors, male chastity and a rejection of women/sexuality/body were valued. I reference Tertullian's "use of the image of the soldier ... to defend the manliness of Christians"[29] to help them see how male chastity was positioned as strength and power

---

28 I often use the chapter from Michael Kimmel's *The Gendered Society* called "Ordained by Nature: Biology Constructs the Sexes" as a reference for them to understand the ways that the concept of "natural" is used today. Michael Kimmel, *The Gendered Society* (New York: Oxford University Press, 2011).

29 Mathew Kuefler, *The Manly Eunuch: Masculinity, Gender Ambiguity, and Christian Ideology in Late Antiquity* (Chicago: University of Chicago Press, 2001), 112. Kuefler cites Tertullian, *Apology* 50, and *Ad martyras* 3.1–3.

through the use of military metaphors, co-opting earlier Roman constructions of masculinity. Then we talk about how strength is similarly valued in Louis XIV's representation and is demonstrated through his wearing of a sword and in his elaborate costume (which is greatly at odds with today's performance of masculinity, thus demonstrating a significant shift). The students note that today's dominant masculinity features muscles (strength) and marrying supermodels (virility), as embodied in Levine. Then we consider how demonstrating the constructed, repetitive, yet changeable/adaptable nature of masculinity points to the possibility of altering its manifestations and disrupting its "natural" connection to patriarchy and misogyny.

Arguments for the inevitability of patriarchy fracture through discussions of its coercive and shifting manifestations. The connection to bystander intervention allows us to joke in class about how they can now intervene when someone makes a stereotypical statement about how women are *naturally* monogamous and men are *naturally* promiscuous. I tell them to just say, "But St. Jerome argued the exact opposite and he is considered one of the fathers of Christianity." Students start to see that stereotypical statements about women's sexuality are coercive, deceptive constructs that serve to maintain patriarchy and rape culture across the centuries, and then we can perhaps brainstorm other ways to intervene in situations like this that don't open them up to mocking for being a nerd by referring to ancient saints. This understanding that patriarchy is not inevitable, and that boys don't have to just be boys, can also help to deconstruct the frequent Otherizing that occurs when discussing these texts.

#NotAllMen

In addition to demonstrating that patriarchy is not "natural," I also want to make sure that students don't Otherize ancient, patristic, and medieval discourse in such a way that they dismiss it as alien from their lives, and thus ignore the parallels with today and the ways in which such discourse continues to construct and maintain rape culture. One particular passage in the *Malleus* frequently inspires the tendency to Otherize. Kramer and Sprenger expound at length about "How, as it were, they [witches] Deprive Man of his Virile Member," and include the following passage:

> And what, then, is to be thought of those witches who in this way sometimes collect male organs in great numbers, as many as twenty or thirty members together, and put them in a bird's nest, or shut them up in a box, where they move themselves like living members, and eat oats and corn, as has been seen by many and is a matter of common report?[30]

In Spring 2014, a male student started a discussion thread in response to this passage as part of the forum about the *Malleus*:

> Did anyone find the text to be SO exaggerated in what it says that it was almost like reading The Onion, or something satirical like it? I found myself laughing

---

30 Kors and Peters, *Witchcraft in Europe*, 203.

actually quite a bit while reading it, it was simply too much. Witches stealing our penises made the biggest impression on me by far (made me laugh the hardest too); it kind of points to some odd repressed feelings of insecurity in the writers.[31]

As many professors know, such reactions are common when teaching disparate and yet similarly misogynistic authors such as Ovid and Tertullian. This student's comment points directly to the issue of Otherizing medieval and ancient history and literature. However, using bystander intervention techniques can allow the instructor and students to engage in discussions of these texts that confront this tendency to Otherize.[32]

To facilitate this discussion, I reference Jackson Katz's twenty-first-century work on violence and masculinity to provide examples of how Otherizing works today.[33] Katz analyzes news stories about incidents of gun violence like those in Newtown and Columbine and points out how problematic it is when the media focus on causes such as mental illness and video games rather than masculinity. In fact, as Katz notes, mainstream news sources rarely, if ever, refer to the perpetrators' sex or gender in these cases.[34] Instead, news stories regularly Otherize the perpetrator and help us to ignore the ways that our culture's construction of masculinity produces, at its extreme, such incidents of violence. For example, a *Huffington Post* article from December 2012 about the Newtown Shootings references both perpetrator Adam Lanza's psychological issues and his fascination with first-person shooter video games. In fact, the article begins with the sentence, "He was an awkward, peculiar kid who wore the same clothes to school every day."[35]

This discussion has a strong link to sexual violence prevention because an analysis of Otherizing helps explain why so much focus today is still on risk reduction and

---

31 It must be noted that my student's reaction to the "penis-stealing" has been a common one since at least the sixteenth century (see Reginald Scot's 1584 *Discoverie of Witchcraft* cited in Moira Smith, "The Flying Phallus and the Laughing Inquisitor: Penis Theft in the *Malleus Maleficarum*," *Journal of Folklore Research* 39 (2002): 90. But as Smith argues, using these passages to dismiss the *Malleus* results in "Otherizing" the text, thus allowing us to dismiss it as ridiculous.)

32 I do not want to single out this student because at least ten other students in this class either agreed with him or made similar comments, albeit not quite so humorously.

33 Jackson Katz, *The Macho Paradox: Why Some Men Hurt Women and How All Men Can Help* (Naperville: Sourcebooks, 2006).

34 Jackson Katz and Jennifer Siebel Newsom, "After Newtown, besides Guns, Let's Talk about Gender," *San Jose Mercury News*, December 19, 2012. In fact, the discussion needs to also intersect with discussions of race and religion. For example, the new coverage of the January 2015 *Charlie Hebdo* shootings in Paris by "Islamic extremists" versus the almost non-existent coverage of the January 2015 bombing of the Colorado Springs, CO, NAACP offices by a "balding white man in his 40s." See Elizabeth Plank, "One Tweet Perfectly Sums up the Big Problem with How We Talk about Terrorism," *World. Mic*, posted January 7, 2015, accessed January 8, 2015, http://mic.com/articles/107926/one-tweet-perfectly-sums-up-the-big-problem-with-how-we-talk-about-terrorism.

35 Katie Zezima, "Newtown Shooting Details Emerge in Aftermath of Sandy Hook Tragedy," *Huffington Post*, posted February 22, 2012, accessed January 7, 2015, www.huffingtonpost.com/2012/12/22/newtown-shooting-new-details_n_2351594.html.

how women can protect themselves from stranger rape, even though stranger rapes are a small percentage of sexual violence. While risk reduction serves a purpose, the problem with many manifestations of it is that it Otherizes the perpetrators of sexual violence as crazed lunatics lurking in bushes and parking garages and allows us to ignore how dominant constructions of masculinity participate in rape culture. Thus, in support of maintaining an unexamined, dominant masculinity, this tendency to Otherize perpetrators of gender-based violence appears in many places, from how we react to misogynistic texts like the *Malleus* to the rise of modern social media movements like #NotAllMen.

While teaching WGSS 163L in Spring 2014, the #YesAllWomen/#NotAllMen social media movements started a dialogue (in class and nationally) in the wake of the Elliot Rodger's misogynistic rampage in Santa Barbara about how problematic it is when SOME men object to bystander intervention efforts that seek to include ALL men because they personally are not rapists.[36] I talked with my students about how when we make statements like "not all men," we are excusing sexist and misogynistic behaviour as not our problem. In bystander intervention training, we contend that we need to hold everyone to a higher standard, and teach everyone how to intervene when we witness low-risk, high-frequency behaviours such as sexist jokes so that the world becomes uncomfortable for that small number of men at the extreme who perpetrate the vast majority of acts of physical and sexual violence and make ALL men look bad. When we laugh dismissively at the *Malleus*, we are participating in a similar process. We are Otherizing overt expressions of misogyny, which allows us to more easily ignore the subtle forms that surround us every day.

Understanding how and why Otherizing occurs allows students to actively engage with, rather than dismiss, the misogynistic writings of the church fathers and the *Malleus*. For example, one discussion thread began with a student commenting about how Tertullian and St. Jerome's condemnation of Eve equated to a condemnation of all women. This condemnation of all women through Eve fits well with a discussion of the #NotAllMen phenomenon in its counterpart of #YesAllWomen—not all men cat-call women but almost ALL women have experienced street harassment; not all medieval men were misogynistic witch-hunters, but all women are guilty by association because of the views expressed in the best-selling *Malleus*.[37] This discussion allowed the students to ask questions about how the condemnation of all women manifests itself today, in ways directly related to their readings of the Bible and the church fathers:

> The reason I find [patristic views of women] interesting is because I come
> from a very religious christian background and I think that some of these

---

36 Jess Zimmerman, "Not All Men: A Brief History of Every Dude's Favorite Argument," *Time Magazine*, April 28, 2014. See also Nolan Feeney, "The Most Powerful #YesAllWomen Tweets," *Time Magazine*, May 25, 2014. It is important to note that the Santa Barbara County Sheriff referred to Rodger as a "madman" (Plank, "One Tweet").

37 The *Malleus* went through approximately twenty-five printings between 1487 and 1669. See P. G. Maxwell-Stuart, trans., *The Malleus Maleficarum* (Manchester: Manchester University Press, 2007), 34.

beliefs still exist, even if they are not intensely broadcasted. While I don't think most of the men in the church would come out and declare that women should bear guilt their whole lives because they are part of Eve who brought sin into the world, I do hear jokes about this topic and supposed light hearted comments like, "Well, Eve DID eat the apple first you know?" So I think that there definitely might be some men who still harbor feelings of blame and resentment towards women in the church. What do you think?

One student stated in reply:

I don't know that men use the story of Adam and Eve to make women feel guilty. In my experience, men use the fact that Eve was "tricked" by the serpent to claim that women are lesser and more gullible. Men have claimed that women are the lesser sex and that they are the reason for all of the suffering of mankind because Eve was "too stupid" to follow the one rule in the Garden of Eden. Or worse, there are men who will "justify" Eve's actions by saying, "Well, yeah of course she took the apple—she didn't have Adam there to tell her it was wrong!"[38]

So what was for St. Jerome and Tertullian a serious discussion of woman's inherent inferiority and guilt due to Eve's "transgression" has shifted today to a joke, but a joke that still fulfils the same purpose as the patristic misogyny—it posits all women as lesser because of Eve. All women are positioned as inferior because of the words of a few men, and some of those men are regularly included in reading lists of college courses. Knowledge of bystander intervention techniques allows us to disrupt the dominant discourse (i.e. intervene) when we are presented with classroom readings that parallel the high-frequency, low-risk behaviours on the continuum of violence and allows us to better understand why many of us argue that we live in a rape culture.

Conclusion

One measure I am using of the success of the integration of bystander intervention in the humanities classroom is out-of-class participation in related events. In the years I have taught this class (2008–present), I have always offered untraditional forms of extra credit, building on Learning Outcomes 1 and 2. Many of my 2014 students attended events like the lecture given at UM by activist and actress Laverne Cox and *The Vagina Monologues* for extra credit, but they have often done so in the past as well. One of the new extra credit opportunities I offered to this class in Spring 2014 was the possibility of volunteering with the Missoula organization Make Your

---

38 The students in the class have already read Genesis 1–4, and thus we have already discussed what the Genesis creation stories actually state in opposition to what we think they say. In particular, students are always shocked to learn that there are two creation stories, that Adam was with Eve in the garden, and that Adam actually comes across as more gullible, at least in certain readings of the text.

Move. This group has produced nationally recognized advertising campaigns aimed at ending sexual violence through bystander intervention.[39] Another aspect of Make Your Move's bystander work includes a photo booth at community and campus events where passers-by can fill out a white board that says "My Best Move to End Sexual Violence Is _____" (Figure 1). Five of my students from this class signed up and took the training to help staff the photo booth during campus events, including the student who made *The Onion* reference in regards to the *Malleus*. While I must state that a number of my students came into the class already volunteering at organizations like SARC and the UM Women's Resource Center, this group of five were not already actively involved in activism of this sort. To me, that is the best sign that the message about ending violence against women being a community issue is working through these coordinated and concerted efforts, both inside and outside the classroom.

Bystander intervention is one of the most promising ways to engage campuses and communities in violence prevention. Victoria Banyard's article "Friends of Survivors: The Community Impact of Unwanted Sexual Experiences" demonstrates that providing students with bystander intervention training is essential because one in three female students and one in five male students will have another

---

39 Megan Kelly, "Six Creepy Overused Sentences That I Wish Always Had These Surprise Endings," *Upworthy*, 2012, accessed December 30, 2014, www.upworthy.com/6-overused-creepy-sentences-that-i-wish-always-had-these-surprise-endings.

student tell them about an experience of sexual violence during their time on campus.[40] But students do not just experience rape culture in social settings outside of the classroom. Analyses of misogynistic discourse in literary texts and historical documents read and discussed in humanities classrooms provide another place to integrate violence prevention on campus. Such discussions give students more exposure to the ideas presented in bystander intervention trainings. My future plans for this course include brief exercises that give them tools to not just understand these readings in more nuanced ways but to actually intervene in discussions in empowering ways. I am developing a classroom activity where the students will brainstorm effective ways to intervene in a class where, for example, Aristotle's misogyny is ignored.[41] My prompts for this exercise will push the students to find ways to intervene, not by challenging Aristotle's inclusion in the syllabus or rejecting the class/professor because of the erasure, but to find ways that would acknowledge this tension as an important part of what the study of the canon should provide. In addition, I plan to test some of these pedagogical techniques in my other first-year literature courses which are not Women's and Gender Studies classes (LSH 151 and LSH 152) where more men are enrolled to see if the use of bystander intervention insights in the humanities classroom can be effective with a broader range of students with different experiences of privilege and oppression. Ultimately, continued discussion of, exposure to, and training in violence prevention efforts in multiple venues, such as the classroom, will result in a safer campus for us all.

Works Cited

Banyard, Victoria, Moynihan, Mary M., Walsh, Wendy A., Cohn, Ellen S., and Ward, Sally K. "Friends of Survivors: The Community Impact of Unwanted Sexual Experiences." *Journal of Interpersonal Violence* 25 (2010): 242–56.

Barz, Diane. "Investigation Report." www.umt.edu/president/docs/DBarzInvestigation Report.pdf (accessed January 20, 2015).

Bhargava, Anurima, and Gary Jackson. Letter from U.S. Department of Justice and U.S. Department of Education to President Royce Engstrom and Lucy France, re: DOJ Case No. DJ 169-44-9, OCR Case No. 10126001. www2.ed.gov/documents/ press-releases/montana-missoula-letter.pdf (accessed January 20, 2015).

---

40 Victoria Banyard et al., "Friends of Survivors: The Community Impact of Unwanted Sexual Experiences," *Journal of Interpersonal Violence* 25 (2010): 242–56.

41 For this exercise, I plan to present the students with a quote from Mary Pipher's book *Reviving Ophelia: Saving the Selves of Adolescent Girls* (New York: Riverhead Books, 1994), 42:

> I was a reader and I remember the trouble I had with misogynistic writers. I loved Tolstoy, but it broke my heart to realize when I read *The Kreutzer Sonata* that he detested women. Later I had the same experience with Schopenhauer, Henry Miller, and Norman Mailer. My daughter, Sara, read Aristotle in her philosophy class. One night she read a section aloud to me and said, "This guy doesn't respect women." I wondered what it means to her that one of the wisest men of the ages is misogynistic.

Bloch, R. Howard. *Medieval Misogyny and the Invention of Western Romantic Love*. Chicago: University of Chicago Press, 1991.

Christine de Pizan. *Book of the City of Ladies*, translated by Rosalind Brown-Grant. New York: Penguin, 1999.

Eckstein, R. P., M. M. Moynihan, V. L. Banyard, and E. G. Plante. "Bringing in the Bystander: A Prevention Workshop for Establishing a Community of Responsibility." Presentation at the University of Montana. 2013.

Feeney, Nolan. "The Most Powerful #YesAllWomen Tweets." *Time Magazine*, May 25, 2014.

Hildegard of Bingen. *Selected Writings*, translated by Mark Atherton. New York: Penguin, 2001.

Katz, Jackson. *The Macho Paradox: Why Some Men Hurt Women and How All Men Can Help*. Naperville: Sourcebooks, 2006.

Katz, Jackson, and Jennifer Siebel Newsom. "After Newtown, Besides Guns, Let's Talk about Gender." *San Jose Mercury News*, December 19, 2012.

Kelly, Megan. "Six Creepy Overused Sentences That I Wish Always Had These Surprise Endings." *Upworthy*. www.upworthy.com/6-overused-creepy-sentences-that-i-wish-always-had-these-surprise-endings (accessed December 30, 2014).

Kimmel, Michael. *The Gendered Society*. New York: Oxford University Press, 2011.

Kramer, Heinrich, and Jacob Sprenger. Excerpts from the *Malleus Maleficarum*. In Alan Charles Kors and Edward Peters, *Witchcraft in Europe, 400–1700: A Documentary History*, 2nd ed. Philadelphia: University of Pennsylvania Press, 2001.

———. *The Malleus Maleficarum*, translated by P. G. Maxwell-Stuart. Manchester: Manchester University Press, 2007.

Kuefler, Mathew. *The Manly Eunuch: Masculinity, Gender Ambiguity, and Christian Ideology in Late Antiquity*. Chicago: University of Chicago Press, 2001.

Nerbovig, Ashley. "Sexual Assault Timeline." *Montana Kaimin*. www.monta nakaimin. com/article_4d5c63c5-2ae4-53c6-a517-7a9e2914e731.html (accessed January 21, 2015).

Pipher, Mary. *Reviving Ophelia: Saving the Selves of Adolescent Girls*. New York: Riverhead Books, 1994.

Plank, Elizabeth. "One Tweet Perfectly Sums up the Big Problem with How We Talk about Terrorism." *World.Mic*. http://mic.com/articles/107926/one-tweet-perfectly-sums-up-the-big-problem-with-how-we-talk-about-terrorism (accessed January 8, 2015).

Saint Jerome. "Jerome 347–419 AD." www.womenpriests.org/traditio/.

Smith, Moira. "The Flying Phallus and the Laughing Inquisitor: Penis Theft in the *Malleus Maleficarum*." *Journal of Folklore Research* 39 (2002): 85–117.

Tertullian. "Tertullian 155–245 AD." www.womenpriests.org/traditio/.

Wozniak, Danielle, Christine Fiore, and Elizabeth Hubble. "Transforming a Rape-Prone Culture: Community Change in Cyberspace." *The Montana Professor* 23, 2013. http://mtprof.msun.edu.

Wozniak, Danielle, and Elizabeth Hubble. "University of Montana PETSA," 2013. www.umt.edu/petsa/.

Zezima, Katie. "Newtown Shooting Details Emerge in Aftermath of Sandy Hook Tragedy." *Huffington Post*. www.huffingtonpost.com/2012/12/22/newtown-shooting-new-details_n_2351594.html (accessed January 7, 2015).

Zimmerman, Jess. "Not All Men: A Brief History of Every Dude's Favorite Argument." *Time Magazine*, April 28, 2014.

Chapter 5

FROM BYSTANDER TO UPSTANDER: READING THE *NIBELUNGENLIED* TO RESIST RAPE CULTURE

ALEXANDRA STERLING-HELLENBRAND

The concept of rape culture in higher education has come under increasingly close media scrutiny at local, state, and national levels. In this chapter, against a background of heightened awareness and of renewed conversation about campus sexual assault, I would like to frame a discussion of the Middle High German *Nibelungenlied*. I argue that this frame offers an unexpected perspective for reading the *Nibelungenlied* in the context of teaching rape and medieval literature, providing a unique opportunity to create dialogue between thirteenth-century texts and twenty-first-century students/readers. The *Nibelungenlied* is, of course, a wonderfully complex work with an equally complicated reception history from the Middle Ages to the present.[1] As a work of Middle High German courtly literature, it also undeniably participates in the rape narrative that Kathryn Gravdal established as integral to medieval romance.[2] The thirteenth-century text has one episode in particular that offers a direct and immediate connection to issues of concern on a twenty-first-century college campus: the tenth adventure. The tenth adventure describes the double wedding of Burgundian king Gunther and his sister Kriemhild (to Brunhild and Siegfried respectively). This adventure can easily be read by modern undergraduates as a very humorous scene. The much-anticipated bridal

---

1 Otfrid Ehrismann gives an excellent overview in *Nibelungenlied: Epoche—Werk—Wirkung*, 2nd ed. (Munich: Beck, 2002). See also Winder McConnell, Werner Wunderlich, Frank Gentry, and Ulrich Mueller, eds., *The Nibelungen Tradition: An Encyclopedia* (London: Routledge, 2002).
2 Gravdal's *Ravishing Maidens* establishes rape as the basis for medieval romance narrative. The *Nibelungenlied* conflates several older narratives within a framework that undeniably participates in the culture of courtly romance. See also Jerold Frakes, *Brides and Doom: Gender, Property, and Power in Medieval German Women's Epic* (Philadelphia: University of Pennsylvania Press, 1994). More recently, Classen explicitly focuses on the issues of sexual violence in his monograph *Sexual Violence and Rape in the Middle Ages: A Critical Discourse in Premodern German and European Literature* (Berlin: de Gruyter, 2011). The second chapter of Classen's *Sexual Violence* focuses on the *Nibelungenlied*: "*Nibelungenlied*—a Male Poet Reveals His Fear of Women: Violence, Rape, and Political Machinations in the Heroic World," Classen, *Sexual Violence*, 33–52.

night proves challenging for Gunther when his new bride Brunhild unceremoniously hangs him from a nail on the wall of their bedchamber and leaves him there until dawn. The next night, Gunther's new brother-in-law Siegfried dons his cape of invisibility and comes to Gunther's aid, duelling with Brunhild in the king's bedchamber while the king listens under the bed. Siegfried defeats Brunhild and leaves, Gunther takes his place, and the episode ends without further incident.

The audience, medieval or modern, can scarcely deny the humour of a newly married king ignominiously hanging on the wall, bound hand and foot by his bride on their first night together, pleading to be released. The audience is likewise intended to find humour in the king's request for help from his best friend and new brother-in-law to subdue his bride. The second night's wrestling match between Siegfried and Brunhild, however, "resolves" the hitherto slapstick comedy through a violent act of physical force that modern students clearly identify as rape. Here the relatively unfamiliar medieval German text confronts the students with an uncomfortably familiar scene that the alterity of the text cannot disguise. The scene recalls the interpersonal or relationship violence or the threat of sexual assault that students confront daily on campus. They live in a community that demands heightened awareness. Not only do they receive unfortunately regular alert bulletins about assault occurrences from campus police. They also see the strategically placed blue lights with emergency telephones and the prominently displayed number for after-dark transportation with Safe Ride or other kind of campus shuttle specially designated for this purpose. For this audience, then, the episode may bring to mind the threat as well as the various strategies for dealing with interpersonal violence that inform many student development and residence hall programs, aimed particularly but not exclusively at first-year students. Many U.S. campuses will have sidewalks lined with red flags at some time during the year to raise public awareness about interpersonal violence.[3] Programs like these demonstrate a university's public and institutional focus on violence reporting and prevention, specifically targeting bystanders.[4] Thus, the thirteenth-century text of the

---

3 Information on the national Red Flag campaign can be found here: www.theredflagcampaign. org/ (accessed November 13, 2016). The Red Flag campaign is a recent example of an initiative begun in Virginia in 2007 that now has representation in forty-eight states (see map, www. theredflagcampaign.org/map/, accessed November 13, 2016). For over twenty-five years, Appalachian State University has hosted an annual Walk for Awareness as one of its opening activities in the fall semester "to commemorate lives lost to interpersonal violence, to support victims and survivors of violence, and to affirm our commitment to making the Appalachian community safe from interpersonal violence." The first Walk for Awareness was held in September 1990 in memory of Appalachian employee Jeni Gray, who had been raped and killed September 1989. Similar programs are found across the landscape of higher education; names and offices may vary but the goals do not. At my institution, these are programs with names like "Appalachian Cares" and "It's Up to Me" in addition to the Red Flag campaign. The websites can be found at http://appcares.appstate.edu/ (accessed November 13, 2016) and http:// redflag.appstate.edu/ (accessed November 13, 2016); the "It's Up to Me" campaign video is on the appcares site.

4 A quick review of publications such as the *Journal of College Student Development*, the *Journal of American College Health*, or *Violence against Women* reveals an ongoing discussion of bystanders in

Nibelungenlied, read through and beyond the tenth adventure, can offer a surprising connection for students: between medieval literature and contemporary issues, between the classroom and the residence hall, between academics and student life. In the following, then, I wish to locate our reading of the *Nibelungenlied* in this twenty-first-century campus environment that exhorts bystanders to stop standing by and to stand up.

The Tenth *Aventiure*

First, a brief summary of the tenth adventure (*aventiure*) may be helpful. It begins with preparations for a wedding. Gunther, the king of Burgundy, is celebrating his nuptials in the court at Worms. He made a triumphant entrance into his kingdom, having returned successful in his quest to the northern kingdom of Iceland to win its lovely yet fearsomely strong queen Brunhild for his bride. As a reward for his service to Gunther, the hero Siegfried has received the hand of Gunther's sister Kriemhild in marriage.[5]

Thinking "that he would rather be lying with the beautiful lady, and that great joy would befall him because of her" (624), the king retires with Brunhild to their bridal chamber, at the same time as Siegfried and Kriemhild also leave the hall.[6] Each of the men eagerly anticipates a night of pleasure, hoping "to conquer the charming ladies with love" (627). Siegfried's night goes as expected; he caresses his wife "so charmingly with his noble love-making" that she becomes "as dear to him as his life." Gunther, by contrast, has an adventure that gives him no pleasure at all. Indeed, it leaves him to greet the breaking dawn from an unexpected vantage point: he is hanging from a nail on the wall of his bedchamber, hands and feet bound, pleading with his new wife to let him down. Acceding to Brunhild's wish that he leave her alone ("I want to remain a maiden still—be sure you mark this!" 634), Gunther desperately promises not to touch her again in return for his release so that his embarrassment will not be made public when the chamberlain comes to wake them for the next day's festivities.

Gunther is not literally humiliated in public here, of course. No courtiers witness his ignominy and shame; however, *he* is painfully aware of his sexual failure and his dishonour, and this time Brunhild is also.[7] Gunther cannot avoid confiding in

the context of interpersonal violence prevention. This is also in the context of the California "yes-means-yes" campus sexual assault bill that made national headlines at the time this chapter's ideas were being formulated, amid increasingly close media scrutiny of the rape culture in higher education following a highly publicized article in *Rolling Stone* in April 2015. Sheila Coronel, Steve Coll, and Derek Kravitz, "Rape on Campus: What Went Wrong?" *Rolling Stone*, April 23, 2015, 31–37.

5 In the sixth adventure, Siegfried helped Gunther prevail against Brunhild by wearing a magic cape that rendered him invisible so that he could compete at Gunther's side to ensure that Gunther wins the contests.

6 All English text references are from *The Nibelungenlied: The Lay of the Nibelungs*, ed. and trans. Cyril Edwards (Oxford: Oxford University Press, 2010). Citations in text indicate verse numbers in the Edwards edition.

7 She does not know, as he does, the extent of his debt to Siegfried for the victory in the earlier contests that brought her to his bed in the first place. Müller discusses both of these scenes in terms of "the confusion of gazes" both literally and figuratively. Jan-Dirk Müller, *Rules for the Endgame* (Baltimore: Johns Hopkins University Press, 2007), 246–58.

his new brother-in-law Siegfried, however, who solicitously inquires after Gunther's sad demeanour as the day progresses and evening approaches again. Siegfried, learning that he and Gunther "fared unequally" (651) in their respective first bridal nights, volunteers to help Gunther with the aid of his cloak of invisibility: "I will compel your wife to let you make love to her tonight, or else I will lose my life" (654). Gunther gives Siegfried permission to "do otherwise all that you will" emphatically stating, "Even if you were to take her life, I would leave it unavenged." Siegfried should, however, take care not to "make love at all to my dear lady." And Siegfried swears that he will not.[8] To all appearances, he keeps this promise. Siegfried battles with Brunhild in the dark of her bedchamber, with Gunther listening nearby, and they are evenly matched in strength; actually, the poet comments on her "superior strength" (671). She "carried him by sheer force—he had no choice!—and squeezed him roughly between the wall and a chest" (671) and later grips his hands "so tightly that the blood spurted from his nails" (674). Brunhild has the upper hand until she reaches for the braid around her waist, the braid with which she trussed up Gunther the night before. Siegfried's grasp stops her "with such strength that her limbs and all her body creaked" (676). Then the battle ends and "then she became Gunther's wife." Brunhild promises to make "full amends" for her behaviour and "never defy" her husband, as she has seen that he can be a "lady's master" (677). After Siegfried departs, taking Brunhild's girdle as well as a ring from her finger,[9] Brunhild and Gunther consummate their marriage and the tenth adventure concludes happily, "as Gunther the warrior wanted" (689). At this point, there may perhaps have been a collective sigh of relief from the audience that potential disaster has been averted, at least for now.[10]

Reading the Tenth Adventure

When reading the *Nibelungenlied* with undergraduates, I ask them to consider this adventure of the *Nibelungenlied* and its immediate aftermath as arguably the most central events of the Nibelung story. In their responses, the students often mention the fairy-tale, fantasy-like aspects of the tale in the preceding episodes; many students shared the opinion of a student who commented that the story had "seemed to be shaping up into the classic fairy tale … of heroes, princesses and chivalry."[11] Student comments highlighted the similarity to familiar fairy tales. The poem

---

8 Siegfried states firmly in verse 656: "I swear by my loyalty … that I will not make love to her. I prefer your fair sister to all I have ever beheld." And, as important as Siegfried's promise, is Gunther's belief in it: "Gunther readily believed what Siegfried then promised."

9 The poet describes the scene: "Siegfried stood back as if he wanted to take off his clothes, leaving the maiden lying there. He took a golden ring off her finger, without the noble queen ever noticing it. He also took her girdle, a fine braid. I don't know if he did that out of his high spirits. He gave it to his wife; that was to cost him dear" (678–79).

10 This is a tragic epic, after all, and the poet frequently reminds the audience of the disaster that will eventually befall the Burgundians.

11 Specific comments are reproduced with permission of the students who enrolled in my course in fall 2014 that provided the basis for this chapter. Students posted their comments

was "an extended fairy tale full of fair maidens and honorable warriors," and it had a "fantasy like feel and mood" that seemed to absorb the violence for many: "The plot is very violent, but it still feels very fairy-tale like … Had the action been more realistic, then it might have felt abrupt or intruding." In this generation of interactive fantasy games and of continued Disney dominance, students tend, the context of medieval courtly culture notwithstanding, to read the violence in this particular scene as reminiscent of the violence they know from fairy tales.[12] College-age youth also value Siegfried's unwavering friendship and loyalty to Gunther; they tend to take Siegfried at his word when he promises not to sleep with Brunhild,[13] viewing Siegfried's "service" in the bedchamber as further evidence of his friendship. And perhaps any modern tendency to over-contextualize the rape in the tenth episode might also have something to do with modern biases toward not just medieval but also Germanic culture, as we perceive both today.[14]

In the medieval text, however, the bedroom battle that re-establishes the courtly order is brutally physical: Brunhild throws Siegfried out of the bed such that his head bangs loudly against a stool (668), she grips his hands so powerfully that blood spurts from his fingernails (674), all her limbs and her body creak when he finally throws her on the bed and prevents her from reaching her belt (676). We have just witnessed what any interpersonal violence taskforce would undoubtedly consider a brutal assault. Students grasp a shift in tone that they also put in context; after all, the poet has repeatedly warned of the disastrous consequences awaiting all actors in the story.[15] The trappings of fairy tale evaporate in "a tragedy of deceit, treachery and murder" as pride and power become "obsessive" traits of each character. Students also do not hesitate to name what happens in the tenth adventure, as one puts it simply, "when Gunther has Siegfried hold Brunhild down so they could have sex."[16]

---

in an online forum discussion and we devoted the next class meeting to a larger face-to-face conversation about their reactions to the text. While specific to the students of that particular course section, the comments also serve as representative examples of responses from students in the millennial generation.

12 Given the influence of Disney, students often also consider fairy tales as kind of "medieval," albeit ones that exist in a kind of hyperreal "multitemporality of medievalism" where the fictions are perceived as more real than the source texts or historical events they represent. Tison Pugh and Susan Aronstein, eds., *The Disney Middle Ages: A Fairy-Tale and Fantasy Past* (New York: Palgrave Macmillan, 2012), 3.

13 Since the girdle and the ring end up in Kriemhild's possession, the symbolism suggests that Siegfried did not keep his promise. Certainly, even Kriemhild believes that he must have slept with Brunhild, which she insinuates during the quarrel of the fourteenth adventure (840 and 841). Furthermore, the oath that Gunther demands from Siegfried swearing his innocence only addresses the accusation that Siegfried bragged publicly to his own wife about having slept with Brunhild (857). Siegfried is never asked to swear that he did *not* have sex with Brunhild. The ambiguity remains.

14 Renz reminds us that this treatment of Brunhild would not be considered rape according to medieval canon law. Tilo Renz, *Um Leib und Leben: Das Wissen von Geschlecht, Körper und Recht im Nibelungenlied* (Berlin: De Gruyter, 2012), 103.

15 Kriemhild is introduced with the lines: "… she grew to be a beautiful woman. For her sake many knights were to lose their lives" (2). And the foreshadowing of doom returns often.

16 As another student puts it, Siegfried "did do some things that were not very honorable. He helped Gunther cheat to win Brunhild, and did things to Brunhild on the night after the

For a pedagogical moment, I want to capture the honesty of that blunt response and the feeling of discomfort it expresses, because it demands further dialogue, unexpectedly connecting our "dusty medieval texts" (like the fairy tales they seem to resemble) to everyday campus life.[17] This brings us back to a focus on bystanders, enabling students to enter meaningfully into that dialogue in a way that may illuminate both the medieval text and its modern context.

From Bystanders to Upstanders

In the introduction to their volume *Preventing Sexual Violence: Interdisciplinary Approaches to Overcoming a Rape Culture*, Anastasia Henry and Nicola Powell suggest that prevention must be "a shared, community or societal responsibility." An emphasis on shared responsibility and community response, according to Powell and Henry, can shift the focus to "men *and women* as bystanders and supporters of rape culture."[18] Bystanders who stand up and take action may "help motivate other individuals to become part of the critical mass that is needed to pressure existing societal structures" to change.[19] As bystander initiatives are becoming institutionalized locally and regionally, college students represent a population at particular risk.[20] This is why the California bill of September 2014 also required outreach and education.[21]

As readers of the *Nibelungenlied* in this larger environment, as part of the poet's audience, students automatically assume the role of "bystanders" to the action of the narrative. With Gunther, we witness Siegfried's struggle with Brunhild in the tenth adventure. Hiding in the room, Gunther is essentially a bystander, and so are the

---

weddings that shouldn't have been done." Yet another commented: "At the beginning, everyone was honorable, beautiful, loyal, heroic, etc., but here they are falling apart with deception, lies, treachery, murder, family feuding, and generally not caring about anyone but themselves."

17 Kathryn Gravdal, "Chrétien de Troyes, Gratian, and the Medieval Romance of Sexual Violence," *Signs* (1992): 585.

18 Anastasia Powell and Nicola Henry, "Framing Sexual Violence Prevention: What Does It Mean to Challenge a Rape Culture?," in *Preventing Sexual Violence: Interdisciplinary Approaches to Overcoming a Rape Culture*, eds. Nicola Henry and Anastasia Powell (London: Palgrave Macmillan, 2014), 7.

19 Alison C. Cares, Mary M. Moynihan, and Victoria L. Baynard, "Taking Stock of Bystander Programmes: Changing Attitudes and Behaviours towards Sexual Violence," in *Preventing Sexual Violence: Interdisciplinary Approaches to Overcoming a Rape Culture*, eds. Nicola Henry and Anastasia Powell (London: Palgrave Macmillan, 2014), 183.

20 See Sarah McMahon, Judy L. Postmus, and Ruth Anne Koenick, "Conceptualizing the Engaging Bystander Approach to Sexual Violence Prevention on College Campuses," *Journal of College Student Development* 52 (2011): 115–30; Sarah McMahon, "Rape Myth Beliefs and Bystander Attitudes among Incoming College Students," *Journal of American College Health* 59 (2010): 3–11; and Victoria L. Banyard, Mary M. Moynihan, and Maria T. Crossman, "Reducing Sexual Violence on Campus: The Role of Student Leaders as Empowered Bystanders," *Journal of College Student Development* 50 (2009): 446–57.

21 In section 1, 13 d and e, the bill stipulates that institutions develop "comprehensive prevention and outreach programs" that can offer strategies such as "awareness raising campaigns" and "bystander intervention." Furthermore, "outreach programming shall be included as part of every incoming student's orientation." The bill lists a number of strategies not limited to those cited here: https://leginfo.legislature.ca.gov/faces/billNavClient.xhtml?bill_id=201320140SB967 (accessed November 13, 2016).

readers.[22] In the contemporary classroom, the language of the text does not allow us to escape the intense physicality of the battle between Brunhild and Siegfried, while Gunther remains in the room listening as "strong Siegfried set about playing his game" and waiting for his own turn when Siegfried finishes. The chamber is also dark and Gunther has locked the three of them inside (663).[23] Gunther's role as voyeur (albeit only in the aural sense) seldom receives attention. The poet does not allow us to forget that Gunther is there; the king

> refrained from speech, concealing himself. Gunther could clearly hear, although he could not see him at all, that nothing intimate passed between them there. They had very little comfort in that bed.
>
> (666–67)

The poet repeats several times that the king can hear the struggle clearly (673 and 675), though he does not speak. The audience listens with Gunther; we literally become complicit in the assault as we essentially "stand by" with him, hidden not by darkness or bedclothes but perhaps by the passage of time and cultural distance. Thus, the question of "witness" joins our campus conversation about bystanders in reactions as contemporary readers of this narrative. With the national spotlight focused on campus sexual violence, many colleges and universitites have put renewed effort and resources into raising awareness among students and faculty and staff, to address the culture and primary causes of interpersonal violence and sexual assault through a focus (evident in current programming) on common responsibility.

I suggest that the thirteenth-century text can bring twenty-first-century students to consider interpretive interventions here, enabling them to consider "standing up" rather than "standing by." The term upstander, though not yet officially in the OED as of this writing,[24] has come to refer to active intervention or even preventative behaviour in the face of injustice rather than passive reaction; in other words, those who stand "up" take action, while those who stand "by" let inappropriate action occur unchallenged. In the context of interpersonal violence prevention, the concept of educating "upstanders" has led to a focus on strategies to support and encourage bystanders to speak up, to take action. In short, as one Red Flag site urges, students must become "upstanders":

> Being an Upstander means that if you see a Red Flag, you will SAY SOMETHING, instead of just letting it slide. A passive bystander hears a friend say something off-base, but chooses to ignore it. An Upstander SAYS SOMETHING.[25]

---

22 Of course, Gunther becomes an active agent not long after he is a bystander.

23 Siegfried extinguishes the lights. And the attendants leave the chamber. "Once that had been done, the powerful king himself locked the door, quickly sliding two very sturdy bolts across it. Quickly he hid the lights under the bedclothes" (663).

24 http://blog.oxforddictionaries.com/2015/07/legislation-lexicography-campaign-upstander/ (accessed November 13, 2016). See also "up'stander, n." OED Online, September 2016, Oxford University Press, http://0-www.oed.com.wncln.wncln.org/view/Entry/220189?redirectedFrom=upstander (accessed November 13, 2016).

25 I cite here the Red Flag campaign from Appalachian State University as a particular local yet representative example of such language used at various institutions in similar contexts: http://redflag.appstate.edu/steps-to-becoming-an-upstander (accessed November 13, 2016).

In this context, we can encourage students to confront the episode in the tenth adventure as "upstanders" and "say something," thereby employing our medieval text as a unique primary prevention strategy. The *Nibelungenlied* can actually move us, in this context, from standing by to standing up.

There are several levels on which we can "say something." First, we should acknowledge our red flag: rape is rape.[26] We must read through the "parodic potential of the courtliness of the episode"[27] although the poet's humour threatens to obscure our modern red flag, underscoring that humour through asides that unambiguously invite the audience to join in.[28] With the poet, the audience actually expects the result of the first night. After all, Gunther may have brought home the bride he desired, but we know that he won that bride only with Siegfried's help and now he must manage on his own. The poet anticipates what is to come with unmistakable irony: "He had often had greater comfort lying with other women ...!" (629). With Siegfried and the poet, the audience should commiserate with the king, share his frustration, understand his embarrassment that he cannot control his wife even in the bedroom. We smile, perhaps we chuckle, because we know what must inevitably come next; we recognize this still familiar plot. In fact, the turning point in Siegfried's struggle with Brunhild further emphasizes the need to re-establish the correct gender hierarchy in the bedroom. After Brunhild pins him "roughly between the wall and a chest," Siegfried considers the fate of all men if he cannot prevail in this struggle:

> "Alas!" thought the warrior. "If I am now to lose my life at the hands of a maiden, then all women will forever be high and mighty in their dealings with their husbands after this, little though they act like that now!"
>
> (672)

At this point, Siegfried feels "greatly ashamed" and begins "to wax wrath," summoning his "monstrous strength" to bring the conflict to an end (674). Order must be maintained, after all, and Brunhild must be put in her place as an example to all husbands and wives. Brunhild is a veritable shrew who must be tamed;[29] this is an all too familiar trope: we must admit our modern complicity in myths that underlie the scene's humour.

As the poet reinforces our complicity, he effectively encourages us to stand by; he does not question the actions taken by Gunther and Siegfried and reminds us of the

---

26 http://redflag.appstate.edu/identifying-red-flags (accessed November 13, 2016). Red flags include a partner's violent behaviour or threats, including forced sex.

27 Frakes, *Brides*, 111. Appalled by the fact that Siegfried "helped Gunther essentially rape Brunhild" and then "stole her personal items and gave them to his own wife," one student (female) voiced the opinions of several, saying "During such scenes, I wondered why Siegfried is even considered a hero. Is such behavior supposed to be admirable or comical ... was sexual violence something to be proud of?"

28 Down to the interjection "hey" that begins the fourth line in verse 681, after Brunhild has yielded at last. Edwards translates it as "Oh" (65), Frakes as "Zowee" (106): "Oh, how much of her great strength abandoned her because of that love-making."

29 Frakes, *Brides*, 107.

serious cultural, social, and political undertones below the episode's comedic sur-face. Gunther is not just any man who cannot control his wife: he is king. Brunhild's strength is not only a challenge to his masculinity; it is also an affront to his royal authority. Male observers (such as Hagen or Siegfried and the poet) see this threat, and the audience is encouraged to see it as well. During the match in Iceland, Hagen calls Brunhild "the very Devil's wife" (438) and, at the sight of her weighty shield, remarks that "she should be the foul fiend's bride in Hell!" (450). Gunther echoes the demonic associations, reinforcing the threat and also connecting the contests on the field with the contests in the bedchamber. Recalling his unfortunate first wedding night to Siegfried the day after, Gunther names her a "foul fiend" (648) and "a terror of a woman" (655) that he has brought home to his house. One might speculate that, because of her roles in older versions of the Siegfried narrative, the figure of Brunhild remained an uneasy interloper in the *Nibelungenlied*.[30] Nevertheless, the situation with Gunther is clearly inappropriate in terms of the text's cultural norms.[31] Brunhild must be subdued and she ultimately gets what she deserves in the marriage bed.[32]

The tenth adventure is a short episode; it ends peacefully, with a celebration, and the story goes on. Though the actual assault seems clearly within the bounds of propriety in the context of the *Nibelungenlied*'s culture, the text and its poet do not stand by as passively as we might expect. The further action of the narrative (murder and disaster result) suggests the extremity of the scene that conceals inappropriate action behind a façade of propriety and courtliness. Siegfried's marriage to Kriemhild depends on the collaborative deception that the men perpet-rate in Iceland when Siegfried holds Gunther's mount for him as visual reinforce-ment of Gunther's superiority over Siegfried.[33] Siegfried's eventual murder is a direct result of the confrontation between his wife and Brunhild on the steps of the cathedral in which Kriemhild reveals that she is wearing the belt Siegfried took as a trophy from Brunhild on the second night. The escalating deception has severe consequences: the girdle Siegfried steals and his action as "vassal" upon arrival in Iceland both lead directly to his demise. They are the subject of the queens'

---

30 This element of the courtly *Nibelungenlied* may be left over from earlier versions of the story, where Brunhild knew Siegfried and may perhaps have been promised to him, as in the old Norse saga of the Volsungs. Recent scholarship by Wakefield and Grimstad suggests that, in fact, both the Nordic and Germanic narratives may have been well known to thirteenth-century audiences.

31 Classen suggests that the king has been made effeminate by his new more "masculine" wife; he is tied up with the "gebende," a term usually used in reference to married women's head-gear. Classen, *Sexual Violence*, 38. Pafenberg suggests that the poem also criticizes Gunther for his apparent transgression of traditional gender roles here; however, only Brunhild must be punished. Stephanie B. Pafenberg, "The Spindle and the Sword: Gender, Sex, and Heroism in the Nibelungenlied and Kudrun," *The Germanic Review: Literature, Culture, Theory* 70 (1995): 109.

32 Both Frakes and Pafenberg argue that Kriemhild also challenges the courtly order and the gendered hierarchy, ultimately meeting a very public and gruesome end at the conclusion of the poem. The implication is that she, like Brunhild, gets what she deserves as well.

33 Gunther proves his suitability to woo Brunhild, who actually has expected Siegfried to arrive in that role.

argument in the fourteenth adventure. Initially, the issue is rank: Kriemhild boasts of her husband's might and Brunhild insists on Gunther's authority. The quarrel is exacerbated by, and it escalates because of, Kriemhild's revelation: Siegfried gifted her with his spoils of the wedding night adventure. This public insult done to Brunhild, with her realization of betrayal and deception, ultimately results in Siegfried's death at the hands of Hagen. In the end, Siegfried pays with his life for his service, his friendship, and his loyalty. Gunther and Siegfried deceived their wives, disenfranchised them, undervalued them.[34] Those wives created, in turn, a public crisis that threatened to destabilize the kingdom.

The poet does not explicitly condemn the men for dishonourable conduct; the demonic epithets are reserved for the women.[35] After all, the men must solve the political crises. Nevertheless, there is space for the modern reader to question the behaviour that obviously leads to such disaster. This is how we may read against the text to subvert and transform for ourselves as readers the rape culture that the text actually seems to affirm. We recognize the violence beneath the courtly (students call it "fairy-tale") façade the text wishes to celebrate; indeed, we can place the violence in cultural context not by erasing it but by recognizing its consequences. We should recognize the negative characteristics that underlie courtly appearances: arrogance, deceit, self-centredness, desire for vengeance.[36] As we look out from our current cultural vantage points, we are asked to consider the issue of "standing by"; we should feel encouraged and empowered to question attitudes of nobility, fairness, and honour. The *Nibelungenlied* deconstructs heroism as an ideal that is "ambivalent" and even "questionable" as Siegfried is repeatedly shown as boisterous, arrogant, and inconsiderate.[37] We read with Gravdal's hope that contemporary audiences will question what they find in the older texts. Sexual violence remains part of the medieval romance narrative. While romance narratives can and often do challenge patriarchal codes, this challenge tends to indulge and accept the status quo: women

---

34 Siegfried and Gunther swear to help one another in their bride quests; these are agreements among the men (331–33). Cowell suggests that women are commodities to be exchanged, ideologically and politically if not economically. Andrew Cowell, *The Medieval Warrior Aristocracy: Gifts, Violence, Performance, and the Sacred* (Cambridge: D. S. Brewer, 2007), 8. Even the gendered grammar of the lovemaking in the tenth adventure reinforces the true relationship between the male subjects and their female "objects" (Frakes, *Brides*, 106–7).

35 Lienert points out that the poet himself never applies these terms to Brunhild or Kriemhild; these terms are used only by male characters to describe the women who confront them. Elisabeth Lienert, "Geschlecht und Gewalt im 'Nibelungenlied,'" *Zeitschrift für deutsches Altertum und deutsche Literatur* (2003): 17.

36 Batt makes a similar claim about Malory's *Morte D'Arthur*, namely that the language of sex, power, and coercion expresses "anxiety, and perhaps disillusion, over the possible comforts for the masculine of the whole Arthurian project." See Catherine Batt, "Malory and Rape," *Arthuriana* (1997): 93–94.

37 Albrecht Classen, "The Downfall of a Hero: Siegfried's Self-Destruction and the End of Heroism in the Nibelungenlied," *German Studies Review* (2003): 308. Classen sees a culmination of this depiction in the final hunt scene before Siegfried is killed by Hagen. Jackson reads the *Nibelungenlied* itself as "the epic of failed violence controls." William H. Jackson, "Court Literature and Violence in the High Middle Ages," in *German Literature of the High Middle Ages*, ed. Will Hasty (Rochester Camden House, 2006), 267.

must still be raped in romance so that men can become heroes, because "rape is not prohibited, rather regulated."[38] The *Nibelungenlied* throws the dilemma of male feudal culture into relief with the treatment of Brunhild by the men around her, notably Siegfried and Gunther. They concoct the story of Siegfried's vassalage and lend visual credence to the ruse by staging the scene in which Siegfried holds the reins of Gunther's steed as the Burgundians disembark in Iceland. They create difficulties for themselves through their own behaviour and both ultimately die because of their deceit, their pride, and their (mis)understanding of honour. The sexual violence that occurs in the bedroom scene is a manifestation of that faulty honour, especially when it later erupts publicly. The violent act itself is not condemned; in fact, it is justified as Siegfried's "defence" of all men against the unruly nature of all women, reinforced by references to Brunhild as the devil's bride. Yet that violent act in the tenth adventure, motivated by pride and greed and selfish desire, leads to complete and utter disaster.

Conclusion

In their article "Teaching about Sexual Violence in Higher Education," Corrine C. Bertram and M. Sue Crowley encourage us to invent strategies for representation and resistance in response to the problems of sexual violence that remain as serious today as in the 1970s. They exhort us to move from theorizing about resistance to engaging in it; sexual violence continues to cross "the borders of complex, multifaceted social positions with relative impunity." And therefore, "Resistance to it must cross those same borders."[39] Resistance, like responsibility, must also cross the borders we construct between time periods, genres, and disciplines. The language of the *Nibelungenlied* does not allow us to escape the brutal physicality of the battle between Brunhild and Siegfried, while Gunther remains in the room listening and waiting for his turn. We are compelled to listen, effectively to stand by. Modern students actually cannot, nor do they wish to, dismiss as comic exaggeration the savagery that seems to underlie the veneer of courtliness, friendship, and loyalty. The violence should feel real to us; it is real, and the text acknowledges this as well. The scope of the larger epic tragedy in the *Nibelungenlied* subsumes this single incident; nonetheless, the tenth adventure calls into question notions of fairness, heroism, and courtliness in ways that we can use to interrogate the larger story, as indeed the narrative actually directs us to do. While the poet cannot prevent patriarchal reality from becoming visible in the text, he also allows us to shape an alternative response to that reality in its medieval context even as we consider remnants of that reality in the twenty-first-century classroom. When we recognize the truly catastrophic

---

38 Gravdal, "Chrétien de Troyes," 583. Here Gravdal applies to the thirteenth century comments on the regulation of rape made by Catherine MacKinnon with respect to twentieth-century attitudes.

39 Corrine C. Bertram and M. Sue Crowley, "Teaching about Sexual Violence in Higher Education: Moving from Concern to Conscious Resistance," *Frontiers: A Journal of Women Studies* 33 (2012): 74.

outcomes of the flawed ideals embodied by the actors in this drama, we can be encouraged to stand up, to say something, to refuse silence, to refute the all too prevalent rape myths we have culturally inherited.[40] I suggest that the medieval text throws into relief the modern issues of interpersonal violence in a way that students do not expect them to appear. In a sense, when we allow them space, our modern attitudes can be good allies in interpretation, even as we listen to the medieval text tell its story. Thus we continue the very real and very relevant dialogue with older texts; the older texts may hold unexpected "promise" in the context of relatively new bystander prevention efforts.[41] In its context and in ours, the tenth adventure of the *Nibelungenlied* can participate in our ongoing attempt to challenge the prevailing rape culture in higher education, to help cultivate a culture of "upstanders."

Works Cited

Banyard, Victoria L., Mary M. Moynihan, and Maria T. Crossman. "Reducing Sexual Violence on Campus: The Role of Student Leaders as Empowered Bystanders." *Journal of College Student Development* 50 (2009): 446–57.

Batt, Catherine. "Malory and Rape." *Arthuriana* (1997): 78–99.

Bertram, Corrine C., and M. Sue Crowley. "Teaching about Sexual Violence in Higher Education: Moving from Concern to Conscious Resistance." *Frontiers: A Journal of Women Studies* 33 (2012): 63–82.

Cares, Alison C., Mary M. Moynihan, and Victoria L. Baynard. "Taking Stock of Bystander Programmes: Changing Attitudes and Behaviours towards Sexual Violence." In *Preventing Sexual Violence: Interdisciplinary Approaches to Overcoming a Rape Culture*, edited by Nicola Henry and Anastasia Powell, 170–89. London: Palgrave Macmillan, 2014.

Cermele, Jill, and Martha McCaughey. "What's Wrong with the CDC's Public Health Model for Rape Prevention." *Journal of Community Med Health* 5 (2015): 387. doi:10.4172/2161-0711.1000387.

Classen, Albrecht. "The Downfall of a Hero: Siegfried's Self-Destruction and the End of Heroism in the Nibelungenlied." *German Studies Review* (2003): 295–314.

———. *Sexual Violence and Rape in the Middle Ages: A Critical Discourse in Premodern German and European Literature.* Vol. 7. Berlin: Walter de Gruyter, 2011.

Cowell, Andrew. *The Medieval Warrior Aristocracy: Gifts, Violence, Performance, and the Sacred.* Cambridge: Brewer, 2007.

Ehrismann, Otfrid. *Nibelungenlied: Epoche—Werk—Wirkung.* 2nd ed. Munich: Beck, 2002.

---

40 Much work remains to be done in the college-aged population to dismantle the acceptance of rape myths. See Kaylee Vance, Megan Sutter, Paul B. Perrin, and Martin Heesacker, "The Media's Sexual Objectification of Women, Rape Myth Acceptance, and Interpersonal Violence," *Journal of Aggression, Maltreatment & Trauma* 24 (2015): 569–87, DOI:10.1080/10926771.2015.1029179.

41 Cares, Moynihan, and Baynard, "Taking Stock," 183.

Frakes, Jerold C. *Brides and Doom: Gender, Property, and Power in Medieval German Women's Epic.* Philadelphia: University of Pennsylvania Press, 1994.

Gravdal, Kathryn. "Chrétien de Troyes, Gratian, and the Medieval Romance of Sexual Violence." *Signs* (1992): 558–85.

———. *Ravishing Maidens: Writing Rape in Medieval French Literature and Law.* Philadelphia: University of Pennsylvania Press, 1991.

Grimstad, Kaaren, and Ray M. Wakefield. "Monstrous Mates: The Leading Ladies of the *Nibelungenlied* and *Völsunga Saga.*" In *Women and Medieval Epic: Gender, Genre, and the Limits of Epic Masculinity*, edited by Sara S. Poor and Jana K. Schulman, 235–53. New York: Palgrave Macmillan, 2007.

Henry, Nicola, and Anastasia Powell. "Framing Sexual Violence Prevention: What Does It Mean to Challenge a Rape Culture?" In *Preventing Sexual Violence: Interdisciplinary Approaches to Overcoming a Rape Culture*, edited by Nicola Henry and Anastasia Powell, 1–22. London: Palgrave Macmillan, 2014.

———, eds. *Preventing Sexual Violence: Interdisciplinary Approaches to Overcoming a Rape Culture.* London: Palgrave Macmillan, 2014.

Jackson, William H. "Court Literature and Violence in the High Middle Ages." In *German Literature of the High Middle Ages*, edited by Will Hasty, 263–77. Rochester: Camden House, 2006.

Lienert, Elisabeth. "Geschlecht und Gewalt im 'Nibelungenlied'." *Zeitschrift für deutsches Altertum und deutsche Literatur* (2003): 3–23.

McCaughey, Martha, and Jill Cermele. "Changing the Hidden Curriculum of Campus Rape Prevention and Education: Women's Self-Defense as a Key Protective Factor for a Public Health Model of Prevention." *Trauma, Violence, & Abuse* (October 16, 2015): *MEDLINE, EBSCOhost* (accessed February 27, 2016).

McConnell, Winder, Werner Wunderlich, Frank Gentry, and Ulrich Mueller, eds. *The Nibelungen Tradition: An Encyclopedia.* London: Routledge, 2002.

McGreevy, Patrick, and Melanie Mason. "California Lawmakers Pass 'Yes-Means-Yes' Campus Sexual Assault Bill." *Los Angeles Times*, August 29, 2014. www.latimes.com/local/lanow/la-me-ln-california-yes-means-yes-sexual-assault-bill-20140829-story.html (accessed 1 March 2015).

McMahon, Sarah. "Rape Myth Beliefs and Bystander Attitudes among Incoming College Students." *Journal of American College Health* 59 (2010): 3–11.

McMahon, Sarah, Judy L. Postmus, and Ruth Anne Koenick. "Conceptualizing the Engaging Bystander Approach to Sexual Violence Prevention on College Campuses." *Journal of College Student Development* 52 (2011): 115–30.

Müller, Jan-Dirk. *Rules for the Endgame: The World of the Nibelungenlied.* Translated by William Whobrey. Baltimore: Johns Hopkins University Press, 2007.

The Nibelungenlied: The Lay of the Nibelungs. Translated and edited by Cyril Edwards. Oxford: Oxford University Press, 2010.

Pafenberg, Stephanie B. "The Spindle and the Sword: Gender, Sex, and Heroism in the Nibelungenlied and Kudrun." *The Germanic Review: Literature, Culture, Theory* 70 (1995): 106–15.

Pugh, Tison, and Susan Aronstein, eds. *The Disney Middle Ages: A Fairy-Tale and Fantasy Past.* New York: Palgrave Macmillan, 2012.

Renz, Tilo. *Um Leib und Leben: Das Wissen von Geschlecht, Körper und Recht im Nibelungenlied.* Berlin: De Gruyter, 2012.

Vance, Kaylee, Megan Sutter, Paul B. Perrin, and Martin Heesacker. "The Media's Sexual Objectification of Women, Rape Myth Acceptance, and Interpersonal Violence." *Journal of Aggression, Maltreatment & Trauma* 24 (2015): 569–87.

Web Resources

Regional/National

www.knowyourix.org: National website for information on Title IX "empowering students to stop sexual violence."

www.chrysalis.com: Site for a Raleigh NC-based innovative workshop facilitator working in fall 2014 and spring 2015 on interpersonal violence training for all supervisors at Appalachian State University.

www.theredflagcampaign.org: Site for the red flag campaign, "a project of the Virginia Sexual and Domestic Violence Action Alliance, and was created by college students, college personnel, and community victim advocates."

www.cdc.gov/violenceprevention/intimatepartnerviolence/: site for the Division for the Prevention of Violence at the Centers for Disease Control. Two sections focus particularly, with bacckground information and resources, on intimate partner violence (IPV) and sexual violence (SV).

www.nsvrc.org/bystander-intervention-background-and-general-information: site for the National Sexual Violence Resource Center with information on bystander intervention.

www.bullybust.org/: definition of an upstander.

https://leginfo.legislature.ca.gov/faces/billNavClient.xhtml?bill_id=201320140SB 967: SB-967: Student safety: sexual assault.

Appalachian State University

www.appcares.appstate.edu: site for wellness, health and safety information, resources, and support for the campus community.

www.redflag.appstate.edu: site for ASU's campus-based campaign designed to raise awareness and educate people about being active bystanders.

Chapter 6

SPEECH, SILENCE, AND TEACHING CHAUCER'S RAPES

TISON PUGH

> At every turn, rape is an interpretive act.
>
> Rachel Warburton, "Reading Rape in Chaucer"[1]

He said/she said: the invariable shorthand for the challenges of deciphering occluded events of violence and violation, in which the question of which story we believe—that of the accused or of the accuser—bears out innumerable consequences related to our conceptions of justice, gender, and sexuality, both in the past and continuing into the present. Chaucer depicts rape and scenes suggestive of rape in several of his *Canterbury Tales*, most notably "The Miller's Tale," "The Reeve's Tale," and "The Wife of Bath's Tale," and in his *Legend of Good Women* as well, particularly in the *Legend of Lucrece* and the *Legend of Philomela*, with these encounters highlighting the ways in which speech and silence formulate readers' reactions to sexual violence. Various medieval theologians and exegetes extol silence as a woman's defining virtue, yet Chaucer's narratives both reinforce this prevailing view and allow readers to consider how male speech either excuses or condemns violent enactments of male sexuality.

By foregrounding in our classrooms the ways in which Chaucer depicts speech and silence as gendered reactions to sexual violence, instructors can illuminate the various ways that literary depictions of rape simultaneously reinforce and undermine medieval constructions of gender. Such a perspective also allows scholars and students to consider the ways in which we choose—or choose not—to speak of Chaucer's vexing identity as a potential rapist in his interactions with Cecily Champaigne—a biographical event in which textuality, speech, and silence converge to haunt our understanding of Chaucer's benevolently paternal image as the "Father of English Literature." In the pages that follow I discuss converging

---

1 Rachel Warburton, "Reading Rape in Chaucer; or, Are Cecily, Lucretia, and Philomela Good Women?," in *Diversifying the Discourse: The Florence Howe Award for Outstanding Feminist Scholarship, 1990–2004*, eds. Mihoko Suzuki and Roseanna Dufault (New York: MLA, 2006), 270.

teaching strategies for addressing Chaucer's depictions of rape that I employ in my classes at the University of Central Florida—a large, metropolitan, public institution with students from a diverse range of backgrounds, with varying previous exposure to medieval literature, to gender theory, and to literary theory.

Speech and silence play constitutive roles in both gender theory and literary theory, and clarifying this confluence for students opens new avenues for their mutual exploration in various texts. Throughout the classical and medieval periods, philosophers praised the virtues of women's silence, thereby constructing gender through a binary of masculine speech and feminine silence. Carolyn Dinshaw's groundbreaking work in *Chaucer's Sexual Poetics* ably documents classical, biblical, and medieval viewpoints advocating women's silence, providing representative statements from Aristotle, Paul, and Thomas Aquinas as evidence of the many variations on this misogynistic theme.[2] Aristotle states, "All classes must be deemed to have their special attributes; as the poet [Sophocles] says of women, 'Silence is a woman's glory'; but this is not equally the glory of man."[3] In the early Christian tradition Paul similarly advocates women's silence: "Let women keep silence in the churches: for it is not permitted them to speak, but to be subject, as also the law saith. But if they would learn any thing, let them ask their husbands at home. For it is a shame for a woman to speak in the church" (1 Corinthians 14:34–5).[4] More than a millennium later, Thomas Aquinas echoes such sentiments, "For what is appropriate for the ornament of a woman or her integrity, that she is silent, proceeds from the modesty which is owed to women; but this does not relate to the ornament of a man, instead, it is fitting that he speaks."[5] He then cites Paul's first epistle to the Corinthians to bolster his point. These classical, biblical, and medieval discourses establish a sharp binary between women's silence and men's speech, one that plays out in various literary texts of concurrent and subsequent eras.

A simple yet effective pedagogical strategy for discussing Chaucer's constructions of gender involves giving students a list of stereotypically male and female characteristics and then asking them to examine a text—"The Wife of Bath's Prologue" works quite well for this assignment—in which they determine how closely the characters adhere to these paradigms. Within medieval binaries of gender, men were perceived as intellectual, active, reasonable, sexually temperate, just, orderly, and truthful, whereas women were perceived as bodily, passive, irrational, lusty, merciful, disorderly, and deceptive.[6] Furthermore, the internal self-contradictions of gendered binaries should become further apparent when

---

2 Carolyn Dinshaw, *Chaucer's Sexual Poetics* (Madison: University of Wisconsin Press, 1989), 19. In this paragraph, I review Dinshaw's examples of such anti-feminist discourse.

3 Aristotle, *Politics*, trans. by Benjamin Jowett (Oxford: Clarendon, 1938), 1260a, at p. 52.

4 Biblical quotations are taken from *The Holy Bible Douay-Rheims Version*.

5 Thomas Aquinas, qtd. in Prudence Allen, *The Concept of Woman: The Aristotelian Revolution, 750 BC–AD 1250* (Montreal: Eden Press, 1985), 400.

6 As necessary, instructors should bring in a variety of primary sources to detail these gender stereotypes more fully. Martha Brozyna's *Gender and Sexuality in the Middle Ages: A Medieval Source Documents Reader* (Jefferson: McFarland, 2005) provides an ample array of appropriate selections.

instructors introduce rebuttals to these prevailing views, such as the complementary gender stereotypes presuming men to be silent and women to be garrulous, even gossipy. Whereas Aristotle, Paul, and Aquinas encourage women's silence, the stereotypes assume their inability to achieve this ambition, as their failure, or refusal to do so, further builds meaning in various literary texts. No binary can capture a character such as the Wife of Bath, and so this assignment highlights both the prevalence of such gendered stereotypes and their limitations for authors seeking to draw characters who reflect and simultaneously transcend the borders between genders. Indeed, as students soon realize, multiple passages recounting Alison of Bath's actions in her Prologue showcase a mixture of male and female attributes, such as her lustiness and her sexual self-control. Soon after she confesses her voracious sexual appetite, in that she "hadde ... many a myrthe" while "walkynge out by nyghte" (3.399, 397), she explains how she exploited male lust for her benefit through restraining her desires:

> I wolde no lenger in the bed abyde,
> If that I felte his arm over my syde,
> Til he had maad his raunson unto me;
> Thanne wolde I suffre hym do his nycetee.
>
> (3.409–12)[7]

Weaving in and out of traditional dichotomies of masculinity and femininity, the Wife of Bath allows students to consider how Chaucer exploits gender stereotypes to enhance her character, depicting her as both marked by and emancipated from discourses of proper female conduct.

As medieval conceptions of gender employ the dichotomy between speech and silence to characterize men and women, literary theory asks readers to consider the contrasting meanings of speech and silence, for the gaps and fissures of a text construct its meaning through what it will not, or otherwise cannot, address. In my personal development as a reader, the words I found singly most illuminating for generating textual interpretations belong to Pierre Macherey: "By speech, silence becomes the centre and principle of expression, its vanishing point. Speech eventually has nothing more to tell us: we investigate the silence, for it is the silence that is doing the speaking."[8] Macherey's words open up new avenues for students learning how texts construct some meanings, camouflage others, or simply cannot broach certain topics because the wider culture could not, or would not, see them. To improve their skills in literary comprehension, all readers must grapple with this inherent tension between text and subtext, speech and silence, or, in another phrasing of an old issue, surface and symptom. Stephen Best and Sharon Marcus

---

7 Geoffrey Chaucer, *The Riverside Chaucer*, edited by Larry D. Benson, 3rd ed. (Boston: Houghton Mifflin, 1987); cited parenthetically.

8 Pierre Macherey, "From *A Theory of Literary Production*," in *A Critical and Cultural Theory Reader*, eds. Antony Easthope and Kate McGowan (Toronto: University of Toronto Press, 1992), 23.

eloquently distinguish between these modes of narrative communication, thereby elucidating their utility as conjoined hermeneutics. A surface reading attends to what "is evident, perceptible, apprehensible in texts; what is neither hidden nor hiding; what, in the geometrical sense, has length and breadth but no thickness, and therefore covers no depth."[9] In contrast, they describe symptomatic readings as ones that "locate outright absences, gaps, and ellipses in texts, and then ask what those absences mean, what forces create them, and how they signify the questions that motivate the text, but that the text itself cannot articulate"; they further hypothesize that symptomatic readings query such binaries as "present/absent, manifest/latent, and surface/depth."[10] When readers search for a text's silences and symptoms, they must pierce through its surface to get a deeper picture of its internal logic, of what is represented but also of what is repressed or silenced. A guiding principle of elementary literary education is that students first learn to read so that they can then read to learn; to advance the objective of critical thinking that is so central to the mission of post-secondary education, we might expand this pithy encapsulation to include that students must learn to read the surface to see what they did not read yet nonetheless perceive in the text's symptoms, which become key to its deeper meaning(s) and to their practice of interpretation.

Further along these lines, the very concept of gender—and the very necessity of gendered analyses—arises in the view of women as symptoms of men, with rape both making these dynamics visible yet also occluding them. The historical devaluation of women as inferior to man, as psychoanalytic criticism demonstrates, boils down to the assumption of signifying potential in the phallus—and the imagined lack of signification through the female body. As Carolyn Dinshaw forcefully avers: "Western society is ordered by a logic that construes the world in terms of one sex and its lack or deviation ... and the act of rape forcibly puts this foundational logic into practice: it insists that woman is—and must be—only what man is not, man's Other, man's lack, a not-man, a no-thing."[11] The longstanding construction of women as Other to men enables rape to communicate gender's raw force to both sexes: rape, in an excrutiatingly horrible sense, simply makes manifest the power dynamics inherent in gender.[12]

In light of this Western tradition we should not be surprised to find that rape so frequently appears throughout Chaucer's corpus, which repeatedly takes as its

---

9 Stephen Best and Sharon Marcus, "Surface Reading: An Introduction," *Representations* 108 (2009): 9.

10 Ibid., 3–4.

11 Carolyn Dinshaw, "Rivalry, Rape, and Manhood," in *Violence against Women in Medieval Texts*, ed. Anna Roberts (Gainesville: University Press of Florida, 1998), 42. For the classical era's one-sex model of human biology and its long reach throughout the medieval era and beyond, see Thomas Laqueur, *Making Sex: Body and Gender from the Greeks to Freud* (Cambridge, MA: Harvard University Press, 1990), 26–62.

12 While Chaucer does not address male–male rape in his corpus (with the possible exception of Absolon and Nicholas, as I discuss shortly), it is worth noting that archaic gender roles resiliently adapt to homosexual rape, with the binary logic of penetrator and penetrated mirroring the overdetermined roles of male and female. The signifying force of the phallus extends to a range of acts and identities beyond the heteroerotic dyad.

subject matter the fraught relations between the sexes. As Jill Mann affirms: "rape remains a constant touchstone for determining justice between the sexes; in the *Canterbury Tales* as in the *Legend* [*of Good Women*] it appears as the definitive form of male tyranny, representing a fundamental imbalance between the sexes which human relationships must seek to redress."[13] And so while I concentrate in this essay on the tales and legends in which rape is clearly suggested or signified—"The Miller's Tale," "The Reeve's Tale," "The Wife of Bath's Tale," *Legend of Lucrece*, and *Legend of Philomela*—it is well worth remembering that many women throughout Chaucer's corpus confront unwelcome erotic advances, undesired marriages, and spousal violence, in such varied texts as the "The Man of Law's Tale," "The Clerk's Tale, "The Franklin's Tale," "The Physician's Tale," "The Second Nun's Tale," and "The Manciple's Tale," as well as many in the *Legend of Good Women*. Studying the fissures between speech and silence illuminates a vast range of sexual encounters in Chaucer's canon, including Emily's marriage to Palamon in "The Knight's Tale" and May's marriage to January in "The Merchant's Tale," in which they do not voice their reaction to their prospective grooms; their silence contrasts sharply with the wife's negotiation of her sexuality (to the profit of her wardrobe) in "The Shipman's Tale," in which speech allows this woman to pursue her desires both erotic and sartorial. Troilus' orchestrated seduction of Criseyde likewise hedges uneasily with rape, especially given Pandarus' flippant advice, after the lovers have been separated, "Go ravysshe here! Ne kanstow nat, for shame?" (4.530). Chaucer's many returns to issues of sexual violence necessitate that instructors confront these encounters in the classroom, and the very frequency of this theme enables students to link otherwise disparate genres, which further illuminates rape's varying yet similar narrative function. Fabliau and romance invert each other's themes and registers almost uniformly, yet in Chaucer's corpus both the humour of "The Miller's Tale" and "The Reeve's Tale" and the courtliness of "The Wife of Bath's Tale" rely on rape to advance their plots. To see that rape shifts as a plot device in these various genres informs students that rape functions discursively—it tells a story, and it is their responsibility to hear it with as much critical acumen as possible.

When students are confronting the difficulties of learning Middle English early in the semester, instructors should forgive them if they miss the allusions to rape in "The Miller's Tale"—especially because the possibility of rape is transformed into the humorous pleasure of adultery in the space of a few poetic lines. After Nicholas aggressively confronts Alison, she vigorously attempts to free herself from what she perceives as her imminent rape:

> And she sproong as a colt dooth in the trave,
> And with her heed she wryed faste awey,
> And seyde, "I wol nat kisse thee, by my fey!
> Why, lat be!" quod she. "Lat be, Nicholas,

---

13 Jill Mann, *Feminizing Chaucer* (1991; Woodbridge: Brewer, 2002), 36.

Or I wol crie 'out, harrow' and 'allas'!
Do wey youre handes, for youre curteisye!"

(1.3282–87)

The taletell words of "out, harrow" and "allas" signify Alison's intention to escape from sexual violence, as she informs Nicholas that she will call out to their neighbours to stop him. The tale avoids rape at this moment, and Nicholas consequently shifts from violent action to honeyed speech in his arsenal of "seductive" tactics: "This Nicholas gan mercy for to crye, / And spak so faire, and profred him so faste, / That she hir love hym graunted atte laste" (1.3288–90). A woman's refusal to be silent allows her to avoid rape, and, in complementary contrast, speech advances Nicholas's desires more effectively than physical force—proving the power of words for advancing this fabliau's farcical plot, which relies on ludicrous speech to succeed when direct action fails.

Rape nonetheless invades "The Miller Tale's" subliteral level, and students should therefore pay attention to the ways in which silence, speech, and sexual violence extend beyond the text's surface significations. Thus, to interpret Absolon's violation of Nicholas at the tale's conclusion—"And he was redy with his iren hoot, / And Nicholas amydde the ers he smoot" (1.3809–10)—as a rape extends the penetrative logic that Nicholas unleashed in the fabliau's beginning. Furthermore, in contrast to Alison's decision not to cry "out, harrow" and "allas" earlier in the tale—that is, in contrast to her choice to remain silent—she joins her lover in publicly crying out these words after he suffers the humiliation of his branding: "Up stirte hire Alison and Nicholay / And criden 'Out' and 'Harrow' in the strete" (1.3824–5). Within the carnivalesque world of this fabliau, Alison's preference for silence over speech allows her the pleasures of her affair, while Nicholas's ready speech first wins him the object of his affections while preparing him for his rival's anal revenge. Readers have long recognized the violence and humiliation meted out to the tale's male characters—John's broken arm, Nicholas's scalded buttocks, Absolon's direct confrontation with thunderous flatulence—while Alison faces no consequences for her erotic transgressions. Here too the narrative encodes an absence—no explanation is given for why Alison escapes punishment—thus asking readers to ponder the ways in which Chaucer's tale opts for silence in its refusal to condemn its female protagonist.

Rape circulates as a potential outcome in "The Miller's Tale," one that Alison avoids and that Nicholas then suffers (at least in the tale's imagery of anal branding). To most modern eyes, rape clearly occurs in "The Reeve's Tale" when Aleyn enters Malyne's bed without her consent, yet, as Holly Crocker cautions of medieval jurisprudence, "Between Aleyn's stealth and Malyne's affection, neither the girl nor Symkyn has a legal claim to rape."[14] In terms of speech and silence, this encounter

---

14 Holly Crocker, "Affective Politics in Chaucer's *Reeve's Tale*," *Studies in the Age of Chaucer* 29 (2007): 246.

alludes to the possibility of a woman defending herself with the same terms as "The Miller's Tale":

And up [Aleyn] rist, and by the wenche he crepte.
This wenche lay uprighte and faste slepte,
Til he so ny was, er she myghte espie,
That it had been to late for to crie,
And shortly for to seyn, they were aton.
Now pley, Aleyn, for I wol speke of John.

(1.4193–98)

With the provocative phrasing "it had been to late for to crie," the narrator encodes the possibility that, if Malyne had had sufficient time to cry out, she would have done so and thus averted her fate. The cultural history of rape—indeed, the logic of rape, if one can concede the possibility of logic coinciding with such brutal violence— requires silence, and Malyne's quiet at this pivotal moment obfuscates for readers her reaction to the unfolding events. The tale's genre of fabliau occludes its sexual politics, in that rape is treated in the same lighthearted tone as Symkin's theft of Aleyn and John's grain, yet it is worth pondering the necessity of women's silence to achieve this narrative goal. If Malyne could speak at this moment, if Chaucer allowed her to do so, what would she say, at this moment of violation, other than no?

"The Reeve's Tale" concerns itself primarily with men's traffic in women, as Aleyn and John, by arrogating to themselves Symkin's wife and daughter for their bodily pleasure, seek revenge against him for stealing their grain, yet the tale also addresses, tangentially yet critically, Malyne's nascent sense of agency. As Nicole Nolan Sidhu posits, "Although rape and the erotic rebellion of a daughter may at first glance appear to be diametrically opposed events, they are unified by their common concern with women's exercise of free will."[15] One of the defining critical cruxes of "The Reeve's Tale," Malyne's silence demands an interpretation that her words do little to clarify. Speechless at the moment of her rape, she voices her desires the following morning:

"Now, deere lemman," quod she, "go, far weel!
But er thow go, o thyng I wol thee telle:
What that thou wendest homward by the melle,
Right at the entree of the dore bihynde
Thou shalt a cake of half a busshel fynde
That was ymaked of thyn owene mele,
Which that I heelp my sire for to stele.
And, goode lemman, God thee save and kepe!"
And with that word almoost she gan to wepe.

(1.4240–48)

---

15 Nicole Nolan Sidhu, " 'To late for to crie': Female Desire, Fabliau Politics, and Classical Legend in Chaucer's *Reeve's Tale*," *Exemplaria* 21 (2009): 4.

Chaucer departs from his primary sources for "The Reeve's Tale" by depicting Malyne's speech after her rape,[16] and so his rewriting of the tale gives this character a new freedom to voice her response to the unfolding events. Through these words, she announces her intention to defy her father, releasing herself from any complicity with his theft of their grain and emancipating herself—in spirit, if not in actuality—from his brutish paternity. Malyne's rape, within the carnivalesque world of Chaucer's fabliau, asks provocative questions about how sexual violence functions narratively: is it funny? Is it empowering, as Malyne finds the agency to disengage from her father after an evening in which "thries in this shorte nyght" Aleyn has "swyved [her] bolt upright" (1.4265–6)? Students should struggle with such challenging questions, yet in analyzing Malyne's speech and silence, they must confront the ways in which genre transmutes trauma into laughter—or at least attempts to do so.

"The Wife of Bath's Prologue" affords students the pleasure of indulging in a torrent of women's words—fast, funny, furious—that Alison then slows to silence as they meet the rape victim of her tale. In multiple registers of discourse and metadiscourse, the Wife of Bath highlights the varying cultural meanings of women's speech and silence, as Suzanne Edwards attests: "At each of its fictive levels—the *Tale*, the *Prologue*, and the story of the Canterbury pilgrimage itself—Chaucer's literary experiment reproduces the formal logic of sexual violence in the late fourteenth century by dramatizing the gap between bodies imagined to have desires and the bodies through which those desires are voiced."[17] In "The Wife of Bath's Tale," rape catalyzes the plot: Chaucer would have no story without it. Foremost, students should recognize a shift in tone in his treatment of rape, primarily as a response to the shift in genre between fabliau and romance. Fabliau revels in plots of violence and sexual transgression, yet romance, as a rule, affirms a world of courtly order, with any disruptions to this state of decorum attended to by the narrative's end. When Chaucer's rapist knight breaks Andreas Capellanus' fifth rule of courtly love—"That which a lover takes against the will of his beloved has no relish"[18]—readers should expect his immediate punishment, and it appears that justice will indeed be meted out to him:

---

16 Chaucer's likely sources for "The Reeve's Tale" include "Le meunier et les. II. clers: Text A" (MS 354 Bibliothèque de Berne, 1275–1300); "Le meunier et les. II. clers: Text B" (Hamilton MS, Berlin, 1275–1300); "Een bispel van.ij. clerken" (MS KB 15.589–623, Royal Library, Brussels "Hulthem Collection," 1350–75); and Boccaccio's *Decameron* (day 9, story 6). These tales feature two men tricking their host and sleeping with his wife and daughter and are anthologized in Robert Correale and Mary Hamel, eds., *Sources and Analogues to the Canterbury Tales* (Cambridge: Brewer, 2002), 1.23–73. For further discussion, see my *Chaucer's (Anti-) Eroticisms and the Queer Middle Ages* (Columbus: Ohio State University Press, 2014), 135–45.
17 Suzanne Edwards, "The Rhetoric of Rape, and the Politics of Gender in the *Wife of Bath's Tale* and the *1382 Statute of Rapes*," *Exemplaria* 23 (2011): 23.
18 Andreas Capellanus, *The Art of Courtly Love*, trans. by John Jay Parry (New York: Columbia University Press, 1960), 184. To further complicate, and also to better contextualize, lessons on medieval speech, silence, and rape, instructors can productively explore the world of medieval courtly love, with its multiple and contradictory rules of seduction. Certainly, a key rule of courtly love demands silence: "When made public, love rarely endures" (185).

He saugh a mayde walkynge hym biforn,
Of which mayde anon, maugree hir heed,
By verray force, he rafte hire maydenhed;
For which oppressioun was swich clamour
And swich pursute unto the kyng Arthour
That dampned was this knyght for to be deed.

(3.886–91)

The passage is astonishing for its journalistic brevity, and, more so, for the raped maiden who simply disappears from the tale. Readers never hear her speak nor learn of her reaction to Guinevere's riddle-quest for the knight: "I grante thee lyf, if thou kanst tellen me / What thyng is it that wommen moost desiren" (3.904–5). Arthur's queen demands the rapist knight move from criminal action to courtly speech, and with the assistance of the "olde wyf" (3.1000) who gives him the answer to her puzzle, he wins his life through his words—or, more accurately, through parroting this woman's words: "Wommen desiren to have sovereynetee / As wel over hir housbond as hir love, / And for to been in maistrie hym above" (3.1038–40). Men's actions inflict violence, whereas women's words facilitate mercy and rehabilitation—a tidier dichotomy between speech and silence, between women and men, could hardly be imagined.

Yet tidy dichotomies are rarely effective teaching strategies, for they reinstitute the type of lazy binary thinking that collegiate instruction should undermine in favour of confronting the rich and full complexity of literary interactions. And "The Wife of Bath's Tale" provides students further opportunities to consider the meanings of speech and silence as the rapist knight's new wife upbraids her husband for his cruel words about her ugliness, her age, and her low social class, while echoing in this extended speech (3.1106–218) many of the Wife of Bath's key themes in her Prologue. While rape is a physical violation, words can wound as well, and so it appears at this point that the rapist knight has merely learned to substitute one weapon (his penis) for another (his mouth). In this wife's monologue, readers return to the type of erudition that characterizes "The Wife of Bath's Prologue," proving again the provocative wisdom of women's speech. A cacophony of voices then concludes Alison's tale: the knight's new wife allows her husband to choose between virtuous ugliness and licentious beauty (3.1219–27), the rapist knight speaks only to express his silence (that is, his inability to decide [3.1230–5]), the Wife of Bath curses "olde and angry nygardes of dispence" (3.1263), and even the Friar, as his Prologue begins, attempts to convert the Wife of Bath's imprecation into play: "Ye han seyd muche thyng right wel, I seye; / But, dame, heeere as we ryde by the weye, / Us nedeth nat to speken but of game" (3.1273–5). Through this interplay of voices and silences, Chaucer challenges his readers to consider the richness of communication, of how gender collapses in the battle of words that arises from a woman who never tells the story of her rape.

Whereas Aristotle, Paul, and Aquinas endorse feminine silence and masculine speech, it is the foolishness of men's chatter that instigates the plot of Chaucer's *Legend of Lucrece*. Bored with the tedium of the seige, Tarquinius desires instead the pleasures of conversation: "And lat us speke of wyves, that is best; / Preyse every man his owene as hym lest, / And with oure speche lat us ese oure herte" (1702–4). Tarquinius' idle delight in conversation soon sparks his lechery, and after witnessing Lucrece's fidelity to her husband Collatinus, he proceeds with his plan to rape her. Speech and silence again afford an index to track gender's manipulations, for his brute force renders her speechless:

> No word she spak, she hath no myght therto.
> What shal she seyn? Hire wit is al ago.
> Ryght as a wolf that fynt a lomb alone,
> To whom shal she compleyne or make mone?
> What, shal she fyghte with an hardy knyght?
> Wel wot men that a woman hath no myght.
> What, shal she crye, or how shal she asterte
> That hath hire by the throte with swerd at herte?
> She axeth grace, and seyth al that she can.
>
> (1796–804)

The classical and medieval traditions that praise women's silence are here achieved only through the violence of a sword's sharp edge, illustrating the ways in which speech and silence serve as arenas in which brute force strips away pretensions of masculine honour. For some women, speech must cede to prayer, in Lucrece's silent call for grace to endure her ordeal.

Yet Lucrece finds her voice following her rape, as the narrator reports: "But atte last of Tarquyny she hem tolde / This rewful cas and al thys thing horryble. / The woo to tellen were an impossible" (1837–9). Chaucer here stresses the paradox of speech, in that even as Lucrece talks, words cannot capture the impossible pain she experienced. But speech affords agency in this legend as well, as Elizabeth Robertson clarifies: "Lucrece's liminal position as a raped woman suggests a paradox: the very event, rape, that defines a woman as an object, reveals her to be a subject for just after rape, a woman's subjectivity is released from the social constraints that determine not only her value or worth as property, but also her identity."[19] The text moves quickly to its conclusion, as Lucrece speaks her final words—" 'Be as be may,' quod she, 'of forgyvyng, / I wol not have noo forgyft for nothing" (1852–3)—and then slays herself. Lucrece's rape results in the birth of the Roman republic, as several commentators have noted, with speech and silence playing key roles in how this violation unfolds in its conception, enactment, and consequences.[20] Indeed, the narrator reports that Lucrece's story commands male speech, both for his own purposes—"I telle hyt" (1874)—as he then compares his words to Jesus's:

---

19 Elizabeth Robertson, "Public Bodies and Psychic Domains," in *Representing Rape in Medieval and Early Modern Literature*, eds. Elizabeth Robertson and Christine Rose (New York: Palgrave, 2001), 285. See also Louise Sylvester, "Reading Narratives of Rape: The Story of Lucretia in Chaucer, Gower, and Christine de Pizan," *Leeds Studies in English* 31 (2000): 115–44.
20 For a masterful reading of the ways that the Western "humanistic tradition ... has celebrated Lucretia's rape as a prologue to republican freedom" (5), see Stephanie H. Jed, *Chaste Thinking: The Rape of Lucretia and the Birth of Humanism* (Bloomington: Indiana

For wel I wot that Crist himselve telleth
That in Israel, as wyd as is the lond,
That so gret feyth in al that he ne fond
As in a woman; and this is no lye.

(1879–82)

Men's speech, a font of corruption, depravity, and violence in the legend's beginning, is reborn as the words of the narrator's saviour, inspiring a moral lesson from a pre-Christian woman who metamorphoses into a Christian saint ("she was holden there / A seynt" [1870–1]). In their multiple and shifting registers, speech, silence, and prayer unite to reveal male depravity, which, in Chaucer's Christological context, can only be redeemed through the Word: "In the beginning was the Word, and the Word was with God, and the Word was God" (John 1.1). The Divine Word is the ultimate wellspring of language and meaning, and it emerges in this legend's conclusion to be contrasted with Tarquinius' vile degradation of truth.

Chaucer's characters barely speak in *Legend of Philomela*—a lacuna that hints at the significance of silence in a tale about Philomela's rape and, through Tereus' hideous act of cruelty in cutting out her tongue, speechlessness. Other than Pandion's six lines to Tereus requesting his daughter Philomela's safe passage to her sister Procne, the legend contains only three additional lines of dialogue. Sensing the violence about to befall her at Tereus' hands, Philomela nervously asks, "Where is my sister, brother Tereus?" (2315), and after the rape, the narrator reports that she utters a few additional words: "She cryeth 'Syster!' with ful loud a stevene, / And 'Fader dere!' and 'Help me, God in hevene!'" (2328–9). Following these emotionally charged words, Chaucer registers the fact that neither Procne, Pandion, nor God can aid her in her distress: "Al helpeth nat" (2330). Whereas in "The Reeve's Tale," Chaucer, in contrast to his sources, bestows speech upon Malyne following her night with Aleyn, in *Legend of Philomela* he encodes a silence, ending his narrative as Procne learns the truth of her husband's cruel duplicity, which renders her equally speechless: "No word she spak, for sorwe and ek for rage" (2374). Rendered mute when Tereus cuts out her tongue to enforce her silence, Philomela must adapt to this violence wrought upon her, and so she communicates through her weaving, proving the protean resilience of women's silence. As Kathryn Sullivan Kruger details, "When Philomela decides to weave her story, she reconstitutes her position in terms of her society, so that instead of remaining an object or body used, silenced, and discarded, she becomes a subject, an artist reclaiming her voice and her forbidden story."[21] Women's silence does not correlate with women's inaction in Chaucer's classical sources, yet once again, silence demands interpretation, for Chaucer's decision to omit Procne and Philomela's gruesome revenge, as they serve Tereus a dinner cooked of his son

---

University Press, 1989), as well as Melissa Matthes, *The Rape of Lucretia and the Founding of Republics: Readings in Livy, Machiavelli, and Rousseau* (University Park: Pennsylvania State University Press, 2000).

21 Kathryn Sullivan Kruger, *Weaving the Word: The Metaphorics of Weaving and Female Textual Production* (Selinsgrove: Susquehanna University Press, 2001), 60.

Itys, encodes an interpretive gap that readers must confront. As Rachel Warburton observes, "The omission of the women's revenge is a double-edged sword. On the one hand, Chaucer removes that which readers might find difficult to sympathize. Under erasure in Chaucer's version, the women's revenge is both absent and present simultaneously, and renders them ambiguous victims at best."[22] Victims, or victims turned victimizers, or perhaps even an escape from the binary logic of victim and victimizer? Chaucer's Procne and Philomela, enveloped in the textual silences that accompany this rape and in Chaucer's metatextual silences that remove the taint of their murderous revenge, exemplify the complexity of interpretation when multiple narratives tell the same story in different ways.

With these brief examples of Chaucer's treatments of rape, and with the many other instances in which he engages with issues of female gender politics, instructors can foreground in their classrooms the utility of gender theories that question artificial distinctions between the sexes, as well as the utility of literary theories of speech and silence as interpretive tools that further enlighten the ways in which gender functions in medieval literature. Theories of gender and of literature must confront the inherent contradictions of binaries that collapse under their own weight, yet these contradictions nonetheless enable readers to construct their own unique interpretations of immensely rich texts. To which does one listen—the speech or the silence? One must hear both, but often one must take precedence over the other. In all "he said/she said" situations, whether literary or not, one must hear through the silences as well as listen to the words that reflect cultural constructions of gender, agency, and violation to discover the truth.

And finally, a particularly troubling silence that arises in the Chaucer classroom surrounds the inscrutable subject of his possible identity as a rapist—as recorded in the legal document testifying to his release from "omnimodas acciones tam de raptu meo tam [sic] de aliqua alia re vel causa."[23] This event offers little hope of interpretive clarity: Richard Firth Green tersely concludes of it, following his exhaustive study of the evidence from medieval quitclaims, that once again "Chaucer is irredeemably elusive."[24] I have argued elsewhere that instructors should engage with this aspect of Chaucer's biography directly, as well as welcoming students to consider the ethical ramifications of deriving textual and other pleasures from historical

---

22 Warburton, "Reading Rape in Chaucer," 279.

23 Martin Crow and Clair Olson, eds., *Chaucer Life Records* (Austin: University of Texas Press, 1966), 343; the passage translates as "all types of actions either regarding my rape or any other matter." Henry Ansgar Kelly documents the various denotations and connotations of *raptus* in "Meanings and Uses of *Raptus* in Chaucer's Time," *Studies in the Age of Chaucer* 20 (1998): 101–65. Christopher Cannon discovered further documentation concerning Chaucer's *raptus* charge than those recorded in *Chaucer Life Records*; see his "*Raptus* in the Chaumpiegne Release and a Newly Discovered Document Concerning the Life of Geoffrey Chaucer," *Speculum* 68 (1993): 79–94, as well as his "Chaucer and Rape: Uncertainty's Certainties," in Robertson and Rose, *Representing Rape*, 225–79.

24 Richard Firth Green, "Cecily Champain v. Geoffrey Chaucer: A New Look at an Old Dispute," in *Law and Sovereignty in the Middle Ages and the Renaissance*, ed. Robert Sturges (Turnhout: Brepols, 2011), 278.

circumstances that appear antedeluvian to modern eyes.[25] To my earlier thoughts on this subject I would only add that the story of Chaucer's rape engages interpreters of literary texts, biographies, and historical documents with insurmountable silences—we simply cannot read legibly through them—and so as readers we are charged with an ethics of interpretation that demands respect for silences and the limits of our ability to understand them. In teaching our students about the cultural meanings of rape in the Middles Ages and Renaissance, moments of silence can assist them in generating their unique readings of Chaucer's and other texts, but the ethics inherent in interpretation will always rest on the shoulders of those who claim knowledge through readings of silence. And to do so, in another paradox constitutive of the human condition, we must speak.

Works Cited

Allen, Prudence. *The Concept of Woman: The Aristotelian Revolution, 750 BC–AD 1250*. Montreal: Eden Press, 1985.

Andreas Capellanus. *The Art of Courtly Love*. Translated by John Jay Parry. New York: Columbia University Press, 1960.

Aristotle. *Politics*. Translated by Benjamin Jowett. Oxford: Clarendon, 1938.

Best, Stephen, and Sharon Marcus. "Surface Reading: An Introduction." *Representations* 108 (2009): 1–21.

Brozyna, Martha. *Gender and Sexuality in the Middle Ages: A Medieval Source Documents Reader*. Jefferson: McFarland, 2005.

Cannon, Christopher. "Chaucer and Rape: Uncertainty's Certainties." In *Representing Rape in Medieval and Early Modern Literature*, edited by Elizabeth Robertson and Christine Rose, 225–79. New York: Palgrave, 2001.

———. "*Raptus* in the Chaumpiegne Release and a Newly Discovered Document Concerning the Life of Geoffrey Chaucer." *Speculum* 68 (1993): 79–94.

Chaucer, Geoffrey. *The Riverside Chaucer*. Ed. Larry D. Benson. 3rd ed. Boston: Houghton Mifflin, 1987.

Correale, Robert, and Mary Hamel, eds. *Sources and Analogues to the Canterbury Tales*. Cambridge: Brewer, 2002.

Crocker, Holly. "Affective Politics in Chaucer's *Reeve's Tale*: 'Cherl' Masculinity after 1381." *Studies in the Age of Chaucer* 29 (2007): 225–58.

Crow, Martin, and Clair Olson, eds. *Chaucer Life Records*. Austin: University of Texas Press, 1966.

Dinshaw, Carolyn. *Chaucer's Sexual Poetics*. Madison: University of Wisconsin Press, 1989.

---

25 See my "Chaucer's Rape, Southern Racism, and the Pedagogical Ethics of Authorial Malfeasance," *College English* 67 (2005): 569–86. Susan Morrison offers an insightful exploration of how Chaumpaigne's occluded history demands a new kind of literary biography—as well as, I would add, a pedagogy reflective of the challenges of recuperating silenced voices, in her "The Use of Biography in Medieval Literary Criticism: The Case of Geoffrey Chaucer and Cecily Chaumpaigne," *Chaucer Review* 34 (1999): 69–86.

———. "Rivalry, Rape, and Manhood: Gower and Chaucer." In *Violence against Women in Medieval Texts*, edited by Anna Roberts, 137–60. Gainesville: University Press of Florida, 1998.

Edwards, Suzanne. "The Rhetoric of Rape and the Politics of Gender in the *Wife of Bath's Tale* and the *1382 Statute of Rapes*." *Exemplaria* 23 (2011): 3–26.

Green, Richard Firth. "Cecily Champain v. Geoffrey Chaucer: A New Look at an Old Dispute." In *Law and Sovereignty in the Middle Ages and the Renaissance*, edited by Robert Sturges, 261–85. Turnhout: Brepols, 2011.

The Holy Bible: Douay-Rheims Version. Charlotte: St. Benedict Press, 2004.

Jed, Stephanie H. *Chaste Thinking: The Rape of Lucretia and the Birth of Humanism.* Bloomington: Indiana University Press, 1989.

Kelly, Henry Ansgar. "Meanings and Uses of *Raptus* in Chaucer's Time." *Studies in the Age of Chaucer* 20 (1998): 101–65.

Kruger, Kathryn Sullivan. *Weaving the Word: The Metaphorics of Weaving and Female Textual Production.* Selinsgrove: Susquehanna University Press, 2001.

Laqueur, Thomas. *Making Sex: Body and Gender from the Greeks to Freud.* Cambridge, MA: Harvard University Press, 1990.

Macherey, Pierre. "From *A Theory of Literary Production*." In *A Critical and Cultural Theory Reader*, edited by Antony Easthope and Kate McGowan, 21–30. Toronto: University of Toronto Press, 1992.

Mann, Jill. *Feminizing Chaucer.* 1991; Woodbridge: Brewer, 2002.

Matthes, Melissa. *The Rape of Lucretia and the Founding of Republics: Readings in Livy, Machiavelli, and Rousseau.* University Park: Pennsylvania State University Press, 2000.

Morrison, Susan. "The Use of Biography in Medieval Literary Criticism: The Case of Geoffrey Chaucer and Cecily Chaumpaigne." *Chaucer Review* 34 (1999): 69–86.

Pugh, Tison. *Chaucer's (Anti-)Eroticisms and the Queer Middle Ages.* Columbus: Ohio State University Press, 2014.

———. "Chaucer's Rape, Southern Racism, and the Pedagogical Ethics of Authorial Malfeasance." *College English* 67 (2005): 569–86.

Robertson, Elizabeth. "Public Bodies and Psychic Domains: Rape, Consent, and Female Subjectivity in Geoffrey Chaucer's *Troilus and Criseyde*." In *Representing Rape in Medieval and Early Modern Literature*, edited by Elizabeth Robertson and Christine Rose, 281–310. New York: Palgrave, 2001.

Robertson, Elizabeth, and Christine Rose, eds. *Representing Rape in Medieval and Early Modern Literature.* New York: Palgrave, 2001.

Sidhu, Nicole Nolan. " 'To late for to crie': Female Desire, Fabliau Politics, and Classical Legend in Chaucer's *Reeve's Tale*." *Exemplaria* 21 (2009): 3–32.

Sylvester, Louise. "Reading Narratives of Rape: The Story of Lucretia in Chaucer, Gower, and Christine de Pizan." *Leeds Studies in English* 31 (2000): 115–44.

Warburton, Rachel. "Reading Rape in Chaucer; or, Are Cecily, Lucretia, and Philomela Good Women?" In *Diversifying the Discourse: The Florence Howe Award for Outstanding Feminist Scholarship, 1990–2004*, edited by Mihoko Suzuki and Roseanna Dufault, 270–87. New York: MLA, 2006.

Chapter 7

CLASSROOM PSA: VALUES, LAW, AND ETHICS IN "THE REEVE'S TALE"

EMILY HOULIK-RITCHEY

As a medievalist, I sometimes find myself encountering the assumption that the issues raised in the texts I study and teach are radically divorced from the concerns of our present day. This is, of course, nonsense, as the controversy surrounding an episode of *Game of Thrones* illustrated with explosive fervour. In 2014, director Alex Graves adapted a scene from George R. R. Martin's novel *A Storm of Swords* that enraged many viewers by apparently transforming an act of consensual sex between characters Cersei and Jaime into a rape.[1] The director and other viewers objected to the viral explosion of criticism about the episode, insisting that the scene as filmed was not a rape at all.[2] Some online commenters intervened into this debate

---

1 Sonia Saraiya, writing for the well-known pop-culture criticism site The A.V. Club, analyzes the scene as filmed by Graves relative to the scene as written by Martin and explores the larger implications of Graves's choices ("Rape of Thrones: Why Are the *Game of Thrones* Showrunners Rewriting the Books into Misogyny?," The A.V. Club, April 20, 2014, accessed January 14, 2015, www.avclub.com/article/rape-thrones-203499).

2 Among the most troubling of Graves's comments is surely his assertion that the sex "becomes consensual" when Cersei opens her legs. For a scathing critique of this position, see Bethany Jones, "*Game of Thrones*, Sex and HBO: Where Did TV's Sexual Pioneer Go Wrong?" (Jezebel. com, June 5, 2014, accessed January 14, 2015, http://jezebel.com/game-of-thrones-sex-and-hbo-where-did-tvs-sexual-pion-1586508636). Jones acerbically retorts: "the incorporation of something into your body might be done in such a way as to minimize the harmful effects of a violent coercive penetration you don't choose, without meaning for a moment that the penetration isn't therefore coercive" ("*Game of Thrones*, Sex and HBO ..."). Jones describes the logic that an act of sex could "become consensual" as a "rapist's reasoning," and delineates it as follows:

1. Desire is a kind of animosity
2. The physical closeness that comes with violence resembles the physical closeness that comes with sex
3. So, the physical closeness of violence will stir similar feelings to the physical closeness that comes with sex
4. If you fight her for long enough, desire will occur
5. Resistance is foreplay
6. Consent is inevitable ("*Game of Thrones*, Sex and HBO ...").

with the opinion that the scene as written in Martin's novel depicted a male rape fantasy that the television version showed more explicitly to be rape. The sexual violence inherent to the fictional world of the show claims a kind of authenticity in its selective cultural mimicry of the violence and patriarchy associated with the medieval world. And indeed, for me the controversy resonated with the Chaucer class I was teaching at the time on women's consent.[3]

Was this scene a rape? Such a question, asked of Geoffrey Chaucer's "The Reeve's Tale," has likewise generated its share of critical controversy.[4] When our texts—literary or visual, ancient or contemporary with us—depict troubling sexual scenes, we have an opportunity to help our students engage the *process* of making decisions about difficult issues. Rape, as well as other forms of violence against women, is inherently a difficult subject. The question, for example, of what precisely happened between Geoffrey Chaucer and Cecily Chaumpaigne that culminated in the exchange of ten pounds and her official release of him from culpability in the matter of her "*raptus*"—variously understood in the medieval period as "rape" and "abduction"—has been troubling scholars since the release's discovery.[5] In response to scholars' attempts to figure out whether the act between Chaucer and Chaumpaigne was or was not a rape, Christopher Cannon cogently argues that it would be difficult for us to make such a determination even if we knew more details. "Sexual violence," Cannon observes, "is itself a crime where ... the very act that might constitute the crime can be variously defined even by those who have identical 'facts' in hand."[6] Therefore, as he astutely explains, "we mistake what this crime *is* when we insist that it has only occurred under conditions of absolute agreement between accuser and defendant or when it has been named and punished by the law."[7] We should expect disagreement (in good faith, even). Yet the existence of disagreement about an act does not disqualify that act as rape. Catherine Mackinnon expands upon the legal implications of such potentially varying accounts of the same sexual act: "The problem is that the injury of rape lies in the meaning of the act to its victim; but the

---

3 I was, at the time, teaching this course at a large public university, to diverse classes of thirty-five mainly traditional age students, many of whom were not English majors. I have also taught it at a small private institution to a racially and ethnically diverse class of eight students, all traditional age, most of whom were English majors.

4 See especially Heidi Breuer, "Being Intolerant: Rape Is Not Seduction (in "The Reeve's Tale" or Anywhere Else)," in *The Canterbury Tales Revisited: 21st Century Interpretations*, eds. Kathleen A. Bishop and David Matthews (Newcastle upon Tyne: Cambridge Scholars, 2008), 1–14; Christine M. Rose, "Reading Chaucer, Reading Rape," in *Representing Rape in Medieval and Early Modern Literature*, eds. Elizabeth Robertson and Christine M. Rose (New York: Palgrave, 2001), 21–60; and Christopher Cannon, "Chaucer and Rape: Uncertainty's Certainties," in *Representing Rape in Medieval and Early Modern Literature*, eds. Elizabeth Robertson and Christine M. Rose (New York: Palgrave, 2001), 255–79.

5 Among the scholars who have addressed Chaumpaigne's release of Chaucer are Derek Pearsall, *The Life of Geoffrey Chaucer: A Critical Biography* (Oxford: Blackwell, 1992); Carolyn Dinshaw, *Chaucer's Sexual Poetics* (Madison: University of Wisconsin Press, 1989); and Christopher Cannon, "Raptus in the Chaumpaigne Release and a Newly Discovered Document Concerning the Life of Geoffrey Chaucer," *Speculum* 68 (1993): 74–94.

6 Cannon, "Chaucer and Rape," 256.

7 Ibid., 257.

standard for its criminality lies in the meaning of the act to the assailant."[8] Legally the presumption of innocence and a tenacious culture of victim-blaming (in which women are seen to give consent through how they dress, whether they choose to consume alcohol, and whether to be out at night) make such cases difficult to prosecute; yet we can know that rape is still rape outside of legal strictures.

The problem is compounded, of course, when the facts themselves are occluded (as in the Chaucer–Chaumpaigne release) or in dispute. For successful prosecution, our legal system depends upon the clear, consistent testimony of rape victims over time—from initial statements made to police, lawyers, and friends, to the testimony offered under oath at trial. And as Susan J. Brison reminds us, the traumatic violation of rape can injure a victim's capacity to recall events with perfect clarity and consistency.[9]

If, then, in certain crucial circumstances, ethics tells us one thing about rape and the law (and its prosecution) tells us something else, how do we, as English instructors, negotiate a classroom conversation that leads students to parse effectively the narratives that touch this subject, in all their ethical and legal complexity? What do we do with difficult literary texts like "The Reeve's Tale," where sexual acts occur that are at once rape and not-rape, because they are read both ways by various parties (the characters involved, the tale's narrator and its author, established scholars in the field of literary studies, and students in the classroom)?[10] How do we get students to listen productively to this very confusion—to attend reflectively to the ways these events are rape and not-rape at the same time? How do we teach these moments ethically to a student body where up to one in five women will experience sexual assault during her college career (horrific enough), and yet additionally cannot count on her institution handling the charges appropriately (as recent Federal investigation into eighty-five U.S. colleges and universities for their mishandling of sexual assault cases brought to national attention)?[11] Not only is

---

8 Catherine Mackinnon, "Rape: On Coercion and Consent," in *Writing the Body: Female Embodiment and Feminist Theory*, eds. Katie Conboy, Nadia Medina, and Sarah Stanbury (New York: Columbia University Press, 1997), 50.

9 Brison further suggests, based jointly on her own experience and her research into this area, that a victim's capacity to heal may in fact depend in fundamental ways upon the re-narration of memories in order to remake a sense of self. See Susan J. Brison, *Aftermath: Violence and the Remaking of a Self* (Princeton: Princeton University Press, 2002); see also Lacy M. Johnson, *The Other Side: A Memoir* (New York: Tin House Books, 2014).

10 For readings that take the sexual encounters in "The Reeve's Tale" to be "seduction," rather than rape, see V. A. Kolve, *Chaucer and the Imagery of Narrative* (Stanford: Stanford University Press, 1984); A. C. and J. E. Spearing, *The Reeve's Prologue and Tale with the Cook's Prologue and the Fragment of His Tale* (Cambridge: Cambridge University Press, 1979); Derek Brewer, "The Reeve's Tale," in *Chaucer's Frame Tales: The Physical and the Metaphysical*, ed. Joerg O. Fichte (Cambridge: Brewer, 1987), 67–81; and Priscilla Martin, *Chaucer's Women: Nuns, Wives, and Amazons* (Iowa City: University of Iowa Press, 1990).

11 The Federal investigations into campus handling of sexual assault began in May 2014 regarding fifty-five colleges and universities. By October 2014 that number had increased to eighty-five. See Tyler Kingkade, "85 Colleges Are Now under Federal Investigation for Sexual Assault Cases," HuffingtonPost.com, October 15, 2014, accessed February 6, 2015, www.huffingtonpost.com/2014/10/15/colleges-federal-investigation-sexual-assault_n_5990286.html.

there a high chance that a college woman will be sexually assaulted; there is the disturbing possibility that her experience of the event will not be taken seriously by her peers, her institution, or the law.

The high numbers of potential rape survivors in college classrooms matters desperately: as Emilie Cox explains, "victims of sexual violence, especially those who have experienced childhood sexual abuse, frequently report that class discussions of rape trigger [traumatic memories, which] cause them to experience dissociation, which explains why victims of sexual abuse sometimes find it difficult to pursue a college degree."[12] Dissociation refers to the disintegration of personality or consciousness as a defensive response to an imminent or remembered threat of bodily harm or death, a state that "prevents emotional processing and learning."[13] This impediment to learning that can arise both from course material and from the classroom dynamic itself necessitates thoughtful pedagogical practices.[14] Therefore, discussions of texts like "The Reeve's Tale" need to actively pursue three goals. First, they should acknowledge the sexual violence against women that they depict. Second, they should make such discussions as safe as possible for students in the classroom who may be or who may know a victim of sexual assault or abuse. Finally, for the purpose of breaking cycles of myth and misunderstanding about what constitutes consent, these discussions should gently push students who interpret the two sexual encounters in "The Reeve's Tale" as consensual to consider the vexed ethics of the tale carefully, without alienating them by adamantly proscribing a particular reading.

"The Reeve's Tale" appears in Chaucer's most famous and canonical work, *The Canterbury Tales*, as part of what is called the "First Fragment"—a grouping of the "General Prologue" and the first four tales of the work.[15] The tales in the "First Fragment" are frequently taught together in sequence, "The Reeve's Tale" forming a direct (and

---

12 Emilie Cox, "Going Rogue: Teaching Rape in the *Reeve's Tale* to Undergraduates," unpublished conference presentation (Medieval Studies Symposium at Indiana University, 2013), 6.

13 Maggie Schauer and Thomas Elbert, "Dissociation Following Traumatic Stress: Etiology and Treatment," *Zeitschrift für Psychologie/Journal of Psychology* 218 (2010): 109. Dissociation can occur in the moment of the threat as well as recurring as a subsequent "replay" of the event, as in Post-Traumatic Stress Disorder. On the disagreement regarding precise definitions of dissociation, despite its simultaneous "appreciated clinical significance," see Schauer and Elbert, "Dissociation Following Traumatic Stress," 110.

14 For example, Corrine C. Bertram and M. Sue Crowley caution instructors to be mindful of what they call the "disguise of openness" regarding representations of sexual assault in our culture today: "the *disguise of openness* about sexual violence places survivors at risk in many college classrooms where their lived experiences are referenced in ways that may expose them to additional, insidious trauma," which "do[es] violence to the soul and spirit" (64, emphasis in original). Bertram and Crowley identify and outline five obstacles to productive engagement with the subject of sexual violence in the classroom, and offer strategies to teach "conscious resistance" to the perpetuation of sexual violence in our society. If I had to choose a single article to recommend to fellow teachers seeking to engage these issues productively in the classroom, it would be theirs. "Teaching about Sexual Violence in Higher Education: Moving from Concern to Conscious Resistance," *Frontiers: A Journal of Women Studies* 33 (2012): 63–82.

15 The "First Fragment" contains, in order, the "General Prologue," "The Knight's Tale," "The Miller's Tale," "The Reeve's Tale," and the fragmentary "Cook's Tale." There are ten "fragments,"

virulent) response by the pilgrim character of the Reeve to a perceived slight in the tale told by the pilgrim character of the Miller. The Reeve tells of another miller, Symkyn, who steals grain from two clerks. In revenge for this theft, the two clerks pursue sexual vengeance against Symkyn upon the bodies of his wife and daughter.

The sexual vengeance is troubling enough, despite the light-hearted voice of fabliau in which this tale is couched. The sex is violent and the two women are not given a chance to consent to it in advance. And yet the details of the story present a complicated scenario.[16] Symkyn and his wife, their daughter Malyne, their infant son, and the two clerks are all sleeping in the same room. The first clerk, Aleyn, explains to his companion, John, that he [Aleyn] will "swyve" the Miller's daughter as legal "esement" for the loss of their grain (4178, 4179).[17] Aleyn jumps upon the sleeping Malyne "er she myghte espie";[18] Chaucer tells us that she is not aware of the sex until it was "to late for to crie" (4195, 4196).[19] Aleyn later boasts that they have had sex three times, and the following morning he offers promises of fidelity before he departs: "Fare well, Malyne, sweete wight! / ... I is thyn awen clerk, swa have I seel!" (4236–9).[20] Malyne responds by calling him "deere lemman" and returning the stolen grain (now baked into a cake) (4240).[21] The other clerk, John, moves the cradle containing Symkyn's infant son from the foot of Symkyn's bed to his own; in the dark of night, this change deceives Symkyn's wife into mistaking the clerks' bed for her own. In a moment of dramatic irony, Chaucer offers us a glimpse into her mental relief at avoiding, as she thinks, the mistake of getting into the wrong bed: "I hadde almoost mysgoon; / I hadde almoost goon to the clerkes bed. / Ey, benedicite! Thanne hadde I foule ysped!" (4218–20).[22] John initiates sex with Symkyn's wife in terms that invoke physical pain and force: "on this goode wyf he leith on soore" and "He priketh harde and depe as he were mad" (4229, 4231).[23] Yet we are also told that the wife enjoys this rough sex—"so myrie a fit ne hadde she nat ful yoore" (4230)—all the while believing John to be Symkyn.[24] Indeed, when she is awakened the next morning by the ruckus of Aleyn

---

or editorial groupings of tales from *The Canterbury Tales*. The fragments are based upon internal links and/or direct references within the tales to each other. The order in which some of the fragments appear varies across manuscripts of *The Canterbury Tales*; for more information see Benson, "The Canterbury Tales," in *The Canterbury Tales Complete*, ed. Larry D. Benson (Boston: Wadsworth Cengage Learning, 2000), 1–3. I use this version when I teach the complete *Canterbury Tales*.

16 Just to clarify my own position, I want to note that these complicating details do nothing to undercut my own conviction that these acts are rapes.

17 Middle English "swyve" means to have sexual intercourse; "esement" is a legal term for compensation.

18 before she could see (him).

19 too late to cry out.

20 Farewell, Malyne, sweet thing! ... I am your own clerk, as I hope to have bliss.

21 dear sweetheart.

22 I had almost gone amiss; / I had almost gone to the clerks' bed / Aye, bless me! Then I would have fared badly.

23 on this good wife he lays on sore; he pricks hard and deep as though he were crazy.

24 she hadn't had so merry a fit for a long time.

and Symkyn fighting, she believes it is the two clerks: "Help, Symkyn, for the false clerkes fighte!" (4291).[25]

The Reeve himself, who tells this tale, is a contemptible figure; yet much of the humour he intends to convey in this fabliau nevertheless translates pretty readily, even into the modern-day classroom. However we may personally react to the events, we understand that the Reeve means this situation to be farcical: Aleyn, who knows nothing of John's removal of the cradle, echoes the wife's mistake, in his case climbing into bed with Symkyn at dawn and, believing Symkyn to be John, confessing his actions. The wife's false impression that John is her husband leads her to strike indiscriminately at the fighting figures that wake her, and she ends up clobbering her husband. We are likewise asked to laugh at the Reeve's final summary of this "jape"[26] of sexual revenge that the clerks take against Symkyn: "His wyf is swyved, and his doghter als. / Lo, swich it is a millere to be fals!" (4207, 4317–18).[27] From the perspective of the Reeve's narrative voice, the wife's enjoyment of the sex with John, and Malyne's apparent love for Aleyn, ought to relieve the reader of the burden of feeling troubled by the way the acts are initiated. At the same time, the Reeve's very unsavouriness as a character can be said to draw into question the fact that he asks us to laugh at these sorts of things. Chaucer's "The Reeve's Tale" calls for careful instruction precisely because all of this is so muddled, and students are likely to respond to these events strongly and diversely. As such, this troubling little tale creates an opportunity to facilitate a productive discussion of the tension between the (il)legality and the ethics of certain sexual acts.

The lesson I use with this tale covers two class periods, which I have overviewed in the table below (Table 1). I cover the tale itself the second day. The first day's lesson frontloads two conceptual frames that we will then use to assess the tale's controversial sex scenes: 1) the tension between (il)legality and ethics, and 2) the constructed nature of gender categories. We use these two conceptual frames to interrogate the issue of violence against women across the texts that this lesson takes up (culminating with "The Reeve's Tale").[28] I issue a content warning, both verbally and in my syllabus's course description, in advance of this two-day lesson plan, for students who may themselves be victims of assault.[29] In

---

25 Help Symkyn, for the false clerks fight!

26 joke.

27 His wife has been slept with, and his daughter as well / Lo, thus it is for a miller to be corrupt. The ethics of glossing this line are vexed. Note how we don't, in Modern English, have a comparable verb for "swyve"—one that is explicit and literal (rather than the metaphoric innuendo of our "sleep with, go to bed with," unromantic (unlike our "make love to") and not profane (our verbs "fuck" or "screw").

28 The first time I taught this lesson, I used solely Day Two's lesson, without the framing discussion of values and ethics. My students have always responded enthusiastically to the lesson on "The Reeve's Tale" and medieval law. I have lately added the values-based activities with the video and the blog post to foster more productive discussion among the students who strongly disagreed with each other about whether the tale depicted rape.

29 Content warnings, or trigger warnings, are an urgent and controversial pedagogical topic in academia. I sympathize with frustrated instructors who cannot hope to anticipate all

Table 1

	Texts Covered
Day One	• Values handout (Table 2) • "Equals" PSA, featuring Judi Dench and Daniel Craig • Julia Caron, "What Is James Bond Doing in Drag? A Sexist Icon Speaking out against Sexism"
Day Two	• Geoffrey Chaucer, "The Reeve's Tale" • Medieval Rape Law (excerpt from Christopher Cannon's "Chaucer and Rape: Uncertainty's Certainties")

most courses I would have alternative assignments and readings ready, should the need arise.[30]

Day One

For the first day of this lesson plan, I assign an advance homework activity in which students rank their top three and bottom three values from a handout in terms of the personal importance they place upon them (Table 2).

---

student triggers, and I appreciate the seemingly slippery slope from truly traumatic triggering experiences to topics that merely make students uncomfortable or that they dislike. However, I remain firm in my conviction that it is appropriate, as well as pragmatic, to warn students when material comes up that engages prevalent traumatic events that students may have experienced themselves or with regard to people close to them: various forms of abuse, rape, suicide, and combat. I continue to teach material that I know may be triggering for my students, but I warn them when that material is forthcoming. I also set very clear ground rules for discussion in my classroom, asking students to be thoughtful and respectful in the comments that they make, and likewise asking students to give each other the benefit of the doubt if they find a comment disturbing. They are encouraged to counter it, but to do so in a respectful way, and to assume that the comment was made with a generous spirit, in an effort to learn. See also Bertram and Crowley's comments on "reflective speech" and "shared discomfort" in "Teaching about Sexual Violence," 69–70. For further reading on the importance (and indeed pedagogical value) of trigger warnings, see Markus Gerke, "In Defense of Trigger Warnings (... as a Practice, not a Policy)," *The Society Pages*, June 19, 2014, Sociology Lens, http://thesocietypages.org/sociologylens/2014/06/19/in-defense-of-trigger-warnings-as-a-practice-not-a-policy/, and "Problems with the trigger warning debate//on being triggered//ableist attitudes about mental health in activist movements," Elusive Healing, Personal blog, June 4, 2014, https://elusivehealing.wordpress.com/2014/06/04/problems-with-the-trigger-warning-debate-on-being-triggered-ableist-attitudes-about-mental-health-in-activist-movements/comment-page-1/#comment-30.

30 In the case of this particular course on consent in Chaucerian texts, the theme of sexual violence and the vexed nature of consent apply to the great majority of texts, making alternative readings impractical. For this reason, I send out an email to students in advance of the course's first class meeting, informing them of the theme so that they can be in contact with me if they have concerns, and so they can make the choice to take the course at a later date under a different theme, should that be necessary. I do not teach a required course focused exclusively on this theme, because of the potentially traumatic nature of so much of the material.

Table 2

Stability	Justice
Empathy	Equality
Predictability	Cooperation
Competition	Self-Reliance
Security	Reconciliation
Spontaneity	Accountability
Care of others	Virtue
Loyalty	Respect for Authority
Freedom	_____
	(add your own value)

In addition to ranking the values, students write out a scenario that illustrates the way they would privilege one of their top three values above another value in the list. The specific values in this list matter less than that they constitute a range. This frontloading activity invites students to ascertain the ways their personal values inform their decisions and reactions. The next part of their homework assignment is to watch the Public Service Announcement "Equals" that aired in the United Kingdom on International Women's Day 2011 (it is now available on youtube).[31] Using the James Bond franchise characters of "007" and "M," "Equals" takes up issues of gender identity, the inequality of women, and sexual violence that are also central to debates about "The Reeve's Tale," and it does so by reifying gender binaries (which "The Reeve's Tale" also does).[32] The PSA garnered a range of positive and negative responses in 2011, largely because it depicts Daniel Craig dressed as a woman. To help students assess both the utility and the limitations of this PSA's contributions to current debates on how we ought to think about gender and sexuality, I assign it in conjunction with Julia Caron's blog post critique of it, "What Is James Bond Doing in Drag? A Sexist Icon Speaking out against Sexism."[33]

In the PSA, Judi Dench's voice-over accompanies a visual of Daniel Craig (dressed initially a suit and tie). Dench, in her role as Bond's boss, "M," the director of MI6,

---

31 "Equals," youtube.com, March 5, 2011, accessed February 13, 2015, www.youtube.com/watch?v=gkp4t5NYzVM.

32 Although see Holly Crocker's essay, "Affective Politics in Chaucer's *Reeve's Tale*: 'Cherl' Masculinity after 1381," for an argument that the tale calls Symkyn's gender identity into question in order to marginalize rural lower-class masculinity (*Studies in the Age of Chaucer* 29 (2007): 225–58).

33 Julia Caron, "What Is James Bond Doing in Drag? A Sexist Icon Speaking out against Sexism," *Shameless*, March 9, 2011, accessed October 20, 2016, http://shamelessmag.com/blog/entry/what-is-james-bond-doing-in-drag-a-sexist-icon-sp.

opens her off-screen monologue with the words, "We're equals, aren't we, 007?" as Craig, impeccably dressed as Bond, swaggers into the spotlighted foreground of an otherwise dark and empty stage. He stands there as the camera slowly zooms in on his impassive visage while "M" begins a stunning statistical lecture of women's inequality, both in the U.K. and worldwide. About a minute into this PSA, "M" says, "For someone with such a fondness for women, I wonder if you've ever considered what it might be like to be one?" Bond at this point breaks the camera's gaze and swaggers off-screen. The PSA then repeats its visual trajectory as Craig swaggers into the focus of the camera and the spotlight again, this time wearing a dress, hose, heels, wig, and earrings. He stumbles slightly in the heels. Dench's monologue regarding gender inequality continues relentlessly; among her citations are the disturbing facts that women do two-thirds of the work worldwide but earn only 10 per cent of total income, that 60 million girls are sexually assaulted on their way to school annually, and that in the U.K. alone two women are killed each week by a domestic partner. Not long into this portion of Dench's lecture Craig breaks his gaze with the camera, pulls the wig off, looking down and to the left, and removes his earrings. "So, are we equals?" Dench concludes, as Craig walks out of the frame: "Until the answer is yes we must never stop asking." The subtext of this PSA, of course, is that even in the U.K. and countries such as the U.S., where women have the right to vote and other legal protections, the social and material realities are far from equal.

Through Dench's monologue, this PSA addresses the legal and social status of women. Elucidating the inequalities and problems facing women, some of which have legal solutions and some of which don't, the PSA reveals the ethical stakes beyond legality. In its auditory components, the PSA thus raises the issue of a tension between ethics and legality that we will take up again the following class period on "The Reeve's Tale" when we examine it through the lens of medieval rape laws. And yet the PSA's assumptions about women in its particular promotion of their equality reveal its investment in gender conformity. This is most immediately apparent in the visual component.

The PSA's decision to have 007 break the expectations we have accrued from generations of films regarding his gender and sexual identity utilizes dressing in drag as a tool to make claims about identity categories that are, finally, hetero- and gender normative. Julia Caron's blog post on this PSA, which I ask students to read in conjunction with it, critiques this reification of rigid, traditional gender categories. As Caron explains,

> Judi Dench, the narrator, posits, "I wonder if you've ever thought about what it means to be a woman?" and Bond trots out in heels and a dress. This is such a reductive view of what it means to be a woman, what it means to be a man, and also serves to erase anyone and everyone who falls outside of those very narrow definitions.[34]

---

34 Caron, "What Is James Bond Doing?"

Caron cogently points out that the PSA is doing problematic things with its representations of gender: imagining masculinity as Craig's version of 007 (short hair, suit, tie) and femininity as breasts, long blonde hair, makeup, earrings, a dress, hose, and heels, the PSA erases transgender, intersex, and nonbinary identities and their concerns from its consideration of worldwide gender inequalities. Caron's critique is generous and thoughtful as well as rigorous; she acknowledges that there are defences to be made of this video, outlines what they are, and then rebuts them. This argumentative mode allows students to discuss the strengths of the PSA— what it is able to contribute to our collective knowledge—as well as to criticize its limitations. As such, Caron's critique models the analytical work I hope to see students produce in my course.

The final piece of their homework assignment for the first day's lesson is to use the values sheet to assess 1) what values underlie the PSA from its creators' perspective, 2) what values Caron asserts underlie the PSA, and 3) what values underlie Caron's article itself. This will enable, during the two class sessions, an ongoing discussion about the ways different cultures and/or time periods have different norms about gender; what values underlie those norms; how we can be self-conscious about our own values as we approach and assess any given representation of gender/sexuality; and what we, as a class, would like our communal values to be.

When students get to class, we begin with an online Socrative "quiz" that allows them to share their values identifications for the PSA and for Caron's essay with their peers.[35] Socrative, a web-based program that is reliable, user-friendly, and free to use, immediately compiles the responses so that the class can view them on a projector screen. We take a few moments to note the differences and correlations among their responses. I then divide them into pairs, assigning each pair one of the three values identification tasks that they completed as homework: 1) the PSA's values from its creators' perspective, 2) the PSA's values from Caron's perspective, and 3) the values underlying Caron's essay. I ask each pair to come to consensus about the top three values that underlie their assigned text and perspective. For example, the group discussing the PSA's values from its creators' perspective might proceed along the following lines. Equality is explicitly valued in this PSA, making

---

35 Students access the online Socrative site through smart phones, mobile devices, or laptops. The instructor organizes an activity (which can be written and saved online ahead of time) that students access during class. I most often use short answer "quizzes"—in this case one that consists of two "questions": 1. list your top three values in order of importance; 2. list your bottom three values. Instructors may set up a free account in advance at socrative.com. The instructor logs into socrative.com under "teacher login," selects the appropriate quiz, or other activity, and starts it. Socrative allows the instructor to control the pacing of the quiz, revealing questions one at a time, or letting students proceed at their own pace through the questions. I nearly always choose the latter. Socrative provides the instructor with a "room number" that the instructor provides to students, who use it to log in under "student login" (also at socrative.com). This takes the students automatically to any quizzes the instructor has initiated. Socrative quizzes automatically ask students to enter their name as the first "question." The program shows the instructor how many students are logged in and are actively taking a quiz at any one time. Once the instructor selects to end the quiz, Socrative provides a series of options for distributing the results.

that a pretty easy choice, yet students must then debate among the relative importance of such values as empathy, cooperation, justice, reconciliation, care of others—
all of which consciously seem to undergird the message. The framing of the message
within the context of James Bond's infamous womanizing, followed by Daniel Craig's
willingness to dress in drag, sends a strong message, both of the necessity for educating men like James Bond, as well as the solidarity with women that Daniel Craig
here expresses. There is no fundamental right answer that I hope students will
ferret out when I challenge them to come to consensus regarding the texts' top three
values. The importance of the lesson lies not in the final ranking they determine, but
in the process of reflection (individual and group) required for them to make those
choices.

The challenge during this deliberation is often helping students to tease out the
positive values underlying negative commentary, whether that is the PSA's scathing
condemnation of a series of negative statistics (such as financial and social disen-
franchisement; the physical violence of rape, abuse, and murder; and M's shaming
of 007 for the social ills of his own sexism), or Caron's condemnation of the PSA's
framing of gender and inequality as a "white, middle-class, cisgender issue."[36] These
negatives grab students' attention. I prompt them to think "backward" from the
negatives to the positive values implicit in each text. For example, again focusing
on the group assessing the PSA's values from its creators' perspective, if students
are stalled I ask them how this video would be different if Daniel Craig stayed in
his impeccably dressed 007 persona the entire time; if Dench and Craig appeared
as themselves rather than in character as "M" and Bond; or if Craig were narrating
rather than Dench. Likewise, what would change about the message and/or its
effects if we both saw *and* heard Dench? These hypotheticals lead students to consider what values are glaringly absent from the situations "M" cites; what values/
emotions seem to prompt Bond's largely blank, direct stare in the first half of the
PSA, and then his evasive gaze and removal of his wig and earrings in the second half;
and what values/emotions undergird Bond's/Craig's willingness to dress in drag.

When students have achieved consensus in their groups of two, each pair joins
with another pair that worked on the same text from the same perspective and
the challenge repeats: to come to consensus again, this time in a larger group. This
process continues, the groups doubling in size each time, until there are only three
groups in the room (one group for each of the values identification tasks).[37] Once
consensus has been reached in the three final large groups, students jigsaw into
new groups of three students each, with one student from each of the consensus
groups. Their task is to explain their prior group's consensus (and the reasoning
on which it is based) to the other two people in their group.

---

36 Caron, "What Is James Bond Doing?"
37 The length of time required to complete this lesson can vary dramatically depending upon
class size. Students don't always manage to come to consensus, mostly because consensus-
building, as a pedagogical practice, takes quite a lot of time. I give this aspect of the lesson as
much time as I can so that they can learn from the process even when they do not reach its
culmination.

There are two goals for this day's lesson. The first is enabling students to see the difference between ethics and law (a distinction that will be crucial during the following day's discussion of "The Reeve's Tale"). Students often see clearly that making an action illegal does not prevent it from occurring (as in the statistics Dench gives about sexual assault and murder of women in the U.K.). This PSA would not exist, such students point out, if the laws that we have in place to promote gender equality were fully successful. Legal recourse has so far proved itself to be insufficient, despite strides over time. But in these instances, I point out to students, what is legal and what is ethical are the same thing; what of when they do not overlap in this way? The example on this point that resonates with many students is the PSA's example of the 30,000 women in the U.K. who lose jobs annually due to pregnancy and childbirth, or the wide gender disparity in terms of property ownership. Once I raise these examples, many students, especially women, will point out that it is unethical for men to own so much more property worldwide than women, even though it isn't illegal. Judi Dench and Daniel Craig appeal to our ethical sensibilities, beyond what we have been legally willing to prohibit/protect, and in so doing they issue a call to action. The PSA thus positions itself rhetorically as a necessary addendum to the illegality of sexual discrimination and assault, as well as to the *legality* of other forms of inequality. In light of Caron's article, students are poised to recognize the vexed ethics of the so-called "Bathroom Bills" (such as North Carolina's House Bill 2, the Public Facilities Privacy & Security Act), the consequent lack of legal recourse many gender nonconforming people have when confronting such discrimination, and the very real damage that this does.[38]

The PSA's ethics are flawed, and a firm understanding of its gender conformity is the second goal for the day's lesson. Craig/007 dresses as a woman as a social experiment, not because he is female (in either persona), nor because he simply prefers to dress in a gender non-conforming way. The rapidity with which he begins to strip away the wig and earrings in the second half of the PSA, and the camera's zooming action which simultaneously cuts off our view of his breasts, heels, and dress, arguably renders such an experiment "safe" for a cisgender audience that may be leery of gender nonconformity. A transgender, intersex, and nonbinary audience will find itself excluded from consideration here, and that matters for a cisgender audience: even cisgender folks who empathize with the inequalities faced by gender nonconforming folks will have their attention redirected elsewhere by the PSA. Violence and discrimination against transgender, intersex, and nonbinary persons is very real.[39] Some students may be disappointed and/or offended by this PSA's

---

38 See, for example, Hayley Miller, "New Study Connects Suicide Rates of Transgender Teens to Bathroom Restrictions," *Human Rights Campaign*, March 18, 2016, accessed October 21, 2016, www.hrc.org/blog/new-study-connects-suicide-rates-of-transgender-teens-to-bathroom-restricti.

39 As Ashitha Nagesh reports, 2016 saw the greatest number of murders of transgender women in recorded history ("2016 is Now the Deadliest Year for Transgender People on Record," *Metro*, October 8, 2016, accessed October 21, 2016, http://metro.co.uk/2016/10/08/2016-is-now-the-deadliest-year-for-transgender-people-on-record-6179912/#item-attachment_6179924).

cross-dressing strategy and its complete disregard of the violence and discrimination that trans women, in particular, face; this, too, should be part of the classroom conversation.

The PSA's normative assumptions are at once its strength and its weakness as a text we can use in conjunction with "The Reeve's Tale." Because it affirms gender conformity, the PSA can help students to address a medieval tale that imagines rigid categories of gender and sexuality in similarly normative ways. A close examination of the PSA and of Caron's critique equips students to notice and analyze such assumptions in Chaucer's tale the following class period. The problematic assumptions that the PSA makes about gender and violence (that it speaks directly only against violence directed toward cisgender women) resonates with the problematic ways that "The Reeve's Tale" manages its representations of gender and violence. What both texts show (perhaps inadvertently) is the vulnerability of women. To be or to appear as a woman—whether one is, like Craig in this PSA, "performing" a woman or whether one *is* a woman (cis or trans)—risks drawing out violence against women. For example, Caron notes that the "Equals" PSA garnered a wide variety of negative responses. Among them were aggressively angry and violent comments on social media that were directly addressed to and/or about Craig, but whose content explicitly threatened trans women: "wtf james bond doing dressing like a tranny? thats a fucked up commercial."[40] In other words, Craig's "performance" of a woman in this PSA, despite its socially experimental and brief nature, nonetheless elicited responses that denigrate women.

Day Two

I alert my students in advance to the fact that "The Reeve's Tale" is a disturbing Chaucerian text—disturbing because its genre asks us to laugh at sexual revenge and even (in many readers' view) at rape. As I give students their advance homework assignment for Day Two, I explain that there has been disagreement among scholars as to whether the two sexual encounters of the tale are rapes or not. But rather than ask my students to tell me whether or not they think the encounters are rape (which could wrongly imply both that this is an easy question to answer and/or that it is a matter of personal opinion), I ask them to chart out the tale's construction of gender identity. What does masculinity look like in this tale? What does femininity look like? To what extent do these categories seem to be rigid or fluid? This directed reading assignment (which I collect) frontloads the tale's construction of gender as one of the issues that is at stake in "The Reeve's Tale," and gives students a focused point of engagement on their first encounter with this difficult text.[41]

---

40 This youtube comment was made by user xtiger357 (quoted in Caron, "What Is James Bond Doing?").
41 The elephant in the room during the discussion of "The Reeve's Tale" can quite easily be Cecily Chaumpaigne's release of Geoffrey Chaucer for *raptus*. My experience has been that at least one student in the room generally knows about the incident and brings it up when

When students get to class I hand out a short excerpt from Christopher Cannon's essay, "Chaucer and Rape: Uncertainty's Certainties," which gives a brief overview of the power and problems with legal definitions of rape in contemporary U.S. law and in late medieval English law.[42] This excerpt works particularly well as an introduction for students new to medieval texts and history, because Cannon's analysis of contemporary U.S. rape law, the thirteenth-century Statutes of Westminster, and the 1382 Statute of Rapes, provides a specific and narrow focus on the topic and gives students a historical framework within which to understand these laws. I group the students in twos or threes, assigning each group a single part of the law code and one of the two events of sexual intercourse in "The Reeve's Tale," ensuring as I do so that at least one group is covering each act of sex from each legal perspective that Cannon surveys. This results in ten possible combinations.[43] The text, I tell them, is their legal evidence, admissible in court. I inform them that they are now legal representatives working on a case; a charge of rape has been brought for their assigned act of sex under their assigned legal definition. I ask them to identify the plaintiff(s) and the defendant(s), imagine the arguments of the prosecution and the defence, and surmise who would be likely to win the suit and what punishment may be forthcoming (if relevant to their law code). Students write out their analysis of the situation, identifying the lines in both Chaucer's text and in Cannon's excerpt on the law codes that support their answers. I collect this at the end of class. I give them a substantial block of time to complete this exercise, and then the groups report to the class. This opens a diverse and fruitful discussion of the tale because

---

the subject of consent in Chaucerian texts is the topic of discussion. I have a few lesson plans that incorporate the incident directly—one on "The Wife of Bath's Tale," and one using the short poem "Chaucers Wordes unto Adam, His Owne Scriveyn." In this Chaucer course on consent, I generally use the latter lesson quite early in the course in conjunction with Rose and Robertson's "Introduction" to *Representing Rape in Medieval and Early Modern Literature*. This lesson takes place before the lesson on "The Reeve's Tale" outlined here.

42 Specifically, I use a selection of his essay starting at the bottom of page 257 and ending at the bottom of page 261 in Robertson and Rose's collection. His essay can also be found in *Studies in the Age of Chaucer* 22 (2000): 67–92. Corinne Saunders has an excellent book on medieval English rape law that could also be excerpted for this purpose, *Rape and Ravishment in the Literature of Medieval England* (Cambridge: Brewer, 2001). I have not sought a comprehensive account of medieval English rape law for this assignment—rather I selected Cannon's essay precisely for the specificity, simplicity, and narrow focus of its discussion; it gives students an accessible first look at medieval rape law.

43 The combinations are as follows: 1) Aleyn/Malyne and contemporary U.S. law; 2) Aleyn/Malyne and Chapter 13 of the first statute of Westminster; 3) Aleyn/Malyne and Chapter 34 of the second statute of Westminster; 4) Aleyn/Malyne and Chapter 35 of the second statute of Westminster; 5) Aleyn/Malyne and the 1382 Statute of Rapes; 6) John/wife and contemporary U.S. law; 7) John/wife and Chapter 13 of the first statute of Westminster; 8) John/wife and Chapter 34 of the second statute of Westminster; 9) John/wife and Chapter 35 of the second statute of Westminster; 10) John/wife and the 1382 Statute of Rapes. Depending on the size of the class, there will be several pairs of students working on each of these (I do insist that students work in pairs, not in larger groups). I have taught this lesson both at large schools with class sizes around thirty-five and at smaller institutions with class sizes ranging from eight to fifteen. For small class sizes, I modify this activity by giving each group one sexual act and multiple law codes.

each law code focuses on slightly different criteria and circumstances, asking the students to attend carefully to the details with which "The Reeve's Tale" describes these events. The same sexual act, students collectively discover, can be interpreted in very different ways depending upon the particular legal framework we bring to our analysis.[44]

This exercise, focusing extensively on the law, helps to bring to the fore the different emphases, and therefore weaknesses, of the different law codes (medieval and modern). The following are a few examples of what students may glean from this exercise. For simplicity's sake, I concentrate here primarily on the sex act between Malyne and Aleyn.

1. **Aleyn/Malyne and contemporary U.S. law:** Though Malyne is given no opportunity to consent to sex with Aleyn, rendering the act rape by modern definitions that hinge upon such consent, the fact that she does not cry out or otherwise resist and that all her actions the next day seem to demonstrate her affection for Aleyn also render this act of rape one that modern U.S. law could have difficulty prosecuting. Though modern law no longer demands "corroborating physical evidence of 'resistance'" (Cannon, 258), modern legal definitions of rape depend upon how one ascertains a woman's internal will.[45] Cannon explains a "definitional failure" in the California Penal Code's definition of "consent," which holds that "consent shall be defined to mean positive cooperation in act or attitude pursuant to an exercise of free will."[46] Cannon explains that "if 'cooperation' must be indicated by 'act,' then any conflicting 'attitude' … may itself be hidden *by means of* a cooperative act" that has been coerced.[47] Consequently, the law has no way to distinguish whether such cooperative acts were coerced or consensual. The ways Malyne appears to cooperate with Aleyn (by not crying out during the sex, by using terms of endearment, and by giving him the stolen grain the next day) could easily be taken by a modern defence attorney and a jury to indicate that her attitude toward sex with Aleyn was likewise positive.[48] Is this rape by modern standards? *Legally*, there is an argument either way. *Ethically*, to presume/ignore Malyne's consent, as Aleyn does, is to rape her.

---

44 This exercise is a thought experiment and does not attempt to address the historical problem that law codes as written do not necessarily reflect actual legal practices. Nor does it attempt to be comprehensive in its attention to medieval and modern rape laws. It necessarily simplifies the legal scene so that students are not overwhelmed either by data or by historical complications regarding archival cases of laws in practice. This is something I tell them directly.

45 Cannon, "Chaucer and Rape," 258.

46 *West's Annotated California Codes*, qtd. in Cannon, "Chaucer and Rape," 259.

47 Ibid. Bethany Jones makes the same point in response to director Alex Graves's assertion that a scene he filmed for *Game of Thrones* between characters Cersei and Jaime was consensual because the woman opened her legs. See note 2 above.

48 Cannon rightly notes that both women in "The Reeve's Tale" would have a case against their rapists according to modern U.S. law (specifically under the code of the state of California). I do not share Cannon's optimism, however, that a modern judgment of rape "would be *easy* by

2. **Aleyn/Malyne and Chapter 13 of the first statute of Westminster:** This part of the fourteenth-century legal code proclaims "that none do ravish nor take away by force any maiden within age, *neither by her own consent,* nor without."[49] On the one hand, this code could allow Malyne to bring a charge of *raptus* (understood as sexual *ravishment* as opposed to abduction) against Aleyn using a similar logic to the modern U.S. code prohibiting rape: because "by the wenche he crepte" while "this wench lay upright and faste slepte" (4193–4), she is not asked for, nor has opportunity to give, her consent.[50] And the law prohibits such *ravishment.*[51] Yet this code would also deem Aleyn's actions to be illegal *ravishment* even assuming that Malyne's attitude toward the sex, once she was aware of it, was positive and cooperative. Her consent, effectively, is taken off the table by this law code, which students often find rather baffling, not least because it renders opaque the identity of our hypo-thetical plaintiff. Students are also not used to considering a definition of forced sexual *ravishment* that legally disregards female consent. This pairing of sexual act and law code raises more questions than it answers.

3. **Aleyn/Malyne (and John/wife) and Chapter 34 of the second statute of Westminster:** Chapter 34 of the second statute of Westminster has two parts relevant to *raptus.* It prohibits *ravishment* "where a woman 'did not consent, neither before nor after' … but, also, where that 'ravishment' occurs 'with force, although [a woman] consent *after.*"[52] This part of medieval law code allows us to interpret Malyne's actions the next day as granting consent after the fact, but to still understand that act as illegal *ravishment.* It also raises the question of how much force Aleyn uses to carry out his plan to "swyve" Malyne (4178), and draws students' attention to the text's descriptions and evasions on this matter. The words "And shortly for to seyn, they were aton" (4197)[53] constitute, from this perspective, a refusal on Chaucer's part that impedes our own interpretation. He evades an opportunity to tell us some of the precise information the legal codes ask for. There is a second part of Chapter 34 of the second statute of Westminster that applies particularly to Symkyn's wife.

---

legal standards of 'force,'" given the current rape culture of this country (Cannon, "Chaucer and Rape," 278, note 34, my emphasis). Even if the case were won, public attitudes toward Malyne might well resemble those toward the victim of the 2012 Steubenville, Ohio rapes. Though the case was prosecuted successfully, it was the victim who received death threats and the rapists who received the most prominent media sympathy, according to an analysis by Erin E. Sweany in "Rape in Popular Culture, Introduction," unpublished conference presentation (Medieval Studies Symposium at Indiana University), 2013, 2–3.

49 Cannon, quoting Statute 1:29, "Chaucer and Rape," 259 (emphasis added by Cannon).

50 he crept up by the maiden; this maiden lay on her back (face up) and slept soundly.

51 Holly A. Crocker interprets the applicability of medieval rape law to Malyne and Aleyn's case differently than I do. See "Affective Politics in Chaucer's *Reeve's Tale,*" 246. See also Pamela Barnett, "'And Shortly for to Seyn They Wer Aton': Chaucer's Deflection of Rape in the 'Reeve's's' and 'Franklin's Tales,'" *Women's Studies* 22 (1993): 145–62.

52 Cannon, quoting Statutes 1:87, "Chaucer and Rape," 260 (emphasis added by Cannon).

53 And shortly for to say, they were at one.

It states that "if a wife willingly leave her husband and go away and continue with her advouterer, she shall be barred forever of action to demand her dower that she ought to have of her husband's lands, if she be convict thereupon" (Cannon, 260, quoting *Statutes* 1.87). Symkyn's wife, as students point out, does not leave her husband and go away with John in "The Reeve's Tale," yet from Symkyn's perspective, she may have been a willing participant in the sex. He might or might not believe her when she insists that she believed John to be Symkyn during the sex, and also didn't realize that it was Symkyn she was aiming at with that club. This law, therefore, provides Symkyn with a potential avenue to bring a case against his wife that would financially disenfranchise her. Students often observe that the tale's account of the "facts" of the case give her a strong defence, but they are also often struck by the way John's sexual deception has the potential to harm this woman financially in a substantial and lasting way, over and above the force and physical pain present in the description of their sex.

4. **Aleyn/Malyne and Chapter 35 of the second statute of Westminster:** Under this statute, Malyne's father and her grandfather (the town parson, who intends to make her his heir) would have a very strong rape case against Aleyn, because the fourteenth century often saw the male guardian of a woman who was raped or abducted as the legal victim of *raptus*. Chapter 35 prohibits the *raptus* of "children, males and females, whose marriage belongeth to another."[54] Cannon explains the rather baffling situation in all of these medieval law codes—that one might have such a thing as "*consensual* 'ravishment' "—by explaining that late medieval law increasingly prosecuted *raptus* (whether understood as rape or abduction) as a crime of property committed against the man with "an interest in the marriage."[55] Sexual consent in the fourteenth century, we find, was granted as much by a woman's male guardians as by the woman herself. In cases where her sexual consent conflicted with her guardian's, it was the guardian's consent that the law defended.

5. **Aleyn/Malyne and the 1382 Statute of Rapes:** The Statute of 1382 throws another wrench into the works, because it provides for the disinheritance of women who consent to *raptus* (usually understood in this context as elopement, but often implying that sexual intercourse, whether forced or consensual, was also taking place). It is still legally *raptus* under this statute if the woman consents because, as we saw previously, medieval law predominantly considers *raptus* to hinge on a father's or other male guardian's consent, rather than on a woman's. This law could use Malyne's actions toward Aleyn the next morning to make her legally culpable in her own *ravishment*. The Statute disinherits women who "after such rape [*raptus*] do consent to

---

54 Cannon, quoting Statutes 1:88, "Chaucer and Rape," 260.
55 Ibid. Corinne Saunders confirms this interpretation of the medieval law codes: "the legal actions available to guardians, based on laws of trespass and custody, became the model for prosecution of *raptus*" in the fourteenth century (Saunders, *Rape and Ravishment*, 61).

such ravishers," of "all inheritance, dower, or joint feoffment."[56] This law code does not provide a way to distinguish between elopement, clandestine sex, or unwanted aggression after which the victim changed her mind. Partly because the medieval law does not attempt to figure out the precise conditions of Malyne's consent at each stage of these events, students are drawn into a reaffirmation of the way these various possibilities matter very much to us today.

In short, no matter what law code (medieval or modern) the students use, and no matter which instance of sexual intercourse they examine (Aleyn/Malyne or John/wife), ethical and legal questions abound. Either the charges of rape (according to modern law) that could be brought would have a hard time in court, or the charges under medieval law would privilege the male guardians of Malyne as victims over Malyne herself, even to the point of holding Malyne legally responsible for a choice Aleyn makes that night, whether or not she is, in the end, amenable to the sex. These are all unsatisfying and troubling scenarios, and here is where the tension between ethics and the law arises, which I help students to parse by returning to the values handout from the previous day. Relegating this discussion to the realm of values coaxes along the students who may not so clearly see the legal inadequacies or the problem with the explicit lack of Malyne's consent at the moment of intercourse. It offers a way to talk about these inflammatory issues that does not rely on judging students' opinions.

In new groups (of two or three students), students brainstorm which values are at work in the various medieval rape laws. Respect for authority may head the list, followed by accountability, stability, justice, and control (recall there is space on the handout to write in values, as needed, and we sometimes find during this second day that we need additional values to cover this scenario). The medieval laws respect and protect the status quo of masculine authority over women's consent, protect the stable transmission of dowries and inheritances to those men selected by male guardians, and attempt to control women's sexual partners. Though the laws have an obvious patriarchal focus with some misogynistic consequences, we can also note that the law disinheriting women who consent to *raptus* (understood as either *ravishment* or abduction), for example, is also a way of financially de-incentivizing acts we would define as rape. As such that law may have also *benefited* women who stood to inherit and so were potential targets for abduction and/or sexual *ravishment*. While this law uses disinheritance to take away female agency to marry outside her family's wishes, it simultaneously helps to prevent men from abducting and raping women to obtain their money. So care for others (specifically women), though it may not look at first like a value held by the law codes, could in fact be at work therein, however subordinated to concerns with authority and financial control/stability. This is precisely the purpose of such exercises—to see how various

---

56 Cannon, "Chaucer and Rape," 261.

values are at play within the laws, and the ethical tensions that arise because laws must inevitably subordinate some concerns to others.

In the lesson's final move, I invite the students to compare Chaucer's construction of gender categories in "The Reeve's Tale" to those of the "Equals" PSA. Students are, by this time, well equipped to note how the logic of the Chaucerian tale's sexual revenge depends upon a fairly rigid gender binary not altogether unlike those promulgated by the James Bond film franchise (and hence by the PSA), and to critique the relationship among genders that such a text imagines. The tale can only imagine these acts as ethically unproblematic, students can now point out, a) when women are imagined as being able to consent to a sex act *after the fact* (as Malyne arguably does when she gives Aleyn the stolen grain); b) when women are figured as beings who inherently desire and enjoy sex in any instance (arguably how we are asked to interpret Symkyn's wife and her enjoyment of the sex John initiates in disguise—perhaps indicting that a constant desire for sex with any partner is part of the way the genre of fabliau constructs "women" as a gender category); or c) when women's consent is positioned as being irrelevant to the ethical question at hand (as when Aleyn reasons that Symkyn owes Aleyn and John legal redress, and that Malyne is equivalent property to the stolen grain). This two-day lesson has taught students to both see and articulate the ways various medieval laws authorized some of these interpretive stances, even as the lesson has also provided them a conceptual and critical vocabulary by which to critique the ethical problems that arise from such values and assumptions.

Teaching Outcomes

My goal as I teach this two-day lesson on "The Reeve's Tale" is to get my students who believe different things about the same descriptive lines of verse to talk productively to each other about rape, consent, gender, ethics, and the law. My abiding hope is that students who are troubled by the sexual violence against women that is depicted in "The Reeve's Tale" find a safe environment in my classroom in which such violence is acknowledged and condemned, while students resistant to this view, without feeling alienated, gain an awareness of the problematic politics of this position and become more sympathetic to the necessity for activism on the matter of sexual assault. It is this ethical higher ground, which in Cannon's and my view trumps the law, that allows us to read the instances of sexual intercourse in "The Reeve's Tale" as rapes, no matter how a law suit based upon those circumstances might play out. By means of "The Reeve's Tale," rape law, and the ethics at stake in, and sacrificed by, both, I envision my classroom as kind of a small live-action PSA— but one where, in contrast to "announcing" or "pronouncing" a judgment, the lesson plan enables productive discussion to take place and sparks greater consciousness.

The issue of rape in the literary canon is central to the analysis and interpretation of texts like "The Reeve's Tale." My lesson produces better readers as it asks students to assess the values that underlie any text's representation of consent and gender and so inform the judgments it encourages its readers/viewers to adopt. The lesson encourages an ethical reading of "The Reeve's Tale" that would see the two sexual encounters as rape, with keen attention to the way that such rapes are subsequently erased within the narrative itself (partly through its construction of gender identity and its invocation of medieval law);[57] using law codes to promote close attention to the complicated details of Chaucer's tale challenges students, even if they disagree with this position, to think their way through the logic and the values that would construe these sex acts as nonconsensual. This activity is, in effect, an object lesson in careful close reading, as students become more aware of the values at work not only in the texts we encounter (medieval or contemporary with us), but also those that motivate our own interpretations.

Works Cited

Barnett, Pamela. "'And Shortly for to Seyn They Wer Aton': Chaucer's Deflection of Rape in the 'Reeve's' and 'Franklin's Tales.'" *Women's Studies* 22 (1993): 145–62.

Benson, Larry D. "The Canterbury Tales." In *The Canterbury Tales Complete*, edited by Larry D. Benson, 1–3. Boston: Wadsworth Cengage Learning, 2000.

Bertram, Corrine C., and M. Sue Crowley. "Teaching about Sexual Violence in Higher Education: Moving from Concern to Conscious Resistance." *Frontiers: A Journal of Women Studies* 33 (2012): 63–82.

Breuer, Heidi. "Being Intolerant: Rape Is Not Seduction (in 'The Reeve's Tale' or Anywhere Else)." In *The Canterbury Tales Revisited: 21st Century Interpretations*, edited by Kathleen A. Bishop and David Matthews, 1–14. Newcastle upon Tyne: Cambridge Scholars, 2008.

Brewer, Derek. "The Reeve's Tale." In *Chaucer's Frame Tales: The Physical and the Metaphysical*, edited by Joerg O. Fichte, 67–81. Cambridge: Brewer, 1987.

Brison, Susan J. *Aftermath: Violence and the Remaking of a Self*. Princeton: Princeton University Press, 2002.

Cannon, Christopher. "Chaucer and Rape: Uncertainty's Certainties." In *Representing Rape in Medieval and Early Modern Literature*, edited by Elizabeth Robertson and Christine M. Rose, 255–79. New York: Palgrave, 2001.

———. "Raptus in the Chaumpaigne Release and a Newly Discovered Document Concerning the Life of Geoffrey Chaucer." *Speculum* 68 (1993): 74–94.

Caron, Julia. "What Is James Bond Doing in Drag? A Sexist Icon Speaking out against Sexism." *Shameless*, March 9, 2011. http://shamelessmag.com/blog/entry/what-is-james-bond-doing-in-drag-a-sexist-icon-sp (accessed October 20, 2016).

Cox, Emilie. "Going Rogue: Teaching Rape in the *Reeve's Tale* to Undergraduates." Unpublished conference presentation. Medieval Studies Symposium at Indiana University, 2013.

---

57 On the narrative's invocation and subsequent erasure of rape, see Breuer, "Being Intolerant," 9–10.

Crocker, Holly. "Affective Politics in Chaucer's *Reeve's Tale*: 'Cherl' Masculinity after 1381." *Studies in the Age of Chaucer* 29 (2007): 225–58.

Dinshaw, Carolyn. *Chaucer's Sexual Poetics*. Madison: University of Wisconsin Press, 1989.

"Equals." youtube.com. March 5, 2011. www.youtube.com/watch?v=gkp4t5NYzVM (accessed February 13, 2015).

Gerke, Markus. "In Defense of Trigger Warnings (... as a Practice, not a Policy)." *The Society Pages*, June 19, 2014. *Sociology Lens*. http://thesocietypages.org/ sociologylens/2014/06/19/in-defense-of-trigger-warnings-as-a-practice-not-a-policy/ (accessed January 14, 2015).

Johnson, Lacy M. *The Other Side: A Memoir*. New York: Tin House Books, 2014.

Jones, Bethany. "*Game of Thrones*, Sex and HBO: Where Did TV's Sexual Pioneer Go Wrong?" Jezebel.com, June 5, 2014. http://jezebel.com/game-of-thrones-sex-and-hbo-where-did-tvs-sexual-pion-1586508636 (accessed January 14, 2015).

Kingkade, Tyler. "85 Colleges Are Now under Federal Investigation for Sexual Assault Cases." HuffingtonPost.com, October 15, 2014. www.huffingtonpost. com/2014/10/15/colleges-federal-investigation-sexual-assault_n_5990286. html (accessed February 6, 2015).

Kolve, V. A. *Chaucer and the Imagery of Narrative*. Stanford: Stanford University Press, 1984.

Mackinnon, Catherine. "Rape: On Coercion and Consent." In *Writing on the Body: Female Embodiment and Feminist Theory*, edited by Katie Conboy, Nadia Medina, and Sarah Stanbury, 42–58. New York: Columbia University Press, 1997.

Martin, Priscilla. *Chaucer's Women: Nuns, Wives, and Amazons*. Iowa City: University of Iowa Press, 1990.

Miller, Hayley. "New Study Connects Suicide Rates of Transgender Teens to Bathroom Restrictions." Human Rights Campaign, March 18, 2016. www.hrc.org/blog/ new-study-connects-suicide-rates-of-transgender-teens-to-bathroom-restricti (accessed October 21, 2016).

Nagesh, Ashitha. "2016 Is Now the Deadliest Year for Transgender People on Record." *Metro*, October 8, 2016. http://metro.co.uk/2016/10/08/2016-is-now-the-deadliest-year-for-transgender-people-on-record-6179912/#item-attachment_6179924 (accessed October 21, 2016).

Pearsall, Derek. *The Life of Geoffrey Chaucer: A Critical Biography*. Oxford: Blackwell, 1992.

"Problems with the trigger warning debate//on being triggered//ableist attitudes about mental health in activist movements." *Elusive Healing*, Personal blog, June 4, 2014. https://elusivehealing.wordpress.com/2014/06/04/problems-with-the-trigger-warning-debate-on-being-triggered-ableist-attitudes-about-mental-health-in-activist-movements/comment-page-1/#comment-30 (accessed January 14, 2015).

Rose, Christine M. "Reading Chaucer, Reading Rape." In *Representing Rape in Medieval and Early Modern Literature*, edited by Elizabeth Robertson and Christine M. Rose, 21–60. New York: Palgrave, 2001.

Saraiya, Sonia. "Rape of Thrones: Why Are the *Game of Thrones* Showrunners Rewriting the Books into Misogyny?" The A.V. Club. April 20, 2014. www.avclub.com/article/rape-thrones-203499 (accessed January 14, 2015).

Saunders, Corinne. *Rape and Ravishment in the Literature of Medieval England.* Cambridge: D. S. Brewer, 2001.

Schauer, Maggie, and Thomas Elbert. "Dissociation Following Traumatic Stress: Etiology and Treatment." *Zeitschrift für Psychologie/Journal of Psychology* 218 (2010): 109–27.

Spearing, A. C., and J. E. Spearing. *The Reeve's Prologue and Tale with the Cook's Prologue and the Fragment of His Tale.* Cambridge: Cambridge University Press, 1979.

Sweany, Erin E. "Rape in Popular Culture, Introduction." Unpublished conference presentation. Medieval Studies Symposium at Indiana University, 2013.

Chapter 8

"HOW DO WE KNOW HE REALLY RAPED HER?": USING THE BBC *CANTERBURY TALES* TO CONFRONT STUDENT SKEPTICISM TOWARDS THE WIFE OF BATH

ALISON GULLEY

I teach Chaucer's "The Wife of Bath's Prologue and Tale" to a variety of students, including sophomores meeting their general education requirements, English majors at both the introductory and advanced levels, and graduate students in a seminar focused on Chaucer's works.[1] For each of my classes I have different pedagogical goals ranging from introducing non-majors and new majors to the greatest hits of medieval and Renaissance British literature and to the pleasures and methodologies of engaging with literary texts, to, with my senior English majors and master's level students in specialized courses, being able to read Middle English with ease and begin themselves to participate in the critical discourse of medieval studies. In all of these settings, however, I begin with the same close reading and basic discussion questions used by most teachers of the text. What do we know about the Wife herself from her Portrait in the "General Prologue" and her own confessional Prologue? What kind of marriage does she prefer? Is the tale appropriate to the teller? Of course, we always weigh in on the Loathly Lady's question to the knight: which type of partner would you prefer, beautiful and faithless or ugly and true? We also discuss Gower's more amusing—to me at least—question of whether one wants a mate beautiful by day or beautiful by night in "The Tale of Florent," Chaucer's probable immediate source.[2] These speculations are fruitful in that they

---

1 Appalachian State University is a large master's-level university in the western mountains of North Carolina, serving about 18,000 mostly in-state traditional students. In my sophomore level course, I use the Prologue and tale in *The Norton Anthology of English Literature*, eds. Stephen Greenblatt and M. H. Abrams, 8th ed. (New York: Norton, 2006). My graduate seminar uses *The Riverside Chaucer*, ed. Larry Benson et al. 3rd ed. (New York: Oxford University Press), 105–22. All references in this essay refer to this edition. Benson's text is also available online, with an interlinear translation, at http://sites.fas.harvard.edu/~chaucer/teachslf/wbt-par.htm.

2 John Gower, "Tale of Florent," in *Confessio Amantis*, vol. 1, ed. Russell A. Peck, with Latin translation by Andrew Galloway, 2nd ed., TEAMS Middle English Texts Series (Kalamazoo: Medieval Institute Publications, 2006), available online at http://d.lib.rochester.edu/teams/publication/peck-confessio-amantis-volume-1.

actively engage students by asking them to consider questions of values and morals in both the text and their own lives. They're also just plain fun. I've had accounting majors try to come up with a numerical matrix that resolves the dilemma once and for all, and other students, in pondering Gower's question, offer some creative solutions to avoid the problem altogether, such as putting a paper bag over your lover's head during the day or keeping the lights out at night. Some suggest that you could make your partner stay at home during the day, while others have said, "Who cares what they look like during the day? I'll be at work!"

The question that tends to stump student readers, however, is that of whether this tale contains both *sentence* and *solaas*, requirements for the storytelling competition that Harry Bailey outlines in the "General Prologue" to *The Canterbury Tales*. Students are usually quick to agree that the Wife of Bath's Tale is full of *solaas*. The *sentence*, however, as with many of the Canterbury Tales, is not so recognizable. Does it, for example, truly illustrate *gentillesse*, the theme expounded upon by the Loathly Lady as she chastises the knight for his ungracious behaviour on their wedding night? Is it a good illustration of a woman's desire for *maistrye*, which is, according to the women in the tale, the thing that "wommen moost desiren"? With further discussion of the intended moral of the story, even the entertainment value may start to dim. A knight rapes a maiden, who disappears immediately from the tale, and not only does he avoid death by agreeing to go on a quest to learn what women most desire, he ends up getting a beautiful, faithful, *and* acquiescent wife, thereby illustrating that *maistrye* isn't really what women desire most at all. This in itself raises a slew of other questions: Why would Guinevere and the other ladies at court be so eager to save a rapist from the prescribed penalty for rape, in this case death? And even more troubling, why would the Loathly Lady be interested in marrying an unrepentant rapist? For whatever one's feelings about whether the knight has learned his lesson, he never expresses remorse for his initial act of rape and we never hear of any reparations to the victim (nor, indeed, to we hear anything further about her). And, most annoying of all, why is he rewarded with the perfect woman?

When I was in graduate school in 1990, Almodovar's *Tie Me Up! Tie Me Down!* was released.[3] The premise of the film is that Ricky, a recent psychiatric patient, has kidnapped Marina, a former porn star with whom he is obsessed, in an attempt to convince her to marry him. Controversially, Marina falls in love with her abductor, who has hit her hard enough to knock her out, and even eventually sleeps with him in the context of what arguably could be a rape.[4] The problem that many noted, however, is that this is a really good sex scene. I raised this issue in a class on literary theory, saying that I really liked the movie, and thought the bedroom scene was really sexy—except that I felt uncomfortable enjoying it because of what it

---

3 *Tie Me Up! Tie Me Down!*, directed by Pedro Almodóvar (1989; Miramax, 1990).

4 For a general discussion of the controversy, see John Hooper, "Sexist or Feminist? Spanish Director Pedro Almodovar Keeps 'em Guessing," *Chicago Tribune* (Chicago) April 14, 1992, accessed May 4, 2013, http://articles.chicagotribune.com/1992-04-14/features/9202030269_1_almodovar-bom-and-other-girls-spanish-film-director-pedro.

implied about women, consent, and sexual violence. One of my classmates said something that has stayed with me, both because it was very funny, but also because it is true: such scenes, whether they appear in a movie or in a book, require, as my classmate termed it, a "willing suspension of disapproval."

As professional and avocational readers, we are called upon frequently to suspend our disapproval and when reading Chaucer this seems especially true of those tales seemingly designed to be all *solaas* and no *sentence*, or at least of highly questionable *sentence*. Kathryn Jacobs, in her essay about audience sympathy toward the rapist knight, reminds us that we are to read this tale as comic, with the audience being in on the joke. Certainly, my students' fun engagement with the knight's dilemma illustrates the humour inherent in the tale, and, in keeping with Jacobs's reading, it's not impossible to see the rape scene and its aftermath as a big wink at the reader. In this scenario, the knight is put in his place by a bunch of ladies and tricked by an ugly woman into the marriage bed, only to find that he's not really expected to have sex with her. Instead, he gets to have sex with a beautiful, faithful wife—a kind of medieval "punking." Jacobs notes the heightened humour of the situation expressed by "the fun of punishing the knight for getting a step ahead of all the other men," which is "accomplished by making him marry a repulsively ugly woman" and then by emphasizing the knight's "appalled reaction" at the prospect. As the joke progresses, we follow him into bed and watch him squirm.[5] And, as she suggests, humour like this wouldn't be possible if the audience wasn't supposed to feel a measure of sympathy for the knight.

The comic value of rape appears elsewhere in *The Canterbury Tales*. The Reeve's Tale *is* funny when the narrator reports that the miller's wife, after having been tricked into having sex with a visiting college student, finds that "so myrie a fit ne hadde she nat ful yoore" (l. 4230), or when the daughter Malyn, having lost her virginity to the other student, also through trickery, says goodbye with the traditional language and emotion of an aubade and then aids the students in repaying her father's thievery through the gift of a cake baked from their stolen grain. And yet we—and I'm including students—have a niggling unsettled feeling too. Evelyn Birge Vitz takes feminist scholars to task for taking scenes of rape in medieval literature too seriously, particularly those that are clearly intended as comic, noting that "We must remember that both men and women have, in the past, laughed at things that we today may not find funny" and that "[the] medieval sense of humor was, by our standards, sometimes harsh and cruel."[6] While this is certainly true, acknowledging that medieval and modern readers contain different sensibilities doesn't mean that readers shouldn't be—and aren't—made uncomfortable by such scenes. To return to the climax of the Reeve's Tale (no pun intended), readers not unreasonably often question the premise for humour: did these women ever consent to sex? And is it

5 Kathryn Jacobs, "Unlikely Sympathies: The Rapist of the Wife's Tale," *Mediaevalia* 29 (2008): 6.

6 Evelyn Birge Vitz, "Rereading Rape in Medieval Literature: Literary, Historical, and Rhetorical Reflections," *Romanic Review* 88 (1997): 1–26.

really funny that the bed trick occurs in order to get back at the dishonest miller, thereby making the women pawns in the action and thus by implication little more than his property?

Another difficulty in addressing medieval literary rape lies with the confusing nature of the act itself. The ambiguity of the rape charge brought by Cecily Champaigne against Chaucer is well known,[7] and some readings of the Wife of Bath's Tale explore the crime in light of contemporary law. For example, Suzanne M. Edwards argues that given the context of the Statutes of Westminster which treated rape and abduction together, since both could "conceivably end in marriage," "the very clarity of the rape scene itself raises questions about the range of acts it might describe; the possibility of the maiden's consent haunts the scene that so clearly invokes her nonconsent."[8]

And yet even those readers who are in agreement that, in the Wife of Bath's Tale at least, rape—as we understand the act—has occurred, still struggle with what to make of the violent act in the context of the rest of the story. Martha Fleming suggests that the rape is not so much rape as a "shameful act, a violation of the knight's vow to protect women," so that his capitulation to the Loathly Lady shows his newly learned ability to honour his vows.[9] Christine Rose proposes that the rape becomes a "transformative act" for the knight so that "[he] learns a lesson about Christian ethics and class divisions, and what it might mean to be forced to have sex without desire (rape), not about the moral consequences of raping and violence."[10] Bernard Huppé, adopting clinical detachment, argued years ago that in order to find an acceptable explanation for the actions of the queen and other ladies, including the Loathly Lady, "we must first enquire as to the status of the raped woman: peasant or lady?" This isn't *my* first question, but I agree that it sheds light on the peculiarities of the tale. Huppé writes:

> [Chaucer's] lines themselves suggest that it is a peasant woman: the "mayde" is walking alone by the river when she is attacked. Because of the rape a great "clamour" and "pursute" is made "unto Kyng Arthour." This is not the description of a nobleman's protest over the rape of his daughter, but the angry outcry of outraged villagers ... This is reinforced if we ask the question

---

7 Christopher Cannon, "Raptus in the Chaumpaigne Release and a Newly Discovered Document Concerning the Life of Geoffrey Chaucer," *Speculum* 68 (1993): 74–94.

8 Suzanne Edwards, "The Rhetoric of Rape and the Politics of Gender in the Wife of Bath's Tale and the 1382 Statute of Rapes," *Exemplaria* 23 (2011): 16. Her larger argument explores the delineation of gender differences and the Wife of Bath's elision of violence and consent, and pleasure and harm. For a thorough discussion of the Westminster Statutes, see J. B. Post, "Ravishment of Women and the Statutes of Westminster," in *Legal Records and the Historian*, ed. J. H. Baker (London: Royal Historical Society, 1978), 150–64.

9 Martha Fleming, "Repetition and Design in the Wife of Bath's Tale," in *Chaucer in the Eighties*, eds. Julian Wasserman and Robert J. Blanch (Syracuse: Syracuse University Press, 1986), 158–59.

10 Christine Rose, "Reading Chaucer Reading Rape," in *Representing Rape in Medieval and Early Modern Literature*, eds. Elizabeth Robertson and Christine M. Rose, The New Middle Ages (New York: Palgrave, 2001), 36.

as to why the Queen protected the guilty knight ... Only if a peasant girl is involved may the Queen's action be explained ... in an entirely satisfactory manner. What in fact the Queen does is to claim the knight as under the jurisdiction of her court—the Court of Love ... By the "statut" of Arthur's realm, the young man had committed a crime, punishable by death. In the law of the Courts of Love he had committed at the most an indiscretion.[11]

The authority for such a reaction, says Huppé, is Andreas Capellanus who, while advising "against love affairs with peasant girls," does allow that a man "overcome by attraction" had "best be brutally abrupt and where persuasion fails have recourse to rape."[12] More recently, Corinne Saunders's analysis of the Wife of Bath's Tale, with particular reference to these same lines from Andreas, shows that the story "does not so much condone rape as enter into a landscape where the rewriting of the rape is possible" by moving "away from the legal detail to depict a fairy-tale world." In this world of romance "rewritten from a woman's perspective," the notion that women most desire control over their men "counters traditional male assumptions that the nature of woman is sensual and material, and particularly that female sexuality ... excuses the action of rape."[13] It is thus possible to understand the Loathly Lady's power over the knight as parallel to the complete power manifested in the rape. For example, Saunders writes,

> The hag becomes the voice of this new order: she is a didactic figure of rational and moral authority in the mould of Boethius's Lady Philosophy or Langland's Holy Church, and her rhetoric is successful in causing the knight to resign his "maistrye," and thus fulfil the female wish for sovereignty ... The hag's carefully constructed discourse on gentillesse illustrates her capacity for reason, and therefore refutes in its very form the anti-feminist texts instanced by the Wife in her prologue, which emphasise the irrationality of women. The plastic nature of romance has allowed for a learning process

---

11 Bernard F. Huppé, "Rape and Woman's Sovereignty in the Wife of Bath's Tale," *Modern Language Notes* 63 (1948): 379.

12 Ibid., 378–79. The relevant lines, from the section headed "De Amore Rusticorum" (The Love of Peasants), read, "Si vero et illarum te feminarum amor forte attraxerit, eas pluribus laudibus efferre memento, et, si locum inveneris opportunum, non differas assumere quod petebas et violento potiri amplexu. Vix enim ipsarum in tantum exterius poteris mitigare rigorem, quod quietos fateantur se tibi concessuras amplexus vel optata patiantur te habere solatia, nisi modicae saltem coactionis medela praecedat ipsarum opportuna pudoris." [But if the love even of peasant women chances to entice you, remember to praise them lavishly, and should you find a suitable spot you should not delay in taking what you seek, gaining it by rough embraces. You will find it hard so to soften their outwardly brusque attitude as to make them quietly agree to grant you embraces, or permit you to have the consolations you seek, unless the remedy of at least some compulsion is first applied to take advantage of their modesty] (I.ix. 222–23). Andreas Capellanus, *Andreas Capellanus on Love*, ed. and trans. P. G. Walsh, Duckworth Classical, Medieval and Renaissance Editions (London: Duckworth, 1982), I.iii, 36–37.

13 Corinne Saunders, *Rape and Ravishment in the Literature of Medieval England* (Rochester: Boydell and Brewer, 2001), 304.

> that rewrites the action of rape, and we are thus able to accept the final
> transformation of the old and loathsome hag into a beautiful young woman.[14]

Amy Vines's reading of the tale puts the knight and his actions at its centre. She reminds us that the setting itself—in a "land fulfild of fayerye," in a time of incubi who might threaten women, and in the kingdom of Arthur who is the result of a rape and who rescues the maiden Helena from rape by the Giant of Mont St. Michel—is "saturated" with rape (III, 859).[15] The rape "provides the grist for the chivalric mill, an inceptive moment from which all [the rapist knight's] future knightly success flows."[16] Contextualizing the rape and quest within the broader set of romances involving violence against women, Vines argues that "it becomes clear that rape and other acts of male aggression against women are not simply rewritten or forgotten in the process of rehabilitating certain knights, but are actually constitutive of knightly development in many cases. Not every romance hero is a rapist, of course, but in many romances, the rapist can become the hero."[17]

My goal in this essay is not to propose a specific way to understand the rape and the subsequent actions of the knight and other characters in the story, but rather to suggest that in addition to offering students academically rigorous ways of reading, we can also help them access the kinds of questions raised by this text and others like it in such ways that acknowledge we're dealing with something that is present in the lives of today's college students. The kinds of readings outlined above are certainly important in helping students understand the literary and cultural milieu of The Wife of Bath's Tale. Ironically, however, by normalizing rape, that is, by showing that the knight's actions can be understood as inherent or even necessary to romance in general and the Wife of Bath's Tale in particular, such interpretations can also serve to obscure even further an act that has already been obscured in the telling, by its very briefness and by the disappearance of the victim from the text, which Rose describes as the "most egregious erasure of rape" in Chaucer's writings.[18] "What is shocking about the rape," writes Brian Lee, "... is the fact that it is apparently not expected to shock. It shocks not simply because it is reported as casually as it happened, its violence muted by an elision of the victim's trauma as complete as the knight's indifference to it."[19]

In my own reading and teaching, I don't find anything ambiguous about what has occurred. The Wife of Bath herself, or rather Chaucer, relates bluntly that a lusty knight "saugh a mayde walkynge him biforn, / Of which mayde anon, maugre hir heed, / By verray force, he rafte hire maydenhed" (III, 886–9). If time permits, I also

---

14 Ibid., 305.

15 Amy N. Vines, "Invisible Woman: Rape as a Chivalric Necessity in Medieval Romance," in *Sexual Culture in the Literature of Medieval Britain*, eds. Amanda Hopkins, Robert Rouse, and Cory James Rushton (Rochester: D. S. Brewer, 2014), 165.

16 Ibid., 165.

17 Ibid., 167.

18 Rose, "Reading Chaucer Reading Rape," 36.

19 Brian S. Lee, "Exploitation and Excommunication in the Wife of Bath's Tale," *Philological Quarterly* 74 (1995): 17.

assign another version of this story, either "The Tale of Florent" or "The Wedding of Sir Gawen and Dame Ragnall," to point out, among other things, that the knight's quest in other versions of the story is not precipitated by a rape. I ask my students to consider whether this particular crime is a necessary element to Chaucer's version and how the meaning of the story changes when the rape isn't included. I was taken aback, then, when a student in my sophomore general education class suddenly blurted out: "How do we know she was raped?" Despite the critical debate surrounding this issue, I'm relatively certain that the student's question did not stem from careful consideration of the legal meaning of rape in this situation (in fact, I'm not even convinced that she did the reading). Instead, my feeling is that she, like many members of a mixed audience, is wary and skeptical when the topic of rape comes up.

Chaucer's contemporary audience, who might very well have been aware of the word's slippery meaning, may have raised this question, but one would hope that for the modern reader, the crime of rape would be more clear-cut—except that frequently it's not. In the court of popular opinion, and in the words of a member of the U.S. Congress, some rapes are legitimate while others are not.[20] The very week that my student popped up with the question of whether or not the knight really did rape the maiden (in March 2013), two male high school students in Steubenville, Ohio were convicted of raping a classmate. The case drew national attention because of the failure of other students to intervene (in fact some took phone shots and disseminated them on social media) and the willingness of adults to cover up the crime. As troubling as the rape itself was, the reaction of the general public and even the media was even more shocking. Many blamed the victim for being drunk and getting herself into the situation, while others, including major news outlets, seemed more focused on the rapists' having squandered their promising futures, which were to include football scholarships and possibly professional sports careers. Such distressing reactions, unfortunately, can be found even among those charged with interpreting and upholding the law: in May 2014, a judge in Texas made national news for handing down a light sentence of probation and community service to a confessed rapist, at a rape crisis centre, no less, noting that it was partly the victim's fault.[21] The topic of rape is a touchy subject in the classroom, then, not least because we know that many of our students, both male and female, hold such views. At the same time, statistics tell us that a class of thirty-six (the size of Appalachian State University's sophomore literature surveys) will likely include several victims of rape or attempted rape and a few rapists too (the oft-quoted

20 I refer to Rep. Todd Akin's comment during his candidacy for Senate in August 2012, that he believed that in a "legitimate rape" a woman's body "shuts down" thereby preventing pregnancy. John Eligon and Michael Schwirtz, "Senate Candidate Provokes Ire with 'Legitimate Rape' Comment," *New York Times*, August 19, 2012, www.nytimes.com/2012/08/20/us/politics/todd-akin-provokes-ire-with-legitimate-rape-comment.html (accessed May 11, 2014).
21 Carol Costello, "Is America Really Clueless about the Meaning of Rape?" May 28, 2014, www.cnn.com/2014/05/06/opinion/costello-understand-what-rape-means/index.html?iref=allsearch (accessed May 28, 2014).

number is that one in four or five women have been the victim, while 8 per cent of men report engaging in activities legally defined as rape).[22]

In his discussion of the ethical dimensions of teaching, Tison Pugh raises some of the issues that emerge in this context. He describes telling his students about the Cecily Chaumpaigne case and explaining that we can only conjecture about these events. "I'm glad we don't know whether Chaucer raped her," one of his students says, "because if he did, I couldn't like him. And I want to like him if I'm going to read him."[23] This kind of statement reminds us that students, most readers really, internalize and personalize the reading experience in ways that literary scholars typically do not when dealing with a text. Pugh takes advantage of this situation by attempting "pedagogically to create a classroom environment sensitive to ethical issues, to model for our students a pedagogical ethos that demonstrates our own difficulties with [a] complex issue, and to encourage our students to explore their own relationships to the past through an analysis of ethics, ethos, and literature."[24] Further, he asks rhetorically, "Does the question of whether Chaucer himself sexually violated a woman really have no bearing on how we view his depiction of women, if not his depiction of rape itself ...? And would the personal experience of reading his works not likely be exponentially more difficult for people who have been raped?"[25]

Common decency requires that in opening up the spaces between the medieval and the present, we don't diminish the real difficulties that certain kinds of texts might present to our students. I'm not suggesting that we adopt "trigger warnings" in the medieval literature classroom (for really, what text doesn't contain something potentially upsetting?) but I am suggesting that we can responsibly help students find the balance between understanding such a text as a cultural document and making it relevant to their own lives in ways that make sense.[26]

In pondering how best to approach the rape in "The Wife of Bath's Tale," particularly in light of my student's completely unexpected query, I realized that I have the tools at hand in materials that I already use. For the past several years, I have been showing certain episodes of the BBC *Canterbury Tales* in all levels of my courses.

---

22 On the likelihood of a college woman being the victim of sexual violence, see C. P. Krebs et al., *The Campus Sexual Assault (CSA) Study* (National Institute of Justice, 2007). For a discussion of men as likely perpetrators, see J. L. Carr and K. M. VanDeusen, "Risk Factors for Male Sexual Aggression on College Campuses," *Family Violence* 19 (2004): 279–89.

23 Tison Pugh, "Chaucer's Rape, Southern Racism, and the Pedagogical Ethics of Authorial Malfeasance," *College English* 67 (2005): 569.

24 Ibid., 571.

25 Ibid., 572.

26 I don't mean to be flippant about this controversial topic. For one approach to using trigger warnings, see Emily Houlik-Ritchey's essay in this volume. The AAUP argues that trigger warnings threaten academic freedom and can hinder effective teaching, and that students suffering from conditions such as post-traumatic stress syndrome can work with student health services and faculty on an individual basis to devise an appropriate plan. See Peter Schmidt, "AAUP Says 'Trigger Warnings' Threaten Academic Freedom," *The Chronicle of Higher Education*, September 8, 2014. In my own classes, I tend to give general alerts so that students will be prepared for any upcoming sex or violence that they might find offensive or disturbing, but I don't provide alternate assignments.

This 2003 mini-series, which includes six episodes (each devoted to one tale), "[aimed] to do in the 21st century what Chaucer did in the 14th and hold a mirror up to society and produce a story with strong characters and an even stronger moral code," according to an article in *Televisual* (a trade publication for those in the TV business).[27] Although sophomore general education students may not have the critical viewing and analytic skills possessed by senior English majors and graduate students, the episode is accessible and enjoyable for all of them and allows for a variety of audience responses.

Before watching the episode, students have spent considerable time with the Wife of Bath. During our discussion of the Wife's Portrait in the "General Prologue," they work in groups of four or five, aided by a reading guide which requires that they carefully read and translate the Middle English and then begin to tease out Chaucer's satire. Students respond to objective questions (What does the Wife look like? How does she dress?), as well as ones that ask them to analyze and require them to use the footnotes, which they are apt to forget to do (What does her "gat-tothed"-ness suggest about Alisoun? Why might she be "out of alle charitee" if someone goes to the offering before her? Why do you think she's going on pilgrimage? Chaucer the pilgrim describes her as a "worthy" woman. Do you think she is?) In preparation for reading the Prologue to the tale, students read biblical passages and excerpts of some of the patristic writings to which the Wife refers, such as Jerome's *Adversus Jovinianum*, Tertullian's *De Cultu Feminarum* or Gratian's explanation of marital *debitum* in the *Decretum*.[28] During our discussion of the Prologue, students note how it informs the Portrait (for example, she is "som-del deef" because Jankyn "smoot" her "on the heed") and also consider how the Wife's use of "auctoritee" responds to prevalent beliefs about women. I ask students to think about the effect of such beliefs on the behaviour of medieval women and whether they think Chaucer is ridiculing medieval anti-feminist beliefs or ridiculing Alisoun by having her so ineptly address them.

My upper division and graduate students take an additional step. In an assignment adapted from one proposed by Candace Barrington, students learn that words that seem familiar often have more than one meaning or may connote several different things, affecting Chaucer's meaning as well as audience response. For example, in thinking about how Chaucer might intend us to perceive of the Wife, a student could look at his use of the word "worthy" in the Portrait, to return to the question above. After consulting the OED, the student might note that the term can have monetary as well as moral meaning, so that our attention is drawn pointedly to the Wife's mercenary discussion of her husbands in the Prologue to her tale. A look at the MED reminds us of other instances of Chaucer's use of the word, for example, to describe the Knight as "a worthy man," this time connoting noble and illustrious

---

27 Qtd. in Kevin J. Harty, "Chaucer for a New Millennium: The BBC Canterbury Tales," in *Mass Market Medieval: Essays on the Middle Ages in Popular Culture*, ed. David W. Marshall (Jefferson: McFarland, 2007), 13.

28 Useful excerpts can be found in Alcuin Blamires, ed., *Woman Defamed and Woman Defended: An Anthology of Medieval Texts* (New York: Clarendon Press, 1992).

virtues, thereby urging a comparison of the two characters.[29] My goal in all of these exercises is to illustrate to the students that our understanding of a medieval text is necessarily hindered by the biases in both the writer's milieu and our own.

While students are predictably shocked by medieval anti-feminism and can see how a character like the Wife is necessarily restricted by her society, they nevertheless express skepticism, not only about the rape in the tale proper, but also about the Wife and her behaviour in general. In one sense they are merely seeing her in the comedic light in which Chaucer casts her, using sex to get her way and lining up her next husband before her current one dies, but in another sense their reading of her reflects the same mistrust that my student's question about rape does. Some are too quick, in my opinion, to find only humour in the blow that Jankyn deals her and even to opine that she deserves it as a comeuppance for her behaviour toward men. The difficulty for the teacher is to encourage and respect student opinions while at the same time noting that such stereotypes can be dangerous.

The BBC "Wife of Bath" provides a way for us to react to both the comedy and the inappropriateness of the characters' behaviour in our own society. Although it is set in the present, both the bawdy humour and the pathos of the Middle English character comes through. Many elements of Chaucer's Portrait, Prologue, and tale are to be found here, and I ask students to tease out those details. Following the in-class viewing, I ask students to evaluate the adaptation in small groups. In response to my query about how the Wife and the Loathly Lady are depicted, students quickly determine that the character of Beth Craddock (played, much to their delight, by Julie Walters, aka Harry Potter's Mrs. Weasley) is a clever blending of Alysoun of Bath in her Prologue and the Loathly Lady of her tale. Many students have already conflated the character, much as people slip up and call Frankenstein's creation "Frankenstein." They also note the effective adaptation of Chaucer's narrative frames. The episode begins with Beth talking about her experiences in love and life for a documentary. Her life is of interest because she, with another nod to Chaucer's use of stories within stories, is the star of a popular soap opera. They quickly identify an echo of the Wife of Bath's first words: "Experience," Beth says, "taught me everything I know." Other plot elements are just as easily identified. We learn that like Chaucer's Alysoun, Beth married early (at a more plausible sixteen) and left school. Also like Alysoun, she has been through four marriages and established herself as a well-respected business woman, in this case as an actress and executive in her own production company rather than cloth-maker. Beth is "gat-toothed," and in fact met husband number four, a dentist, while getting her teeth fixed. When the dentist leaves her after sixteen years of marriage, she seeks solace in the arms of a much younger man, Jerome, whose name evokes Jankyn's Book of Wicked Wives, and who plays opposite her in the soap opera. Just as the character of Alysoun from the Prologue is conflated with the Loathly Lady, Jankyn and the rapist knight are

---

29 For a full explanation of the assignment, see Candace Barrington, "Teaching Chaucer in Middle English: A Fundamental Approach," *Studies in Medieval and Renaissance Teaching* 22 (2015): 21–32.

represented by Jerome and his fictive soap opera counterpart Gary. And just as the rape and victim of the original tale appear only briefly, never to be mentioned again, here the theme of rape is mentioned fleetingly.

In this retelling, we hear about the rape only as a soap opera plotline during a story meeting of the principles in the show-within-a-show. When we first learn of it, the rape has apparently already occurred and the production staff are discussing possible story outcomes. When Beth suggests that her character Roz would not rush to condemn the young male character who has been accused of the crime, the producer protests that they shouldn't forget that a girl really has been raped. Like the invisible rape victim in the Wife of Bath's Tale, the victim's name is never spoken. The erasure of the crime is more complete than in Chaucer's version in that we don't hear what, if any, the legal repercussions are. Instead, one of the writers suggests a compromise: "What if … Roz gets him off the hook? She says to him, 'If I get you off the hook, you have to do anything I ask … if it's within your power.' " The payment, of course, is that Roz wants the young rapist to sleep with her. "Why," the producer asks agitatedly, "would she want to sleep with the rapist in the first place?" "Because," interrupts the writer, "she's feeling old and unattractive."

This exchange mirrors almost exactly the discussions that inevitably arise in a classroom discussion of the Wife of Bath's Tale. Having already connected the Loathly Lady to the Wife of Bath, students begin to consider new ways of understanding or interpreting Alisoun's marital experience in the Prologue with reference to the role of violence in the tale. Of course, many students consider that the rape is nothing more than a plot device to send the knight on his quest, but those students who are bothered by the quick introduction and dismissal of the crime quickly identify a parallel in the way that the TV characters react. Despite the doubts of the producer that a woman would find a rapist attractive, the dominant female voices—those of Beth, her makeup artist, and a production assistant—fully support Roz's forgiveness of and subsequent coupling with Gary, the rapist. In discussing the original plan to have Roz condemn Gary's actions, her hairdresser exclaims, "It's so wrong! … Roz wouldn't do that." "She'd believe Gary," agrees the assistant. "She'd sympathize with him. She'd get him off the hook even if he had raped Lauren." In the course of a scene, the rape has gone from fact, as stated by the producer, to merely a possibility. Elaine Tuttle Hanson's description of the aftermath of Chaucer's literary rape is apropos here: "[The] apparent seriousness of the crime is thoroughly undercut by the breathless, offhand manner in which it is reported … [The] rape is just as quickly erased: the knight is reprieved as swiftly as he was condemned, thanks to the intervention of the queen and ladies. Their response seems to confirm what the Wife alleged in her prologue, that women really love a violent man."[30] But what Beth's

---

30 Elaine Tuttle Hanson, "Of his love daungerous to me: Liberation, Subversion, and Domestic Violence in the Wife of Bath's Prologue and Tale," in *Geoffrey Chaucer, The Wife of Bath: Complete, Authoritative Text with Biographical and Historical Contexts, Critical History, and Essays from Five Contemporary Critical Perspectives*, ed. Peter Beidler (Boston: Bedford, St. Martin's, 1996), 280–81.

character in the BBC retelling illustrates is that it's not simply that women love a violent man, it's that a woman in search of true love will *put up* with a violent man. Just as the soap opera character of Roz, feeling old and unattractive, pursues a relationship with Gary, Beth, feeling unloved in the wake of her fourth failed marriage, quickly marries Jerome. And, reflecting Alysoun's beating at the hands of Jankyn, he—in retaliation for what he sees as Beth's controlling nature—beats Beth up.

Kevin Harty finds little to sympathize with here:

> Beth is not nearly so sympathetic a character [as the Wife]. If [Alysoun] is profoundly human, mixing weakness with fortitude as she goes about fictional daily life in the fourteenth century, Beth seems more venal ... Unlike Beth, Jerome seems content to settle down. But, like her Chaucerian counterpart, Beth wants to be in charge, both of her life and her career—and unfortunately Jerome's as well. Their breakup is caused not by spousal infidelity, as had been true of her marriage to James [the dentist], but by her lying to Jerome. If Chaucer's Wife pleads her case for understanding to her own advantage, the same cannot quite be said of Beth.[31]

He notes that after the episode of abuse, Beth undergoes plastic surgery in order "to retain her youthful looks" and is on the lookout for husband number six. Some of my students agree with Harty's estimation and characterization of Beth (and the Wife); for me, however, and many other students, this version suggests what I have long sensed about the Wife of Bath—part of her enduring popularity is due to her comic bluster but also her vulnerability. Are we really meant, after all, to take her words at face value? Although arguably her deafness and the abuse that caused it are presented in a humorous light, is it possible that someone would sail through such an experience unscathed? And what of the Loathly Lady and the question of her desire to marry a rapist?

The beauty of the BBC "Wife of Bath" is that it raises these issues in ways that are recognizable and accessible to a modern audience and sophisticated enough for a meaty class discussion. When I ask my class if the interaction of Jerome and Beth following the beating is realistic, many students are quick to point out that their language and actions reflect those of a batterer and a battered wife. Appropriately chagrined and tear-stained, Jerome explains pleadingly to the police officers who take his statement after arresting him, "I shouldn't've hit her. See, I was drunk. I didn't know what I was doing. I love her and I've always loved her." When he learns that she has dropped the charges against him, he shows up at her house and apologizes profusely for his actions, as he hands her a comically large bouquet of flowers: "I'm sorry. Do you hate me? You can't hate me more than I hate myself." When he asks his wife, "Why didn't you press charges?" she answers, "Because I didn't want you to hate me." As Harty notes, she *has* undergone plastic surgery

---

31 Harty, "Chaucer for a New Millennium," 17.

since the attack, but not because she merely wants to retain her looks, and certainly not because she wants to retain *maistrye* over her young husband or because she's on the prowl for husband number six. Instead, like her soap opera counterpart Roz, Beth has been feeling old and unattractive (in fact Jerome in his drunken rage tells her that she's "fat and ugly" and will die alone). Post-surgery, she tells him she's done it for him so that she won't look like his mother. As his medieval counterpart does, Jerome promises that he has changed, saying, "I will never piss you off again. I'll do everything you tell me to do." Like Alysoun who is willing to forgive and forget, Beth clearly wants love, saying, "Promise me you won't go away again. Promise me you'll never leave me."

Harty confuses the need to be loved with the inability to maintain a good relationship. He argues, "Chaucer's Wife of Bath and Beth share a dilemma: they seem unable to live with or without men."[32] On the surface one might suppose the Loathly Lady is also unable to live without a man—even one who has never expressed remorse or even acknowledged that he's done something wrong. And the premise that what women truly desire is *maistrye* in marriage is quickly shown to be a red herring: remember that upon hearing the "right" answer, "she obeyed hym in every thyng / That myghte doon hym plesance or likyng" (III 1254–5). The modern Beth, despite all her material success and power, likewise is still at the mercy of someone or something else, as the case may be. As Kathleen Forni explains it, "Beth ... may have little concern about ecclesiastical opinions regarding female sexuality. But she does face a cultural ladder of perfection that is equally pernicious: the Western cult of youthful physical beauty," which is "not unlike the Wife of Bath's exposure of the misogyny underlying authoritative interpretations of scripture."[33]

Our own students, both male and female, often feel these kinds of stricture in their own lives—on their behaviour, their physical movement, and their ability to be loved. Perhaps my student's question about whether the knight really raped her stemmed from an unrecognized or unarticulated place of uncertainty. Edwards suggests that "[in] making visible masculine aggression and feminine suffering, the [rape] scene [in the Wife of Bath's Tale] makes it possible to see the pervasive social inequalities linked to gender difference."[34] In our supposedly post-feminist world, people often deny that such inequalities exist, and women, especially young women, may be reluctant to acknowledge the possibility that they may not always be in control. Pairing an example from the seemingly foreign Middle Ages with an example from our own familiar world can allow students to address some of the most complex and interesting, if uncomfortable, moments in the classroom.

---

32 Ibid., 16.
33 Kathleen Forni, "Popular Chaucer: The BBC's *Canterbury Tales*," *Parergon* 25 (2008): 185.
34 Edwards, "The Rhetoric of Rape," 4.

Works Cited

Andreas Capellanus. *Andreas Capellanus on Love*. Edited and translated by P. G. Walsh. Duckworth Classical, Medieval and Renaissance Editions. London: Duckworth, 1982.

Barrington, Candace. "Teaching Chaucer in Middle English: A Fundamental Approach." *Studies in Medieval and Renaissance Teaching* 22 (2015): 21–32.

Blamires, Alcuin, ed. *Woman Defamed and Woman Defended: An Anthology of Medieval Texts*. New York: Clarendon Press, 1992.

Cannon, Christopher. "Raptus in the Chaumpaigne Release and a Newly Discovered Document Concerning the Life of Geoffrey Chaucer." *Speculum* 68 (1993): 74–94.

Carr, J. L., and K. M. VanDeusen. "Risk Factors for Male Sexual Aggression on College Campuses." *Family Violence* 19 (2004): 279–89.

Chaucer, Geoffrey. "The Wife of Bath's Prologue and Tale." In *The Norton Anthology of English Literature*, edited by Stephen Greenblatt and M. H. Abrams, 8th ed., 282–410. New York: Norton, 2006.

———. *The Riverside Chaucer*, eds. Larry Benson et al. 3rd ed., 105–22. New York: Oxford University Press.

Costello, Carol. "Is America Really Clueless about the Meaning of Rape?" May 28, 2014, www.cnn.com/2014/05/06/opinion/costello-understand-what-rape-means/index.html?iref=allsearch (accessed May 28, 2014).

Edwards, Suzanne. "The Rhetoric of Rape and the Politics of Gender in the Wife of Bath's Tale and the 1382 Statute of Rapes." *Exemplaria* 23 (2011): 3–26.

Eligon, John, and Michael Schwirtz. "Senate Candidate Provokes Ire with 'Legitimate Rape' Comment." *New York Times*, August 19, 2012, www.nytimes.com/2012/08/20/us/politics/todd-akin-provokes-ire-with-legitimate-rape-comment.html (accessed May 11, 2014).

Fleming, Martha. "Repetition and Design in the Wife of Bath's Tale." In *Chaucer in the Eighties*, edited by Julian Wasserman and Robert J. Blanch, 158–59. Syracuse: Syracuse University Press, 1986.

Forni, Kathleen. "Popular Chaucer: The BBC's *Canterbury Tales*." *Parergon* 25 (2008): 171–89.

Gower, John. "Tale of Florent." In *Confessio Amantis*. Vol. 1, edited by Russell A. Peck, with Latin translation by Andrew Galloway, 2nd ed., TEAMS Middle English Texts Series. Kalamazoo: Medieval Institute Publications, 2006. Available online at http://d.lib.rochester.edu/teams/publication/peck-confessio-amantis-volume-1.

Hanson, Elaine Tuttle. "Of his love daungerous to me: Liberation, Subversion, and Domestic Violence in the Wife of Bath's Prologue and Tale." In *Geoffrey Chaucer, The Wife of Bath: Complete, Authoritative Text with Biographical and Historical Contexts, Critical History, and Essays from Five Contemporary Critical Perspectives*, edited by Peter Beidler, 280–81. Boston: Bedford, St. Martin's, 1996.

Harty, Kevin J. "Chaucer for a New Millennium: The BBC Canterbury Tales." In *Mass Market Medieval: Essays on the Middle Ages in Popular Culture*, edited by David W. Marshall, 13–27. Jefferson: McFarland, 2007.

Hooper, John. "Sexist or Feminist? Spanish Director Pedro Almodovar Keeps 'em Guessing." *Chicago Tribune* (Chicago), April 14, 1992, http://articles. chicagotribune.com/1992-04-14/features/9202030269_1_almodovar-bom-and-other-girls-spanish-film-director-pedro (accessed May 4, 2013).

Huppé, Bernard F. "Rape and Woman's Sovereignty in the Wife of Bath's Tale." *Modern Language Notes* 63 (1948): 378–81.

Jacobs, Kathryn. "Unlikely Sympathies: The Rapist of the Wife's Tale." *Mediaevalia* 29 (2008): 1–13.

Krebs, C. P., Krebs, C. P., Christine H. Lindquist, Tara D. Warner, Bonnie S. Fisher, and Sandra L. Martin. *The Campus Sexual Assault (CSA) Study*. National Institute of Justice, 2007.

Lee, Brian S. "Exploitation and Excommunication in the Wife of Bath's Tale." *Philological Quarterly* 74 (1995): 17–35.

Post, J. B. "Ravishment of Women and the Statutes of Westminster." In *Legal Records and the Historian*, edited by J. H. Baker, 150–64. London: Royal Historical Society, 1978.

Pugh, Tison. "Chaucer's Rape, Southern Racism, and the Pedagogical Ethics of Authorial Malfeasance." *College English* 67 (2005): 569–86.

Rose, Christine. "Reading Chaucer Reading Rape." In *Representing Rape in Medieval and Early Modern Literature*, edited by Elizabeth Robertson and Christine M. Rose, 21–60. The New Middle Ages 36. New York: Palgrave, 2001.

Saunders, Corinne. *Rape and Ravishment in the Literature of Medieval England.* Rochester: Boydell and Brewer, 2001.

Schmidt, Peter. "AAUP Says 'Trigger Warnings' Threaten Academic Freedom." *The Chronicle of Higher Education*, September 8, 2014.

Tie Me Up! Tie Me Down! Directed by Pedro Almodóvar. 1989; Miramax, 1990.

Vines, Amy N. "Invisible Woman: Rape as a Chivalric Necessity in Medieval Romance." In *Sexual Culture in the Literature of Medieval Britain*, edited by Amanda Hopkins, Robert Rouse, and Cory James Rushton, 161–80. Rochester: Brewer, 2014.

Vitz, Evelyn Birge. "Rereading Rape in Medieval Literature: Literary, Historical, and Rhetorical Reflections." *Romanic Review* 88 (1997): np.

Chapter 9

TEACHING THE POTIPHAR'S WIFE MOTIF IN MARIE DE FRANCE'S *LANVAL*

ELIZABETH HARPER

The mid-twentieth-century folklore scholar Stith Thompson lists motif K2111 as "Potiphar's Wife" and describes it as follows: "A woman makes vain overtures to a man and then accuses him of attempting to force her."[1] This motif is very widely known, appearing not just in Genesis and the Koran (where it derives its name), but in ancient texts from across the world. It remains a mainstay of Western storytelling, appearing in narratives as disparate as Alexandre Dumas's *The Three Musketeers*, Harper Lee's *To Kill a Mockingbird*, and Gillian Flynn's *Gone Girl*. Less entertainingly, it also appears whenever the subject of acquaintance rape is discussed in the American media. To some segment of the populace, it is both possible and likely that women who accuse men of rape are doing so out of vengeful motivations—and this perception has been apparently validated by such high-profile cases as the Tawana Brawley case in 1987, the Duke lacrosse case in 2006, and the story published by *Rolling Stone* in 2014 under the title "A Rape on Campus."

The academic study of literature has largely moved beyond simply identifying motifs in narrative, yet the popularity of websites like TVtropes.org suggests that ordinary audiences still find this form of analysis useful and accessible. In this essay, I will suggest that the analysis of motifs should still be a tool for medievalists in the classroom. Reading and analyzing Marie de France's *Lanval* in the light of literary motifs can help our students examine elements of American rape culture.[2] Central to the plot of *Lanval* is the queen's false accusation that the male protagonist has made sexual advances to her—a charge which is patently unbelievable not only to the audience of the poem, but also to the other characters in the story. In the context of literary study, the queen's accusations take on a more violent subtext, reflecting

---

1 Stith Thompson, *Motif-Index of Folk-Literature: A Classification of Narrative Elements in Folktales, Ballads, Myths, Fables, Medieval Romances, Exempla, Fabliaux, Jest-Books, and Local Legends*, rev. ed. (Bloomington: Indiana University Press, 1955), www.ruthenia.ru/folklore/thompson/index.htm.
2 Throughout this essay, I will assume an American context for my arguments, and I will be confining my comments to male-on-female rape allegations.

the Potiphar's Wife motif. My central suggestion in this essay is that the motif reflects one way of making sense of a real epistemological dilemma. Moreover, I will argue that this motif performs a certain sort of cultural work, allowing readers to enter into a fantasy inversion of normal gendered power dynamics that allows true allegations to be safely ignored or discredited. Lastly, I will explore several different ways that we can use *Lanval* to help college students recognize the motif, analyze its function in Marie's text, and connect it to the culture in which they move.

The Problem of False Allegations

Actual false allegations of rape are quite rare. Several studies have shown that such allegations compose between 2 and 8 per cent of all accusations of rape, which is on par with false accusations of other crimes such as burglary or arson.[3] Moreover, more than 90 per cent of rapes go unreported, a fact which, if factored into the above statistics, makes the proportion of false allegations to actual rapes much, much lower (in the neighborhood of .05 per cent).[4] Considering these very low figures, why are false rape allegations the locus of so much anxiety and public worry?[5] The answer, I think, lies in a legitimate epistemological problem that we face when discussing a charge of acquaintance rape (the most common type of rape). This epistemological problem has three parts. First, unlike stranger rape, the woman who alleges acquaintance rape is always accusing a specific person or people of the crime. Second, our society claims to believe in presuming innocence until proven guilty. Third, because of the nature of the crime, it is extremely unlikely that someone alleging acquaintance rape has identified the wrong rapist(s). The person who hears an allegation of rape is suspended between two apparently equal possibilities: the accuser is either telling the truth or deliberately lying. So when we hear

---

3 Lawrence A. Greenfeld, *Sex Offenses and Offenders: An Analysis of Data on Rape and Sexual Assault* (U.S. Department of Justice, Office of Justice Programs, Washington, DC, 1997), www.mincava.umn.edu/documents/sexoff/sexoff.pdf, accessed April 3, 2014; Philip N. S. Rumney, "False Allegations of Rape," *Cambridge Law Journal* 65 (2006): 125–58; Joanne Belknap, "Rape: Too Hard to Report and Too Easy to Discredit Victims," *Violence Against Women* 16 (2010): 1335–44. To complicate matters, some police departments classify as "false" or "unfounded" all accusations for which there is no physical evidence available. As one study puts it, "[I]n general the greater the scrutiny applied to police classifications, the lower the rate of false reporting detected." See David Lisak, Lori Gardinier, and Ashley M. Cote, "False Allegations of Sexual Assault: An Analysis of Ten Years of Reported Cases," *Violence Against Women* 16 (2010): 1331.

4 Belknap, "Rape."

5 See, for instance, the many recent attempts to differentiate between false and true rape allegations based on the content of the accusation. Russell Norton and Tim Grant, "Rape Myth in True and False Rape Allegations," *Psychology, Crime & Law* 14 (2008): 275–85; Lisak, Gardinier, and Cote, "False Allegations of Sexual Assault"; Liz Kelly, "The (In)credible Words of Women: False Allegations in European Rape Research," *Violence Against Women* 16 (2010): 1345–55; Laura Hunt and Ray Bull, "Differentiating Genuine and False Rape Allegations: A Model to Aid Rape Investigations," *Psychiatry, Psychology & Law* 19 (2012): 682–91.

about a charge of rape, our expectations of justice ask us to simultaneously believe and disbelieve the accuser.

This is a complex position to hold. Rape culture offers to resolve the difficulty for us by offering the myth that women frequently "cry rape" falsely, either to avoid responsibility for consensual sex or to take revenge. This belief is a key component in the rhetoric that surrounds media and popular discussions of sexual violence.[6] In both the Duke lacrosse case and the case covered by *Rolling Stone*, investigations eventually showed that the accused could not have done what their accusers alleged had been done. Both stories are now routinely cited by some people as reasons to be skeptical of all rape allegations. And this underlines for us the double harm that false allegations of rape do: they obviously harm the falsely accused, but they also harm the real survivors of rape whose credibility is undermined by association.

The Outlines of the Potiphar's Wife Motif

The Potiphar's Wife motif appears in Western texts as diverse as the Joseph narrative of Genesis, the story of Bellerophon in the *Iliad*, and the story of Hippolytus in book 15 of Ovid's *Metamorphoses*.[7] Although the details change with the context, in each case, the narrative emphasizes that the woman is exploiting the man's social vulnerability (his age or lack of social status) to ensure that she, not he, is believed. As a result, the narrative invites readers to sympathize with the hapless male victim. We should note that the man in each story has some obligation to the woman's husband which precludes his sexual involvement with the woman. In Genesis, the additional prohibition is Joseph's servile status; in the *Iliad*, it is the fact that Bellerophon is a guest and thus obligated to his host; in the *Metamorphoses*, it is Phaedra's marriage to Theseus, Hippolytus' father, which makes her his stepmother and thus subject to the incest taboo.

---

6 See, for instance, Clare Gunby, Anna Carline, and Caryl Beynon, "Regretting It After? Focus Group Perspectives on Alcohol Consumption, Nonconsensual Sex and False Allegations of Rape," *Social & Legal Studies* 22 (2013): 87–106.

7 Thompson, *Motif-Index of Folk-Literature*. Thompson's identification of this motif is congruent with the examples discussed in Frederic E. Faverty, "The Story of Joseph and Potiphar's Wife in Mediæval Literature," *Harvard Studies and Notes in Philology and Literature* 13 (1931): 81–128, though Faverty includes *Lanval* in his list and Thompson does not.

Although Faverty and Thompson list many examples, the motif does not seem to have received sustained attention in later scholarship except in treatments of the ancient Near East; see Susan Tower Hollis, "The Woman in Ancient Examples of the Potiphar's Wife Motif, K2111," in *Gender and Difference in Ancient Israel*, ed. Peggy L. Day (Minneapolis: Fortress, 1989), 28–42; Shalom Goldman, *The Wiles of Women/the Wiles of Men: Joseph and Potiphar's Wife in Ancient Near Eastern, Jewish, and Islamic Folklore* (Albany: State University of New York Press, 1995). Marie de France would of course have been familiar with Genesis, and her writing indicates a deep and sophisticated engagement with Ovid's *Metamorphoses*: see Robert T. Cargo, "Marie de France's Le Laustic and Ovid's Metamorphoses," *Comparative Literature* 18 (1966): 162–66; SunHee Kim Gertz, "Transforming Lovers and Memorials in Ovid and Marie de France," *Florilegium* 14 (1996): 99–122; Sun Hee Kim Gertz, "Echoes and Reflections of Enigmatic Beauty in Ovid and Marie de France," *Speculum* 73 (1998): 372–96; Emanuel J. Mickel, "Marie de France and the Learned Tradition," in *A Companion to Marie de France*, ed. Logan E. Whalen (Leiden: Brill, 2011), 31–54.

Marie de France's *Lanval* follows the structure of motif K2111 very closely, although rape itself is present only by association.[8] In the central external conflict of *Lanval*, the queen tries to initiate a sexual relationship with the hero, using language that suggests she can't imagine her offer being turned down. Lanval replies bluntly, "I have no desire to love you, for I have long served the king and do not want to betray my faith. Neither you nor your love will ever lead me to wrong my lord!"[9] Offended, the queen accuses him of homosexuality, and he in turn retaliates by describing his fairy mistress and comparing her favorably to the queen. The queen complains of this treatment to King Arthur, but crucially, she covers her sexual aggressiveness toward Lanval by accusing him of the same behaviour she is guilty of: "[The queen] said that Lanval had shamed her. He had requested her love and because she had refused him, had insulted and deeply humiliated her. He had boasted of a beloved who was so well-bred, noble and proud that her chambermaid ... was worthier than the queen" (77). Lanval then faces a kangaroo court from which he is rescued by his fairy lover's timely appearance and taken off to the magical land of Avalon. The similarities are obvious here. In place of a physical struggle, we have a battle of words, in which Lanval and the queen exchange sexually charged insults, but otherwise the elements are all present: a married, high-status woman, trying to initiate a taboo sexual encounter, a socially inferior man with prior commitments to both her husband and to his own lover; the false allegation as retaliation, with an emphasis on the shamefulness of the violation; a justice system stacked in favour of the powerful woman. Medieval audiences would have recognized the plot; and so, I think, do most modern students reading the story.

What is striking to me about the false allegation motif is how perfectly it mirrors the real conditions surrounding acquaintance rape throughout history. Each of these stories occurs in a narrative context that includes many more instances in which noble men sexually exploit socially inferior women within their domains, and these fictional incidents reflect a terrible reality.[10] Remember also that until the

---

8 Pointed out by Faverty, "Potiphar's Wife in Mediæval Literature," 90, and subsequently taken for granted, as in Mickel, "Marie de France and the Learned Tradition," 37. Few scholars besides Faverty have examined the Potiphar's Wife motif in *Lanval*, although the *lais* obviously lend themselves to folklore studies more broadly. See, for example, the discussions in Emanuel J. Mickel, *Marie de France*, Twayne's World Authors Series 306 (New York: Twayne Publishers, 1974), 72–94; Glyn Burgess, *The Lais of Marie de France: Text and Context* (Manchester: Manchester University Press, 1987); Judith Rice Rothschild, "Marie de France and the Folktale: Narrative Devices of the Marchen and Her Lais," in *In Quest of Marie de France: A Twelfth-Century Poet*, eds. Chantal A. Maréchal and Glyn S. Burgess, Medieval and Renaissance Series 10 (Lewiston: Edwin Mellen, 1992), 138–47.
9 Glyn S. Burgess, trans., *The Lais of Marie de France*, 2nd ed. (Harmondsworth: Penguin Classics, 1999), 76. All citations from the *Lais* will be taken from this translation.
10 For instance, see Marie's lai *Equitan*, in which the steward's wife expresses a fear of being exploited by the king who is initiating an adulterous affair:

"You are a king of great nobility; I am not wealthy enough to be the object of your love or passion. If you had your way with me, I know well and am in no doubt that you would soon abandon me and I should be very much worse off ... Because you are a

advent of DNA testing and other scientific methods of crime investigation, an accusation of rape was largely a question of his word against her word. When it comes to the question of consent, it still often is. And the words of seventeenth-century jurist Matthew Hale, at one time often used to instruct juries, makes clear just how those two words would be received: "rape … is an accusation easily to be made and hard to be proved, and harder to be defended by the party accused, tho never so innocent."[11] In other words, the motif itself is a mirror image of the actual problem of a rape accusation. We have a socially powerful aggressor trying to break a basic human rule for the sake of sexual gratification; a potential victim whose lack of social status is exploited by the aggressor; an explosive accusation that cannot be disproved by evidence but that has the power to ruin reputations; and a system of justice stacked against the potential victim. The difference is that the genders are switched.

In our own cultural context, and particularly within the context of the college campus, this motif is a double-edged sword. On the one hand, we know that false allegations of rape, however rare, have serious consequences for those falsely accused, and this motif is a way of imagining those consequences in a literary way. On the other hand, when students encounter this motif uncritically, they can interpret it in ways that allow it to take on malign and oppressive significance. As with so many other cultural narratives, this motif can be adopted as an unconscious explanation of how the world works, and so students who encounter it may mentally take it as confirmation that women do "cry rape" falsely. Accepted uncritically, it valorizes these other common beliefs in rape culture thinking: that accusers are typically not credible; that they had or sought consensual sex and then regretted it; that they are lying out of villainous motives such as vengefulness or malice; that the act of accusing someone automatically victimizes him.

Literature as a Tool for Truthfulness

So how to deal with the problem I have raised? I want to clarify that I am not suggesting that we stop teaching such material: as college teachers of literature, our mission is to help students understand the literature, not censor it. Moreover, we want our students to see the connections between medieval literature and their own cultural context. So I propose that we read this material in a way that will recover it for feminist purposes—to reframe the motif so that it does constructive work rather than destructive work. In what follows, I will suggest several possible ways to help our students critically process the motif and its cultural work. My comments are

---

powerful king and my husband is your vassal, you would expect, as I see it, to be the lord and master in love as well"

(58)

The steward's wife here articulates a keen awareness of her powerlessness in the relationship, and her behaviour in the rest of the *lai*, although wicked, appears to be motivated by this same awareness.

11 Quoted in Nicola Gavey, *Just Sex? The Cultural Scaffolding of Rape* (Hove: Psychology Press, 2005).

based on my four years teaching *Lanval* at a regional comprehensive university in the rural South, but I think that what I say here can translate easily to most college campuses (including my own new institution, a selective liberal-arts college in the urban South).

First, and simplest, we need to help our students recognize the false allegation motif *as* a literary motif. This method works especially well in courses that already use comparative methods, as medieval literature classes tend to, but it's well adapted for any literature course. When I read this text with my students, I found it helpful to point out the motif for my students in lecture, connecting *Lanval* with the narratives from Genesis, the *Iliad*, and the *Metamorphoses* in just a sentence or two, and labelling it a motif. Many of my lower-division students were avid but uncritical consumers of narrative in the form of television and movies. They came into my classes treating all narrative as entertainment without thinking much about the ways in which it shaped their ethical commitments or their assumptions about gender and power. But once my students became aware of the literary false allegation *as* a pattern, they (and I) could recognize it as an object of inquiry as well. The motif became available for us to analyze and interpret in the same way that we analyzed and interpreted other literary motifs, such as the bed trick or the "fair unknown" motif. More sophisticated readers, often students who already knew Genesis or Greek mythology, found it helpful to think of Marie as in conversation with those earlier texts, adopting and adapting freely with her own agenda in mind.

Second, we have to be aware that a depressingly high number of our students are likely to be survivors of sexual assault. I know there has been a lot of debate over the merit of trigger warnings, but I do use them, and here is how: when we talk about rape in class, I flag the subject matter at the start of the discussion and explicitly acknowledge the statistic that indicates that one in four college women has experienced some sort of sexual assault during her lifetime. I then point out that this statistic includes only female survivors (at this point, the whole class settles down to a kind of startled silence as they all mentally do the math for their class of thirty). I then say that anyone who can't stand to engage with the material is welcome to tune out for the duration, promising that I will rely only on volunteers for class discussion rather than cold-calling on the inattentive as I normally do. In my experience, this makes for an especially lively discussion, as students think of their contributions as potentially helping out someone who does not wish to talk. In short, I use the trigger warning as an opportunity to educate all students and to engage their empathy in constructive ways.

Third, we need to make sure that our students take a long look at agency in *Lanval*. My students invariably read this *lai* as a fairy tale, and in discussions they talk about how surprised they are at Lanval's passivity from start to finish. In the six semesters that I taught *Lanval* to undergraduates, I have never needed to guide my students in this direction. When I opened class by asking what interested or surprised them about the text, someone always pointed out that Lanval behaves more like a stereotypical damsel-in-distress than he does like the questing, rescuing knights that they expect to find in an Arthurian tale. They note that the fairy maiden initiates the relationship with Lanval and sets its terms, that Lanval pines and mourns for her when she disappears unilaterally, and that in the end she rescues him. This was a great time to confirm their perception: I contrasted Lanval with the Pearl-Poet's Gawain or Malory's Lancelot, both of whom express submission to a lady while at the same time embarking on adventures in which they act decisively and assertively. My students then felt more confident in describing Lanval as unusually passive, and often concluded that Marie is deliberately reversing gender roles in the *lai*. When I heard them make this leap, I then asked them to articulate the gender expectations they have in mind. Many of my students came to class with stereotyped expectations of a woman's role, and those students in particular needed to articulate those expectations before comparing and contrasting the different depictions of female sexual desire within the *lai* itself. While Marie depicts the queen in terms that connect her sexuality with her opportunism, ego, and vengefulness, Marie's fairy maiden is just as sexually assertive, but in ways that demonstrate the courtly virtues of nobility, generosity, and forgiveness. When she first appears, for instance, Marie describes her this way:

> She lay on a very beautiful bed—the coverlets cost as much as a castle— clad only in her shift. Her body was well formed and handsome, and in order to protect herself from the heat of the sun, she had cast about her a costly mantle of white ermine covered with Alexandrian purple. Her side, though, was uncovered, as well as her face, neck, and breast; she was whiter than the hawthorn blossom.
>
> (74)

Here the maiden's beauty is inextricably bound up both with her provocative clothing and her rich surroundings, all of which she offers to Lanval. Marie de France, far from being critical, is celebrating the maiden's assertiveness. We went on to discuss the maiden's behaviour throughout the rest of the poem, and students began to understand that, to Marie, the queen's problem was neither her sexual desires nor her assertiveness but her predatory behaviour.

Fourth, we can help our students understand how the false allegation motif functions as part of the social critique built into this *lai*. In my experience, students can readily identify the queen's shortcomings, but they rarely pick up on the larger social critique that Marie embeds into the story. As a result, they come to class assuming that the queen is the only villain in the story. To remedy this, I spent about five minutes describing medieval ideals of kingship, particularly the expectation that a good king would generously reward his loyal followers with wealth and lands. I then pointed out the failure of Arthur to do just this at the start of the story, noting that Gawain and his followers in the court don't befriend Lanval until he has become independently wealthy. In particular I pointed them to Gawain's comment, "In God's name, lords, we treat our companion Lanval ill, for he is so generous and courtly, and his father is a rich king, yet we have not brought him with us" (76), which highlights the court's focus on external rather than internal qualities. I then suggested that the queen's interest in Lanval seems to begin at the same time and for the same reasons. I ended by suggesting that Marie de France depicted Arthur's court as a shallow, unjust, and materialistic society, failing to measure up to the ideals that it was often treated as embodying. This short lecture prepared students to look for more social critique in the *lai*, which I often asked them to do in discussion groups of four or five. At this point, many groups noted the false allegation and the kangaroo court that follows as important abuses of power by both the queen and King Arthur. In the discussion that followed, I responded to their observations by noting that in many cultures women risk their reputations if they go public with a rape accusation, and I asked students what makes it safe for the queen to accuse Lanval. They quickly pointed to her privileged social station and married status, which protect her reputation from the consequences that a younger, less noble woman might face. Students thus began to register that rape is not, after all, "an accusation easily to be made," in Hale's words, but rather an accusation that lays the accuser open to attack on many levels.

Lastly, we need to listen carefully to our students' reactions. This topic is a scary and challenging one for many undergraduates, and it's important to both respect their reactions and challenge them where they need challenging. Obviously this means being prepared to listen to rape survivors who self-identify in or out of class, and to direct them to the resources they most need. But it also means listening to and interacting constructively with those students who voice dissent. For example, when one group of my students were discussing the false allegation motif, a male student expressed disbelief that any man would turn down the chance to have sex with an attractive woman. While I wanted to roll my eyes at this stereotyped thinking, I was grateful that he was willing to voice skepticism because it allowed me an opening to describe back to him what I thought he was describing: the common image of the sex-obsessed man. Then, rather than responding directly to him, I asked the rest of the class whether this was a neutral stereotype. With a little help, the students were able to isolate two important ways in which that stereotype was harmful to both women and men: first, by affirming that men are slaves to their sexual desires (and thus not responsible for their actions), and second, by shaming and silencing male victims of rape. I went out of my way to treat my skeptic's opinion as worthy of serious investigation, rather than trying to shut him down, because it allowed my other students to question his ideas themselves.

Medievalists have a two-pronged mission in the classroom: first, we want to help students understand medieval literature in historical and cultural context; and second, we want them to become more aware of their own historical and cultural context. Asking students to analyze the Potiphar's Wife motif in Marie de France's *Lanval* can help with both of those tasks because it reminds students that Western literature relies on shared narratives. Those narratives can make sense of our lived experience, but they can also falsify our perceptions, particularly when we enter into the difficult work of judging guilt and innocence. Reading and discussing *Lanval* with our students will not solve this problem, but it can help us raise our students' awareness and understanding of the issue. And that is a good start.

Works Cited

Belknap, Joanne. "Rape: Too Hard to Report and Too Easy to Discredit Victims." *Violence Against Women* 16 (December 2010): 1335–44.

Burgess, Glyn S., translated by *The Lais of Marie de France*. 2nd ed. Harmondsworth: Penguin Classics, 1999.

———. *The Lais of Marie de France: Text and Context*. Manchester: Manchester University Press, 1987.

Cargo, Robert T. "Marie de France's Le Laustic and Ovid's Metamorphoses." *Comparative Literature* 18 (1966): 162–66.

Doucet, David. "L'affaire DSK, un 'troussage de domestique'? Kahn s'excuse." l'express.fr. www.lexpress.fr/actualite/politique/l-affaire-dsk-un-troussage-de-domestique-kahn-s-excuse_994399.html (accessed October 3, 2014).

Faverty, Frederic E. "The Story of Joseph and Potiphar's Wife in Mediæval Literature." *Harvard Studies and Notes in Philology and Literature* 13 (1931): 81–128.

Gavey, Nicola. *Just Sex? The Cultural Scaffolding of Rape*. Hove: Psychology Press, 2005.

Gertz, Sun Hee Kim. "Echoes and Reflections of Enigmatic Beauty in Ovid and Marie de France." *Speculum* 73 (1998): 372–96.

———. "Transforming Lovers and Memorials in Ovid and Marie de France." *Florilegium* 14 (1996): 99–122.

Goldman, Shalom. *The Wiles of Women/the Wiles of Men: Joseph and Potiphar's Wife in Ancient Near Eastern, Jewish, and Islamic Folklore*. Albany: State University of New York Press, 1995.

Greenfeld, Lawrence A. *Sex Offenses and Offenders: An Analysis of Data on Rape and Sexual Assault*. U.S. Department of Justice, Office of Justice Programs, Washington, DC, 1997, www.mincava.umn.edu/documents/sexoff/sexoff.pdf (accessed April 3, 2014).

Gunby, Clare, Anna Carline, and Caryl Beynon. "Regretting It After? Focus Group Perspectives on Alcohol Consumption, Nonconsensual Sex and False Allegations of Rape." *Social & Legal Studies* 22 (2013): 87–106.

Hollis, Susan Tower. "The Woman in Ancient Examples of the Potiphar's Wife Motif, K2111." In *Gender and Difference in Ancient Israel*, edited by Peggy L. Day, 28–42. Minneapolis: Fortress, 1989.

Hunt, Laura, and Ray Bull. "Differentiating Genuine and False Rape Allegations: A Model to Aid Rape Investigations." *Psychiatry, Psychology & Law* 19 (November 2012): 682–91.

Kelly, Liz. "The (In)credible Words of Women: False Allegations in European Rape Research." *Violence Against Women* 16 (December 2010): 1345–55.

Lisak, David, Lori Gardinier, and Ashley M. Cote. "False Allegations of Sexual Assault: An Analysis of Ten Years of Reported Cases." *Violence Against Women* 16 (2010): 1318–34.

Mickel, Emanuel J. *Marie de France*. Twayne's World Authors Series 306. New York, NY: Twayne Publishers, 1974.

———. "Marie de France and the Learned Tradition." In *A Companion to Marie de France*, edited by Logan E. Whalen, 31–54. Leiden: Brill, 2011.

Norton, Russell, and Tim Grant. "Rape Myth in True and False Rape Allegations." *Psychology, Crime & Law* 14 (August 2008): 275–85.

Rothschild, Judith Rice. "Marie de France and the Folktale: Narrative Devices of the Marchen and Her Lais." In *In Quest of Marie de France: A Twelfth-Century Poet*, edited by Chantal A. Maréchal and Glyn S. Burgess, 138–47. Medieval and Renaissance Series 10. Lewiston: Edwin Mellen, 1992.

Rumney, Philip N. S. "False Allegations of Rape." *Cambridge Law Journal* 65 (2006): 125–58.

Thompson, Stith. *Motif-Index of Folk-Literature: A Classification of Narrative Elements in Folktales, Ballads, Myths, Fables, Medieval Romances, Exempla, Fabliaux, Jest-Books, and Local Legends.* Revised edition. Bloomington: Indiana University Press, 1955. www.ruthenia.ru/folklore/thompson/index.htm.

Chapter 10

SEXUAL COMPULSION AND SEXUAL VIOLENCE IN THE *LAIS* OF MARIE DE FRANCE

MISTY URBAN

While the *Lais* of Marie de France contain no explicit instances of rape, these twelve short Anglo-Norman poems dating to the later twelfth century abound with episodes of infidelity, indiscretion, sexual compulsion, and sexual violence. Lovers pursue affairs that imperil their lives and often end in their violent deaths together; knights or their go-betweens are frequently dismembered by jealous husbands; and overwhelming passion compels all manner of secret plotting and betrayal. Even the tales with ostensibly happy endings demonstrate how firmly Western conventions of romantic love link desire and suffering, passion and violence, masculinity and aggression, femininity and threat.[1] Kathryn Gradval identifies the medieval romances of Chrétien de Troyes as the source of these "ideological couplings that will become key in Western literature and culture," but Marie's Breton *Lais* share the same tendency "to obscure, rationalize, or sentimentalize sexual violence against women."[2] While key moves like privileging heteronormative desire, celebrating the devotion between lovers, and describing the conquering, indeed overpowering, nature of love all strike familiar chords with modern readers of the *Lais*, a discussion of these narrative moves ought also to observe the frequent commodification of the female body, the patriarchal regulation of sexuality, and the erotics of suffering, all of which demonstrate the many ways in which rape culture in so-called courtly literature coheres with present-day constructions on sex and gender.[3] Approaching Marie as a foundation for our modern tropes of sexual love is one way to make the Middle Ages accessible to students, and at the same time defamiliarize our own cultural assumptions about sex, love, desire, and power.[4]

---

1 R. Howard Bloch explores the basis and proliferation of these themes in *Medieval Misogyny and the Invention of Western Romantic Love* (Chicago: University of Chicago Press, 1991).

2 Kathryn Gradval, "Chrétien de Troyes, Gratian, and the Medieval Romance of Sexual Violence," *Signs* 17 (1992): 561 and 585.

3 Gradval, "Medieval Romance of Violence" and *Ravishing Maidens: Writing Rape in Medieval French Literature and Law* (Philadelphia: University of Pennsylvania Press, 1991).

4 Elizabeth Robertson and Christine M. Rose argue in *Representing Rape in Medieval and Early Modern Literature* (New York: Palgrave, 2001) that violence toward women is "deeply

Teaching "Lanval" in Brit Lit I

In the early segment of the British Literature survey, I paired the poetic translation of "Lanval" in *The Norton Anthology of English Literature* along with the excerpt from Malory's *Morte Darthur*[5] as an introduction to the genre of medieval romance. My introductory lecture typically included a brief illustration of sociohistorical context[6] and some sense of critical reception before we proceeded to student-led discussion, which was grounded on textual analysis and designed to address some thematic element with which students could engage. Having discussed masculinity and heroism in *Beowulf* and the literary stereotypes of female sexuality debated in Chaucer's "The Wife of Bath's Tale," I invited students to consider the attitudes toward love and sex that prevailed in the romance texts, along with the corresponding demands made on gender roles and their function as an aspect of economic and political power. I proposed they consider in what ways the conventions of the romance might authorize, question, or subvert the gender roles we had so far seen established as tropes of medieval literature, especially considering that, like the fairy queen in "The Wife of Bath's Tale," Lanval's mysterious *amie* seems to exercise unchallenged agency along with her sexual appeal.[7]

---

implicated in the social and epistemological structures of Western culture" (3). Marilynn Desmond in *Ovid's Art and the Wife of Bath: The Ethics of Erotic Violence* (Ithaca: Cornell University Press, 2006) describes "the everyday violences that work to organize gender and sexuality" and asserts that " 'violence against women' ... performs the category maintenance work of contemporary heterosexualities by naturalizing hierarchy and power" (4).

5 Marie de France, "Lanval," in *The Norton Anthology of English Literature*, 8th ed., vol. 1, eds. Greenblatt et al. (New York: Norton, 2006), 141–55. Sir Thomas Malory, "Morte Darthur," in ibid., 438–56.

6 One of the ways I attempted to characterize ecclesiastic attitudes was to summarize Jerome's ranking of women's sexuality, with virgins as most pleasing to God, followed by abstinent widows and then continent wives, as expressed in his *Adversus Jovinianum*; see Ralph Hanna and Traugott Lawler, eds., *Jankyn's Book of Wikked Wyves* (Athens: University of Georgia Press, 1997). I suggested that the book of Genesis served as the key text for authorizing common beliefs about the biological if not spiritual inferiority of women and "the curse of Eve," justification for all manner of female subjugation to male authority. To summarize legal attitudes I briefly outlined the categories of *feme sole* and *feme covert*, as defined in *Women and Gender in Medieval Europe: An Encyclopedia*, ed. Margaret C. Schaus (New York: Routledge, 2006).

7 If I didn't bring it up, a student in their own reading usually discovered Chaucer's real-life rape charge, which allowed us to discuss *raptus* as a legal term conflating sexual assault with the property crime of theft (Gradval, "Chrétien," 564–68 and *Ravishing Maidens*). Barbara A. Hanawalt, *"Of Good and Ill Repute": Gender and Social Control in Medieval England* (New York: Oxford University Press, 1995) contains much useful information on English rape law. Robertson and Rose in *Representing Rape* also note the conflation of terms in the legal definition of *raptus*, saying it reflects "shared basic legal understandings of women as marriageable commodities subject to damage as male possessions through rape" (7). Caroline Dunn's *Stolen Women in Medieval England: Rape, Abduction and Adultery 1100–1500* (Cambridge: Cambridge University Press, 2012) gives a full-length treatment of this subject. Jocelyn Catty in *Writing Rape, Writing Women in Early Modern England: Unbridled Speech* (London: Macmillan, 1999) notes that the Latin meaning of *raptus* as "theft" obtains into the early modern period in England, meaning "either abduction, seduction or rape" (1–2).

To the Norton headnote, which speculates on the identity of Marie and the general form and content of the Breton lay,[8] I added, as preface to our discussion, a highly abbreviated account of the *romanz* as a popular vernacular form that relied upon conventions of *fin' amor*, courtly conduct, the marvellous or supernatural, and a vaguely historicized treatment of contemporary norms and attitudes. If the discussion leader didn't introduce them, I prompted students to consider the power of the women in the love relationship, the ways in which the fairy world reflects and comments on Arthur's court, and the significance of Marie's neat reversal on the imperiled-woman trope, so that, like Malory's Guinevere tied to the stake, we find Lanval, the foreign knight, on trial for his life because of his presumed sexual misconduct.

Our discussion typically proceeded through a close reading of certain key passages that establish the terms of gendered power in the world of the poem. From the initial glance at a foreign threat from without, the action moves swiftly to private concerns that ally gender performance to economic status. Lanval is disadvantaged because he cannot participate in the rituals of gift-giving and hospitality, making him nominally impotent. There is also the suggestion that he is envied for his "handsomeness," a hint of sexual jealousy or competitiveness that leads to his exclusion (l. 21). Arthur's feudal gifts of "Wives and land" (l. 17) group women under the category of valuable and alienable property, subject to male dispensation, and signal the ongoing ways in which sexual and economic registers converge in this poem. In contrast to the rules that this opening establishes as governing the masculine, homosocial world of Arthur's court, the countryside into which Lanval escapes is a female-populated world wherein a splendid and powerful but unnamed fairy mistress offers to remedy Lanval's situation through sexual and economic largesse.

The power of Lanval's lady cannot be separated from her extraordinary wealth, which in turn enhances her value as a sexual object. Her self-presentation, reclining in a sheer gown upon a sumptuous bed in an equally magnificent tent, looks like a modern-day advertisement for high-end home furnishings, conflating the beauty of her material goods with her superlative personal beauty, a connection that rests on the audience's understanding that wealth is sexy and a beautiful woman is a luxury good. In an inverse parallel to Arthur's distribution of wives and land, the lady grants Lanval access to herself and her bank account in return for his pledge of loyalty and agreement to her terms of secrecy. Lanval, marvelling at his good fortune, is eager to comply, and the terms of his consent provide an interesting point for discussion. "He promised her that he would do / Whatever thing she told him to" (ll. 149–50), in return for which she presents "him her heart / and her body, every part" (ll. 129–30). This otherwise crude exchange of sex for money is romanticized and authorized by the language of love; the lady declares "I love you over everything" (l. 114), and for Lanval's part, "Love pierced his eyes with its bright rays, / Set fire to and scorched his heart" (ll. 116–17). One can pause to note

---

8 "Lanval," *Norton Anthology*, 141–42. Line numbers from the poem will be hereafter given in parentheses.

here that there is no question Lanval will not accept either the lady's sexual favours or economic gifts; at play is the assumption that a healthy male is always available and ready for sex, and will take any opportunity offered him.

Guinevere's approach to Lanval, who catches her eye due to the popularity granted him by his improved economic status, must be read in parallel to the lady's, and yet students tend to interpret it with an entirely different tone. It is worth noting that in the original Anglo-Norman, Guinevere's declaration to Lanval follows the same pattern as the lady's: she declares her love, consents to be his mistress, and promises him the benefit of joy, if not money.[9] In the Norton translation, Guinevere's sentiments are named by the narrator as "passion" (l. 260),[10] though she herself calls it love, and whether passion or lust get accorded a different status than love, then or now, deserves consideration. Likewise students should be questioned as to why they find it logical, and also hilarious, that Guinevere, finding her advances spurned, should immediately respond to Lanval with the accusation that "women are not what you prefer" (l. 278). Adultery poses no barrier to courtly love, and since a healthy male is presumably disposed to sex at every opportunity, as noted above, Guinevere assumes Lanval rejects her because his sexual preferences lie elsewhere; her desirability is not in question until he claims that his girlfriend is prettier than she is. The retaliation the queen takes—and how this remark of Lanval's gets turned into treason—proves the crux upon which a full understanding of the poem's codes of gender and power rest.

The queen's legal charge puts less emphasis on Lanval's fabricated overtures to her, a claim that would, in the legal atmosphere of the day, in fact constitute treason.[11] Instead, the personal insult that Lanval claims a secret lover "[so] chic, noble, and proud ... That even her lowliest chambermaid, / The poorest one that might be seen, / Was worthier than she—the queen" (ll. 319–22) turns into a charge of defamation, slander, and therefore treason. Decoding the logic behind this offers a fruitful conversation about the hierarchy of beauty established in the poem and its valuation of female attractiveness. For both the fairy mistress and Guinevere, having a court of beautiful women enhances their own stature, though their personal beauty of course is superior. Suggesting his wife is not the fairest in the land somehow translates as an insult *to Arthur*, either of his masculinity, his authority, or his own sexual potency. What would be fodder for a literary Court of Love—whose girlfriend is prettier—becomes a matter of public dispute in a court of law, presided over by

---

9 See the *Lais de Marie de France*, based on the edition by Karl Warnke and trans. into modern French by Laurence Harf-Lancner (Paris: Le Livre de Poche, 1990): ll. 263–6.

10 The line reads: "All the passion that she [Guinevere] feels," a faithful rendering of the corresponding line in the Warnke edition, which reads "tut sun curage li mustra." Harf-Lancner gives a more romantic translation: "pour lui révéler le secret de son cœur" [she revealed to him the secret of her heart] (l. 264, pp. 146–47).

11 Treason—which came by the time of Edward I to include not just plotting against the king's life but abusing the king's wife or family, falsifying the king's coin, or counterfeiting the king's seal—was automatically a felony and answerable by death. See J. G. Bellamy, *The Law of Treason in England in the Later Middle Ages* (Cambridge: Cambridge University Press, 1970), 23–24.

all of Arthur's knights and barons.[12] To be pardoned, Lanval must prove he spoke "without base intent" (l. 458) by producing a girlfriend who is, in point of fact, sexier than the queen.

The final scene is wonderfully rich in the way it settles the "hot or not" contest, and demands to be examined for the ways in which it makes male evaluation of female beauty not just a privilege but in fact an obligation, one which regards female sexual desirability as an objective measure upon which consensus is possible. The initial approach of the beauteous damsels in their purple gowns "with nothing underneath" again conflates material wealth and nobility with sexual allure; "The men took pleasure in these sights," the narrator observes, validating that the display of feminine beauty is a performance designed to impress and move the viewing male (ll. 477–9). The descriptions of the *bel amie* herself establish the magical power of female sexual allure: "Her beauty quieted jest and laughter" (l. 582) and warms "the heart of every single knight ... with sheer delight" (ll. 585–8), a nice euphemism for sexual arousal. The general agreement that Lanval's girl wins the beauty contest releases him from the charge of slander but further emphasizes the prerogative of the male to determine sexual appeal, which corresponds directly to female worth. This custom will not shock any population of college students, who are habituated to a culture that makes female sexuality the object of discussion, legislation, judgment, and scorn, while male virility is admired and the satisfaction of male heterosexual desire drives entire industries of marketing and entertainment. If nothing else, a close reading of "Lanval" reveals to students that our present-day culture's assumptions about male virility, female objectification, and gendered power have a long history.

Jane Chance provocatively suggests that Marie's poem puts her male knight, Lanval, in a feminine subject position,[13] and a debate over the extent to which students find this true offers a useful way to close classroom discussion of this poem. Why do we read Lanval as feminized because he is the recipient, rather than the initiator, of sexual advances? Why does it feminize him that, like Malory's Guinevere or modern-day celebrities, his sex life is a matter of public concern and debate, and moreover his fate depends not just on the decision of a jury but the key witness testimony of a woman? Why does the end of the poem, when he mounts her horse behind his beloved and she carries him off to Avalon, read as a reverse *raptus*,[14] in which the victorious woman carries off her prize? That we so easily identify the objectified, disempowered, victimized, or silenced as a *feminine* position should

---

12 A footnote in the Norton on p. 150 observes that Arthur's legal proceedings reflect actual twelfth-century practice.

13 "Marie de France versus King Arthur: Lanval's Gender Inversion as Breton Subversion," in *The Literary Subversions of Medieval Women* (New York: Palgrave Macmillan, 2007), 41–61. Chance finds the fairy queen unambiguously positive and powerful, a reading I find complicated by the narrative conflation of her material wealth and beauty with her social and aesthetic value.

14 Chance points out that Marie uses the Old French *raviz* to describe Lanval's removal to Avalon ("Marie de France," 53). Harf-Lancner translates Warnke's line "la fu raviz li dameiseals" (l. 662, p. 166) into the more stately "le jeune homme a été enlevéé" (l. 662, p. 167).

give us pause. The translation of feminine as passive offers a teaching moment that makes visible the ways that violence against women is constitutive of the Western ideology of romantic love.

Teaching the *Lais* in Medieval Lit

In organizing a senior seminar in Medieval Literature around the theme Myths of the Middle Ages, I used Busby and Burgess's prose translation of the *Lais* to introduce the topic of romantic love, along with selected lyrics of the troubadours, excerpts from Andreas Capellanus' *Art of Courtly Love*, and selected correspondence of Abelard and Heloise.[15] My introductory lectures on socio-historical background tended to be more in-depth than in the survey,[16] but our student-led class discussion was still generally based on textual analysis, with some recourse to literary theory to offer various critical lenses. In my introduction to the *Lais* I briefly described the rise of French vernacular poetry and their tropes of *fin 'amor*, then showed images from British Library MS Harley 978 and read to the class in the Anglo-Norman to establish a sense of the *lai* as a performative oral literature as well as a material object of study, the creation of a specific moment in historical time.[17]

My goal in teaching romantic love as a cherished myth with its foundations in the medieval literature of Western Europe was to address the social constructedness behind Marie's ideas about romance, love, desire, and gender roles. One such notion surfaces from Busby and Burgess's observation in their introduction that love in Marie has "an almost inevitable association with suffering" (28), best stated by the narrator herself in "Guigemar": "Love is an invisible wound within the body and, since it has its source in nature, it is a long-lasting ill" (49). The *Lais* abound with instances of sexual violence and compulsion, as well as the insistence that passion overrules all else, including reason. I suggested to my students that the *Lais* offer not straight praise but rather a critique of romantic love in their portrayal of passionate love (and sex) as socially as well as personally disruptive. The use of violence as a critical lens offers a further series of questions with which students can engage: the purpose of the frequent objectification of women's bodies, the limiting of women's agency to their selection of sexual partner, and the ways in which violence is

---

15 Glyn S. Burgess and Keith Busby, *The Lais of Marie de France*, 2nd ed. (New York: Penguin, 1986). Page numbers from this text will hereafter be given in parentheses. To represent the troubadours I selected lyrics by William IX, Marcabrun, and Bernard of Ventadour from Alan R. Press's *Anthology of Troubadour Lyric Poetry* (Austin: University of Texas Press, 1971). I also assigned Andreas Capellanus, *The Art of Courtly Love*, trans. John Jay Parry (New York: W. W. Norton & Co., 1969), 177–86 ("The Rules of Love") and *The Letters of Abelard and Heloise*, trans. Betty Radice (New York: Penguin, 1974), 64–78, 96–102, 112–18, 122–25, 129–36, and 145–54, which excerpt Abelard's *Historia calamitatum* and the first four "personal" letters.
16 I also assigned Andrew Galloway's *Medieval Literature and Culture* as background reading (New York: Continuum, 2006).
17 Burgess and Busby's second edition contains three *lais* edited from H 978: "Lanval," "Laüstic," and "Chevrefoil," which can give students a sense of the original composition.

naturalized, even romanticized, to the point that love and violence, desire and suffering are constitutively linked.

A discussion of the first *lai* in the collection, "Guigemar," will serve here to suggest how the ubiquitous sexual violence can become a critical interpretive lens for examining how Marie constructs and perpetuates the terms of masculinity, femininity, love, and desire in her poems. From this, students can be encouraged to turn the same deconstructive lens on their own world, its very similar gender norms, and its similar forms of sexual violence.

"Guigemar" offers a lesson not just in the uses of violence but in compulsive heterosexuality as the foundation of Western romantic love. The first half of "Guigemar" describes the hero's initiation into heteronormative sexual relationship as part of his broader journey to a legitimate and respected social position. Guigemar is introduced as a knight to whom "Nature had done ... such a grievous wrong that he never displayed the slightest interest in love" (44), despite the number of noble and beautiful women who offer themselves to him. It's worth asking students precisely what Nature's requirements of sexual normalcy are and why Guigemar's showing "no visible interest in love" makes him a "lost cause" (44), for the language itself performs the logic of connecting the social and cultural requirements of heterosexuality to biological desire in ways that get coded as either "natural" or "unnatural." Guigemar, thus established as a queer sexuality—asexual, virgin, or other—engages with his first trial in the act of hunting, a typically masculine and knightly pursuit, and his quarry is similarly queer: a "hind with its fawn," a beast "completely white with the antlers of a stag on its head" (44). The rebounding arrow that pierces Guigemar "in the thigh and going right through into the horse's flesh" (44) opens a wound that can be read in a number of ways, but most suggestively as a castrating wound delivered by "the androgynous hind, the monstrous horned mother."[18] The magical hind inflicts a further wound on Guigemar in the form of a curse that he can only be healed "by a woman who will suffer for your love more pain and anguish than any other woman has ever known, and you will suffer likewise for her" (44). Guigemar's reparation for injuring this ambiguously gendered animal and the cure for his presumed sexual deficiency can only be rendered through the imposition of unparalleled emotional suffering on a currently unknown and otherwise innocent woman.

Guigemar's removal to the sea-enclosed keep made of green marble, accomplished by the technique of the rudderless boat, raises the same questions of sexual agency and feminization introduced in "Lanval." So jealously is this mysterious lady enclosed by her aged husband that the old priest appointed to serve

---

18 Susanne Klerks, "The Pain of Reading Female Bodies in Marie de France's 'Guigemar,'" *Dalhousie French Studies* 33 (1995): 5 and 11. Klerks positions Marie de France more generally within a "culture desensitized to antifemale violence" and suggests she "reveals women's marginalized positions within courtly literature" and "exposes the complicity of a courtly culture predicated on aggression" (8–10). Klerks's analysis of what she calls the raping/reading paradigm established in "Guigemar," while germane to the theme of this volume, gains more from reading the *lai* in the Anglo-Norman; this trope of a reading as a type of rape does not emerge in the Busby and Burgess translation.

her can only be trusted because "he had lost his lower members" (46). The moral of the painting on the walls of the lady's chamber, depicting the goddess Venus tossing Ovid's *Ars Remedia* into a fire (46), offers either a remark on the reasons why female sexuality must be contained, or a remark on why male constraint on female sexuality can and perhaps must be defeated; students can decide.

But the mural leads to the third step in the sexual tutelage of Guigemar, delivered by the lady's handmaiden and the narrative voice of Marie, informing Guigemar and the reader that a "right and proper" love thrives on fidelity, physical beauty, nobility, and obedience to the beloved's demands (49). Guigemar, previously wounded by his own arrow, finds that "love had now pierced him to the quick," a second penetration that reorients his suffering, for "the lady had wounded him so deeply" that "he felt no pain from the wound in his thigh" (48).

Love likewise tortures the lady, who has a similar ardour "kindled within her heart" (48). But the seeming mutuality of their love and suffering is tempered by the speech which Guigemar, emboldened by love "to reveal his feelings to her," subsequently makes (49). Though he is washed ashore, wounded, and at her mercy, the tone of Guigemar's speech quickly moves from the typical lover's complaint—"I am dying because of you … If you are not willing to cure me, then it must all end in my death"—to a lecture on the obligations of a female addressee: "a woman who is always fickle likes to extend courtship in order to enhance her own esteem," Guigemar, suddenly an expert on the ways of love, informs her. "But the well-intentioned lady, who is worthy and wise, should not be too harsh towards a man, if she finds him to her liking; she should rather love him and enjoy his love" (49–50). The young matron, taking to heart this instruction that a good girl does not keep a man in agony, "recognized the truth of his words and granted him her love without delay" (50). Once he kisses her, Guigemar "henceforth was at peace," his painful sexual frustration finding its proper resolution, and he and his beloved spend the next year and a half in "great delight" (50). His queerness is corrected, his wound healed, and her isolation remedied by mutual pleasure, which reaffirms the "naturalness" of heterosexual passion, though adulterous and kept secret.

The nature of the love pledges that Guigemar and his lady exchange deserves a careful reading for what they reveal about male privilege and access to the body. The lady ties a knot in the tail of Guigemar's shirt and gives him leave "to love the woman who can undo the knot and untie it" (50). This item of raiment allows Guigemar, once he returns to his homeland, to duplicate his previous indifference to love, for there is no lady or maiden who can undo the shirt, though many make the attempt. The lady's pledge, in return, is "a belt which she would gird about her bare flesh and draw tightly around her loins. He encouraged her to love any man who could open the buckle without tearing or severing it" (50). While Guigemar can don or dispense with his love test at will, he has in effect given his lady love a chastity belt, different from the "tower of dark-hued marble" in which her husband encloses her only by matter of degree (52). The fidelity of the male partner is a matter of choice, while female loyalty can be compelled and access to her body controlled by the tokens or barriers imposed by the man who lays claims to her.

A difference of degree likewise prevails in the sorrow the lovers feel at being parted, for while Guigemar is "sad and downcast," refusing to marry, the lady in her tower "suffered during the day and at night it was worse. No man on earth could describe the great pain, agony, anguish and grief which the lady experienced" (51–2). Their eventual reconciliation presents her further pain, when after her own sea voyage she is taken in by the lord Meriaduc, who, on the basis of her beauty and nobility, falls in love with her. Guigemar is besieged by maidens eager to unknot his shirt, but the lady suffers a more direct physical attack: the spurned Meriaduc "took her in his arms, cut the lacing of her tunic, and endeavoured to open the belt, but to no avail. Afterwards all the knights in the land were summoned to make the attempt" (53), a strategy that cannot read as other than an attempted gang rape, prevented only by the previous claim of a rival male upon her.

Meriaduc reads as another version of the jealous husband who breaks down the door to the lady's chamber, but whether Guigemar's form of masculinity presents any variance on or correction to this hyper-masculine type is a matter of debate. Guigemar's obstacle during the recognition scene is that, to him, "women look very much alike" (53), a statement that demands decoding for its understanding of females as an undifferentiated and indistinguishable collection of objects presenting themselves for male entertainment. The lady's agency in reclaiming her preferred sexual partner is further reduced in the recognition scene, for when the shirt is brought to her, "her heart was too full of anguish" to self-identify (53); instead, she unties the knot only when Meriaduc orders her to. Even so Guigemar insists on ocular proof, cajoling her to "let me see your body and the belt with which I girded you." Only when he "placed his hands on her hips and found the belt" does he believe she is his beloved (54). The mutuality of suffering proceeding from the curse of the hind suggests that Guigemar's sighs and heartaches are somehow equivalent to the forced imprisonment, suicidal impulses, and attempted serial rape of the lady, whose body is literally passed from hand to hand until her "true" or "proper" mate appears.

A full reading of the violence in the poem rests on the way its final reunion of the lovers is achieved through Guigemar's masculine aggression. When Meriaduc refuses to surrender the lady, claiming that "I found her and I shall keep her and defend her against you" (53), Guigemar responds by assembling his men and recruiting Meraiduc's rival in a siege that "starved all those inside"; then he "captured and destroyed the castle and killed the lord within," and "took away his beloved" (54–5). True love prevails, with the help of a breathtaking episode of war that leaves a fairly high body count as the cost of bringing the fated lovers together.

If one is to read "Guigemar" as idealizing a certain kind of love, as some critics do,[19] then one must deal with the ways in which Guigemar's acquisition of secure

---

[19] As does Benjamin Semple in "The Male Psyche and the Female Sacred Body in Marie de France and Christine de Pizan," *Yale French Studies* 86 (1994): 164–86. In contrast, Renee L. Curtis in "Physical and Mental Cruelty in the *Lais* of Marie de France" observes a plentitude of anti-social, "unprincipled and quite unacceptable behavior" in the poems, presenting love as a corrosive rather than constructive force (*Arthuriana* 6 (1996): 22–35).

social position and chosen sexual partner relies on his transformation from asexual, impotent hero "healed" through enthusiastic hetero sex to full, potent manhood, which first requires him to outperform the older, jealous husband and then annihilate the more virile rival male. We can also ask whether this "ideal" glosses over any particular injustices to the lady, who, while given thought and expression, functions largely as a possession of various men. Her agency extends to devising a test to ensure her chosen partner's fidelity. This supposedly idealizing lay defines love as a tormenting, debilitating, possibly fatal physical condition and, despite a brief interlude of bliss at the woman-run castle by the sea, ultimately sorts its lovers into a feudal, patriarchal world that endorses masculine aggression and female compliance, valorizes suffering, and models a man-as-hunter, woman-as-prey paradigm that students might easily identify in contemporary "rules" about courtship.[20]

"Guigemar" lays out themes that can be traced through the remainder of the *Lais*, amplifying and extending ideas about the necessity of suffering to love, the function of women as exchangeable goods, and the uses of violence to secure, obstruct, or redress a proper love relationship. In some cases it takes effort to sensitize students to what actually counts as violence, so accepted are certain outcomes in the narrative logic of the poems. Examples include the conclusion of "Equitan," in which the betrayed seneschal pitches his wife into the tub of boiling water she had prepared to kill him. Curiously enough, rather than face the enraged husband, her lover the king part hops into the boiling pot after her "[t]o conceal his wickedness" (60). We ought to ask why we so easily accept murder and suicide as the price for sexual misconduct, and whether capital punishment really is a fair sentence for adultery. Likewise, students are generally entertained by the husband's revenge at the end of "Bisclavret," when he bites off the nose of the wife who trapped him in his lupine form (69). Yet we should pause to consider what exactly is signified by her punishment, which manifests evidence of her switch in sexual allegiances in the visible marker of her noseless offspring.[21]

Equally puzzling and subtle moments of violence include the slander against twins in "La Fresne," which leads a mother to abandon one of her twin daughters in order to protect her reputation from a charge she herself invented; the refusal of the young lover in "Les Deux Amanz" to take the magical strength-imbuing potion the princess secures for him, which results in his death and hers; the refusal of the lady in "Chaitivel" to prefer any one knight, which leads to death and suffering for them

---

20 Helen Benedict in "The Language of Rape" claims that a rape culture "portrays women as sexual objects, fair prey for the hunter-man" (*Transforming a Rape Culture*, 101). bell hooks in "Seduced by Violence No More," in the same volume, likewise points out that "the heterosexist framework … condones male erotic domination of women" and that by refusing to submit to it, "females would be actively disempowering patriarchy" (356).

21 As an aside, this facial mutilation is on the books as legal remedy for female sexual misconduct in twelfth-century England. According to the laws of King Cnut, ca. 1030, a woman proved guilty of adultery shall "lose both her nose and her ears"; see A. J. Robertson, ed. and trans., *The Laws of the Kings of England from Edmund to Henry I* (Cambridge: Cambridge University Press, 1925), 202–3.

all; and the booby-trapped window in "Yonec," which destroys the hawk-knight, a death Yonec later punishes by murdering his stepfather once he learns of the tale. And the spectre of rape haunts the whole of "Laüstic," in which the slaughter of the poor nightingale, as stand-in for the lady's forbidden lover, functions as a symbolic murder/castration of the bachelor knight, a symbolic rape and/or violent assault on the lady (whose breast is spangled with the blood of the bird), and an allusion to the rape and dismemberment of Philomel, who in the myth was turned into the bird and her voice restored in its song.[22]

Dwelling on these moments of violence in Marie's *Lais* brings to light how readily passionate love is perceived and even valorized for its anti-social tendencies. Desire oversets and is the antithesis to reason; lovers are ennobled by death in one other's arms, remaining entwined like the hazel and honeysuckle as described of Tristan and Isolde in "Chevrefoil"; and sexual compulsion explains and justifies all manner of social, legal, or feudal trespasses. That suffering for love becomes synonymous with romance as both literary genre and affective experience is a chief myth of the "romantic literature" that deserves some serious interrogation, especially when, as the letters of Heloise show, this myth provides a framework for actual women to reconcile themselves to the woes brought upon them by love.

If, as Suzanne Klerks suggests, Marie is out to expose the "antifemale violence" of the courtly register,[23] an antidote can possibly be found in the end of "Eliduc," which moves the conversation about love into a spiritual register that repairs and corrects the tangled love triangle into which earthly passions lead the central characters. Eliduc's first wife, Guildelüec, in first saving the life of the maiden Guilliadun and then removing herself from her marriage to let her husband marry the younger and prettier girl, performs an ennobling gesture of sacrifice that seems to epitomize selfless femininity, and which employs selflessness and piety to neutralize the otherwise violent and painful outcomes of his bigamy. That the tale concludes with all three characters pursuing lives of spiritual devotion seems Marie's happiest ending yet, and divine love offers a resolution to the sufferings attendant on sexual passions.

Reading Marie's *Lais* as a whole text provides, in the end, a wealth of evidence to support the argument that Marie makes visible the ways in which compulsion, violence, and suffering are not just indicative but constitutive of Western romantic love, and that not only does sexual violence result in consequence of these celebrated passions but violence is also used to remedy the supposed threats that unrestrained desires pose to reason, logic, and social order. We likewise see that the cultural rhetoric of the romance confines women's chief concerns to selection and pursuit of desired sexual partner, ignoring their influence in any other than strictly private,

---

22 Robertson and Rose in *Representing Rape* think that Marie makes an anti-rape statement in her fable "The Fox and the Bear," which describes the "sinister" violation of a female bear by a fox, with the moral "that even the wise and virtuous cannot escape the wiles of the wicked" (16–17n10).
23 Klerks, "Female Bodies," 2.

domestic, affective realms.[24] Whether these conventions of romantic love qualify as medieval misogyny or violence against women offers grounds for fruitful classroom debate. But a reading of Marie's *Lais* through the critical lens of sexual violence and compulsion yields moments when the ideology of romantic love makes visible its constitutive moves: its valorization of erotic love as a private good; its characterization of sexual desire as powerful, even destructive; its erotics of suffering; and the easy progression from male prerogative to aggression to sexual violence. These historically distant poems dramatize a twelfth century which links love with violence, desire with compulsion, and show us how much the "cultural law of male power and female powerlessness"[25] persists in our own day, legitimizing continued violence against women and perpetuating a rape culture that harms us all.[26]

Works Cited

Chance, Jane. "Marie de France versus King Arthur: Lanval's Gender Inversion as Breton Subversion." In *The Literary Subversions of Medieval Women*, 41–61. New York: Palgrave Macmillan, 2007.

Classen, Albrecht. *Sexual Violence and Rape in the Middle Ages: A Critical Discourse in Premodern German and European Literature.* Berlin: De Gruyter, 2011.

Curtis, Renee L. "Physical and Mental Cruelty in the *Lais* of Marie de France." *Arthuriana* 61 (1996): 22–35.

Desmond, Marilynn. *Ovid's Art and the Wife of Bath: The Ethics of Erotic Violence.* Ithaca: Cornell University Press, 2006.

Dunn, Caroline. *Stolen Women in Medieval England: Rape, Abduction and Adultery 1100–1500.* Cambridge: Cambridge University Press, 2012.

---

24 Women's enduring interest in matters of courtship, sexual pairing, and relationship are often cited as reasons for the current popularity of the genres of women's fiction, chick lit, and romance. Pamela Regis reaches this conclusion in *A Natural History of the Romance* (Philadelphia: University of Philadelphia Press, 2003), though she in no way suggests that women's interests are exclusively limited to the finding and retention of a mate.

25 Gradval, "Chrétien de Troyes," 585.

26 Though it didn't arise in our classroom discussions, the question of consent necessarily pairs with any analysis of sexual compulsion. Evelyn Vitz, "Rereading Rape in Medieval Literature," *Romanic Review* 88 (1997): 1–26, suggests that rape is a thorny issue to prosecute because "no" might mean "yes," and women might enjoy being "forced" to undergo something they wanted anyway. Vitz doesn't address how women's desires might be conditioned to the point that a pervasive cultural eroticization of violence might teach women (and men) to find violence a turn on. Robertson and Rose effectively deconstruct her argument in *Representing Rape*, 12–13. Still, these same confusions about the question of will inhibited medieval judgments on rape (Hanawalt, *"Of Good and Ill Repute,"* 136) and continue to hamper rape prosecution in our own day, as discussed in Mary E. Williams and Tamara L. Roleff, eds., *Sexual Violence: Opposing Viewpoints* (San Diego: Greenhaven Press, 1997). The belief that the violation of rape is remediated or even justified if conception results might be traced to Britton, who recommended that rape not be prosecuted as a felony if the victim conceived (Hanawalt, "Repute," 127), presumably due to the prevalent medieval belief that women's sexual pleasure was a condition of conception.

Edwards, Suzanne. *The Afterlives of Rape in Medieval English Literature.* New York: Palgrave Macmillan, 2016.

Gilbert, Dorothy, ed. and trans. *Marie de France.* New York: Norton, 2015.

Gradval, Kathryn. "Chrétien de Troyes, Gratian, and the Medieval Romance of Sexual Violence." *Signs* 17 (1992): 558–85.

——. *Ravishing Maidens: Writing Rape in Medieval French Literature and Law.* Philadelphia: University of Pennsylvania Press, 1991.

Hanawalt, Barbara A. *"Of Good and Ill Repute": Gender and Social Control in Medieval England.* New York: Oxford University Press, 1995.

Hanning, Robert, and Joan Ferrante, trans. *The Lais of Marie de France.* Durham, NC: Labyrinth Press, 1978.

Kinoshita, Sharon, and Peggy McCracken. *Marie de France.* Woodbridge: Boydell, 2012.

Klerks, Susanne. "The Pain of Reading Female Bodies in Marie de France's 'Guigemar.'" *Dalhousie French Studies* 33 (1995): 1–16.

Robertson, Elizabeth, and Christine M. Rose, eds. *Representing Rape in Medieval and Early Modern Literature.* New York: Palgrave, 2001.

Saunders, Corinne. *Rape and Ravishment in the Literature of Medieval England.* Rochester: Brewer, 2001.

Semple, Benjamin. "The Male Psyche and the Female Sacred Body in Marie de France and Christine de Pizan." *Yale French Studies* 86 (1994): 164–86.

Vitz, Evelyn. "Rereading Rape in Medieval Literature." *Romantic Review* 88 (1997): 1–26.

Warnke, Karl, ed. *Lais de Marie de France.* Translated by Laurence Harf-Lancner. Paris: Le Livre de Poche, 1990.

Williams, Mary E., and Tamara L. Roleff, eds. *Sexual Violence: Opposing Viewpoints.* San Diego: Greenhaven Press, 1997.

Chapter 11

TROUBADOUR LYRIC, *FIN'AMORS*, AND RAPE CULTURE

DANIEL E. O'SULLIVAN

The term "rape culture" was coined relatively recently, but its salient features are perceptible throughout history. Definitions vary, but most critics describe it as a culture in which people consider rape a "fact of life," a society that implicitly or explicitly promotes sexual violence. First applied to all of American society by second-wave feminists in the 1970s, the notion has many detractors. Men's rights organizations believe feminism and political correctness have wrongfully transformed traditional forms of romance into excuses for man-bashing; furthermore, they allege the judicial system overrides due process by favouring victims' rights over those of the accused.[1] Others claim that the notion trivializes female sexual empowerment: ours is not a rape culture but a hook-up culture in which both women and men seek "no strings" sexual relationships. Consequently, they argue, our ideas of what is considered socially acceptable must evolve.[2] Even prominent feminists like bell hooks believe that rape culture must be analyzed within a broader culture of violence that disproportionately affects minorities, especially women and persons of colour.[3]

Nowhere in American society is the term debated more hotly than on college campuses. Rape statistics have long met with skepticism: government and watchdog agencies rely on statistics voluntarily reported by institutions of higher learning,

---

[1] Articles and op-ed pieces on this and related issues can be found all over the internet. For example, see "False Accusations" on the National Coalition for Men website: http://ncfm.org/2009/01/issues/false-accusations, January 11, 2009.

[2] A recent academic and scientific review of literature and perspectives is Justin R. Garcia et al., "Sexual Hookup Culture: A Review," *Review of General Psychology* 16 (2012): 161–76, and can be found here: www.apa.org/monitor/2013/02/sexual-hookup-culture.pdf, accessed February 20, 2015.

[3] hooks makes many of her first criticisms in *Outlaw Culture: Resisting Representations* (New York: Routledge, 1994), and especially her Chapter 10, "Seduced by Violence No More," 128–33. For recent commentary about hooks's writing and position, see Cynthia Carter, "The Transformative Power of Cultural Criticism: bell hooks' Radical Media Analysis," in *Radical Mass Media Criticism: A Cultural Genealogy*, eds. David Berry and John Theobald (Montreal: Black Rose Press, 2006), 212–33.

and under-reporting has frequently been the norm due to some administrations' allergic reaction to negative press.[4] In September 2014, the Obama administration pushed university administrators to become more proactive in combating sexual violence by taking surveys of students' attitudes and experiences and then charging faculty and staff to create programs to combat the problem.[5] Much of the debate revolves around the issues of coercion and consent. Consent is a freely given, never assumed, agreement to engage in a sexual relationship with a person of equal power (thus students cannot consent to have sex with teachers or players with coaches); moreover, fear or social pressure must not be present, and the influence of drugs or alcohol nullifies any consent.[6] Coercion, on the other hand, denotes the use of force or intimidation to obtain compliance, be it through emotional manipulation, implied or real threats in the form of psychological, verbal, or physical harm.[7] Coercion and consent are, in short, mutually exclusive.

Most recently, it is the notion of affirmative consent that has been debated with particular verve. In California, a law was passed to describe what has been known widely as the "affirmative consent standard" which, according to its proponents, eliminates any ambiguity when it comes to whether or not a person consents to have sex. In the absence of clear, affirmative consent, sexual interaction is rape. As Christine Helwick puts it, positive description of the standard is harder to achieve than one that relies on negatives:

> [Affirmative consent] is *not* silence, lack of protest or resistance, the existence of a dating relationship or previous sexual relations. It can*not* exist when a sexual partner knew, or reasonably should have known, that the other was asleep, unconscious or incapacitated due to drugs, alcohol or medication, or unable to communicate due to a mental or physical condition.[8]

---

4 A 2008 study by the National Institute of Justice that breaks down statistics from the Department of Education and other institutions can be found at www.nij.gov/topics/crime/rape-sexual-violence/campus/Pages/measuring.aspx, October 1, 2008. The situation might be improving according to Tyler Kingkade in the Huffington Post article "Colleges Are Reporting More Sexual Assaults, and That's a Great Sign," in September 2014, www.huffingtonpost.com/2014/10/12/college-sexual-assault-numbers-clery-reports_n_5967412.html, October 12, 2014. Then again, Collin Blinkley, Jill Riepenhoff, and Mike Wagner of The Columbus Dispatch with Sara Gregory of the Student Press Law Center take issue with the Department of Education statistics upon which Kingkade based his report, "Reports on College Crime Are Deceptively Inaccurate," www.dispatch.com/content/stories/local/2014/09/30/campus-insecurity.html, October 9, 2014.
5 See Michael D. Shear and Elena Schneider's *New York Times* article, "Obama Unveils Push for Young People to Do More against Campus Assaults," from which the story and its aftermath may be followed: www.nytimes.com/2014/09/20/us/politics/obama-campaign-college-sexual-assaults.html?_r=0, September 20, 2014.
6 Resources that define and discuss notions of consent vs. coercion online are plentiful. See, for example, "About Sexual Assault," posted by the Center Against Rape and Domestic Violence at http://cardv.org/aboutsexualassault.php, accessed February 20, 2015.
7 Ibid.
8 See "Affirmative Consent, the New Standard," www.insidehighered.com/views/2014/10/23/campuses-must-wrestle-affirmative-consent-standard-sexual-assault-essay, October 10, 2014.

Communication can be verbal or nonverbal, which means that it can take myriad forms: a verbally articulated "yes," a nod, or, well, it's not clear. The lack of apparent clarity has led to criticism of such policies for giving people, especially men, an impossible standard to meet.[9]

Questions of where the line should be drawn can arise not only at fraternity parties and in bars, but also in the classroom. In my medieval French and Occitan literature classes, love, seduction, sexual encounters, and violence do not arise infrequently. Anyone who studies medieval culture knows that popular images of courteous knights and demure damsels in distress represent whitewashed, anachronistic portraits of medieval culture.[10] For example, in the *pastorela* or *pastourelle*, the lyric genre popular first in Old Occitan and then more widely among Old French audiences, a knight happens upon a shepherdess in a field. After addressing her, he attempts to seduce her, at which point the narrative may take several turns: the young woman may give in; she may manage to rebuff her would-be seducer's advances herself or with the help of nearby shepherds; or, if she continues to resist, he might rape her.[11] This is usually not described in detail. For example, the knight of Thibaut de Champagne's "J'aloie l'autrier errant" (RS 342),[12] after pulling his prey into the wood and hearing the approach of nearby shepherds, ends his tale thus:

> Assez fis plus que ne di.
> Je la lais, si m'en fouï;
> N'oi cure de tel gent.
>
> (58–60)[13]

My most naive students may not discern the significance of the pithy dénouement at first, and I have to ask: what "more" did the knight do? It might take a knowing glance before it dawns on them, and many shrink with horror. Moreover, while the notion of physically overpowering a woman and raping her is morally repugnant

---

9 Emily Yoffe addresses the problem in "The College Rape Overcorrection," www.slate.com/ articles/double_x/doublex/2014/12/college_rape_campus_sexual_assault_is_a_serious_ problem_but_the_efforts.html, December 7, 2014.

10 Most recently, Amy N. Vines reassesses the place of rape in courtly romance in "Invisible Woman: Rape as a Chivalric Necessity in Medieval Romance," in *Sexual Culture in the Literature of Medieval Britain*, eds. Amanda Hopkins, Robert Rouse, and Cory James Rushton (Cambridge: Brewer, 2014), 133–47.

11 Kathryn Gravdal provides excellent analysis of the genre in the chapter "The Game of Rape: Sexual Violence and Social Class in the Pastourelle" in her *Ravishing Maidens: Writing Rape in Medieval French Literature and Law* (Philadelphia: University of Pennsylvania Press, 1991), 104–21. A more recent study that includes, but doesn't focus exclusively on, questions of gender and sexual violence, is Geri L. Smith, *The Medieval French Pastourelle Tradition: Poetic Motivations and Generic Transformations* (Gainesville: University of Florida, 2009).

12 In keeping with prevailing scholarly norms, trouvère songs are identified by their Raynaud Spanke (RS) number from Hans Spanke, *G. Raynauds Bibliographie des altfranzösischen Liedes, neu bearbeitet und ergänst* (Leiden: Brill, 1955).

13 The citation of Thibaut's *pastourelle* comes from the edition that the author is currently preparing with Christopher Callahan and Marie-Geneviève Grossel. Readers may also consult the text in Axel Wallensköld, *Les Chansons de Thibaut de Champagne, Roi de Navarre* (Paris: Champion, 1925), 176–79.

to most, if not all, twenty-first-century twenty-somethings, when they learn such songs provided entertainment for the noble class of society, their indignation rises even further.[14]

I teach at a relatively large public university in the conservative southeast of the United States. The vast majority of my students are traditional in terms of both demographics and social attitudes. Terms such as "courtesy," "courteous," and "courting" remain part and parcel of students' vernacular, and homecoming courts persist as socially important institutions. Even more ingrained into the social fabric of universities like mine are Greek associations. These institutions have their own histories and legends, fierce loyalties, codes of social engagement, and, especially when it comes to fraternities, reputations, be they earned or not, for creating spaces in which women are objectified and prey to hypersexual and drunken young men.[15] Sexual tension can run high in social interactions outside of the classroom, so when overtly sexual content comes into the classroom, an instructor has to wonder how best to approach the issues presented. While other authors in this volume focus on this problem, I will instead confront the issue of teaching material in which sexual content is not explicit but implied.

While students may react viscerally to knights nonchalantly raping recalcitrant shepherdesses, they may heave a sigh of relief or melt with a warm, romantic feeling, at least at first, when reading Old Occitan *cansos*, the love songs embodying the very notion of courtly love or *fin'amors* in the High Middle Ages.[16] The concept has been called the precursor to modern conceptions of Western romantic, heterosexual

---

14 A veritable blueprint for such *pastourelles* comes in Andreas Capellanus' *De Amore*, another product of courtly culture. In book I, Chapter 1, "The Love of Peasants," the author advises his noble male readers: "And if you should, by some chance, fall in love with some of their [peasant] women, be careful to puff them up with lots of praise and then, when you find a convenient place, do not hesitate to take what you seek and to embrace them by force," *The Art of Courtly Love by Andreas Capellanus*, with introduction, translation, and notes by John Jay Parry (New York: Columbia University Press, 1990), 150. Whether the treatise is serious or parodic has been long debated, and a recent book-length study that confronts the problem head on is Kathleen Andersen-Wyman, *Andreas Capellanus on Love? Desire, Seduction, and Subversion in a Twelfth-Century Latin Text* (New York: Palgrave Macmillan, 2007). See especially her introduction, 1–33, and her final chapter, "Andreas on Women," 201–35.

15 A recent association between heightened incidents of rape and fraternities came in late 2014 after *Rolling Stone* published a story about an undergraduate at the University of Virginia who claimed she was gang raped at a fraternity party allegedly as part of an initiation ritual among pledges: Sabrina Rubin Erdely, "A Rape on Campus: A Brutal Assault and Struggle for Justice at UVA," www.rollingstone.com/culture/features/a-rape-on-campus-20141119, November 19, 2014. When inconsistencies arose in the story, *Rolling Stone* backed away from it, but the subsequent furore in traditional and social media outlets demonstrates the ongoing association that Americans make between fraternity parties and sexual predation.

16 "Courtly love" or *amour courtois* was a term coined by Gaston Paris in the late nineteenth century, but modern analyses usually begin with Moshé Lazar's *Amour courtois et fin'amors dans la littérature du XIIe siècle* (Paris: Librairie C. Klincksieck, 1964). Frede Jensen includes a short but uncritical review of the concept in *Troubadours Lyrics: A Bilingual Anthology* (New York: Peter Lang, 1998), 17–19. The concept of *fin'amors*, however, has been analyzed and criticized by various scholars, such as Simon Gaunt in his *Gender and Genre in Medieval French Literature* (Cambridge: Cambridge University Press, 1995). An excellent

love.[17] A male poet, hopelessly in love with a woman, extols her as the pinnacle of beauty, grace, and breeding. He may also incorporate motifs from Ovidian love—sickness, sleeplessness, or lack of appetite due to love's pangs—or upon rhetorical ploys such as the indescribability topos where the lady is so beautiful that no one could ever describe her, though the poet will nonetheless try. He also pledges life-long devotion to her: he will never love another, though she may spurn him over and over again, for long-suffering patience is only a testament to the purity and intensity of his love. Furthermore, he swears fealty to her as a vassal does a lord, and if only she would accept him in her retinue—or rather, as we shall see, since he deserves to be accepted and will thereby presumably be accepted—he promises to do anything she might ask. On the surface, these attitudes jibe quite well with notions of courtship that survive in some social circles to this very day. After all, contemporary cinema is replete with romantic comedies featuring young men desperately trying to convince young women to date them.[18] Therefore, due to confirmation bias, my students might make connections between the medieval text and their lived experience, and that is both good and bad.

If students fail to see the veiled sexual violence in short, elliptical pronouncement of the knight at the end of Thibaut's *pastrourelle*, how can they penetrate the dense rhetoric of the *canso* to understand the discursive scaffolding underneath? In the remaining pages, I would like to outline a historically grounded approach that promotes critical thinking through analyses of presuppositions. The sheer rhetorical weight of the troubadour's efforts sometimes appears, I would argue, less like persuasion and more like coercion and, against the backdrop of current (and laudable) efforts on our campus to address rape culture, discussions can quickly turn to notions of agency and consent. Did the troubadour's lady ask to be praised by the poet? Is she free to refuse the advances or is she expected to listen, despite her personal feelings? If the latter, what are the social repercussions? When does seduction cross the line into harassment? Moreover, even if these poems are not historical accounts of encounters,

---

summary and feminist critique of scholarship prior to 2000 comes in E. Jane Burns, "Courtly Love: Who Needs It? Recent Feminist Work in the Medieval French Tradition," *Signs: Journal of Women in Culture and Society* 27 (2001): 23–57, and James Schultz assesses the usefulness of the concept before undertaking his study of Middle High German literature in *Courtly Love, the Love of Courtliness, and the History of Sexuality* (Chicago and London: University of Chicago Press, 2006). A useful reference work comes in volume 2 of *A Cultural History of Sexuality* (Oxford: Berg, 2010): that volume, edited by Ruth Evans, is dedicated to the Middle Ages. Finally, several contributions to *Shaping Courtliness in Medieval France: Essays in Honor of Matilda Tomaryn Bruckner* (Cambridge: Brewer, 2013) incorporate analyses of *fin'amors* in the wider context of courtliness, especially Peter Haidu's essay, "A Perfume of Reality: Desublimating the Courtly," 25–45.

17 The classic, though not unproblematic, historical study of the coupling of romantic love with misogyny from the Middle Ages to today comes in Howard Bloch, *Medieval Misogyny and the Invention of Western Romantic Love* (Chicago: University of Chicago Press, 1991). A review and nuanced critique of studies of *fin'amors* or "courtly love" comes in Burns, "Courtly Love: Who Needs It?" 23–57.

18 See, for example, Chloe Angyal, "Romantic Comedies Teach Women That Stalking Is a Compliment," www.huffingtonpost.com/entry/romantic-comedies-teach-women-that-stalking-is-a-compliment_us_56a8fa1fe4b0f7179928a17d, January 28, 2016.

what values and sexual roles do they promote? If students are going to personalize these expressions of love, it might be best for instructors not to swim against that current, but rather to leverage that tendency so that students will not only dig deeper into the *canso* and traditional assumptions about gender roles, but also apply those lessons to their lives outside of the classroom.

At first, students may think it rather sweet that a man serenades his lady with elaborate love songs in which he pledges his undying love, devotion, and service for which the troubadour hopes to be rewarded. Part of the problem comes from their unfamiliarity with the feudal paradigm and its terminology, all of which undergirds the love ideology of the troubadours.[19] An understanding of the presuppositions of the poet must begin with this basic historical and ideological information. By way of context, the social and political landscape of feudalism and how that becomes appropriated into *fin'amors* is paramount. The feudal political paradigm is hierarch-ical above all: a vassal pledges his fealty and (usually military) service to a lord in exchange for lands, or fief, that he, the vassal, administers. It is this relationship that the troubadour adopts and adapts in the *fin'amor* ethos whereby the woman becomes the lord and the man becomes the vassal. The vassal pledges his service in terms of panegyric song, repeatedly mentions his worthiness, and implies—or outright demands—his reward. Troubadours use terms like *ben*, *onor*, and *gazardo* to describe the compensation they seek. For example, *ben* means "good" generically, as in "goods and services," and the same holds true for *onor*, which can mean simply "honor": such notions appear to harbour hardly any sinister connotations. *Gazardo* is a more specialized term for "reward" and its unfamiliarity means that it carries little cultural baggage for our students. Once the discussion turns to *jauzimen/joi* or "joy," it begins to dawn on some students—naturally, the more astute ones—that these expressions might include less salubrious and platonic nuances than at first glance. *Joi* encapsulates not just emotional euphoria but the erotic and sexual satis-faction that the singer wishes to derive in exchange for his devotion. At this moment, I can see it on my students' faces, especially the women: the song deals not with innocent love and courtship but with the exchange of sexual favours for flattery, praise, and public acceptance.

The instructor, in order to avoid the anachronism of "judging" medieval society according to modern social norms, may wish to establish historical and cultural distance: medieval society was "like that" and we are not; women, especially those who belonged to the aristocracy, i.e., those addressed in these courtly songs, were considered mere pawns in a social game played between men, but now women's roles have evolved beyond these limits. An instructor employing this critical

---

19 The best study of the lexicon of *fin'amors* remains Glynnis Cropp, *Le Vocabulaire cour-tois des troubadours de l'époque classique* (Geneva: Droz, 1975). Non-francophones may con-sult Linda Paterson's chapter, "*Fin'amor* and the Development of the Courtly *Canso*," in *The Troubadours: An Introduction*, eds. Simon Gaunt and Sarah Kay (Cambridge: Cambridge University Press, 1999), 28–46, or Moshé Lazar's chapter, "*Fin'amor*," in *A Handbook of the Troubadours*, eds. F. R. P. Akehurst and Judith Davis (Berkeley: University of California Press, 1995), 61–100.

strategy might turn to a formal approach to the song in order to avoid uncomfortable questions. Occitan poets and their audiences delighted in formal virtuosity: complicated metrical and rhyme schemes, rich and difficult rhyme words, and acoustic play were all par for the course in the Occitan *canso* and the other Romance traditions from which it was derived. Paul Zumthor, discussing the direct line of influence from the Old Occitan troubadours to the Old French trouvères, could then posit the following:

> Les poètes que le langage d'alors désigna du nom de *trouvères* nous ont donné la première poésie « lyrique » qui apparaisse à l'horizon de la langue française: mode de dire entièrement et exclusivement référé à un *je* qui, pour n'avoir souvent d'autre existence que grammaticale, n'en fixe pas moins le plan et les modalités du discours.[20]

By extension, notions of seduction, exchange, and coercion become merely available topoi deployed in an elaborate poetic game. The approach, though old-fashioned, certainly does not lack for intellectual rigour, but the sublimation of content to form is rejected by many scholars today for its lack of historicity.[21] Moreover, the argument is akin to saying after making an off-colour comment, "I was only joking." In other words, "Yes, the content when taken literally may seem offensive, but you're missing the point. See, it's witty, and pleasing to the ear, and you shouldn't take it seriously." The words that the troubadours employed had meaning, no matter how gracefully they were arranged and enhanced by delightful melodies.

At this point, students have a basic historical understanding of the contractual relationship between lord and vassal and how that contract has been assimilated to the affective rapport between men and women. Contracts, however, as I hasten to point out, require two-party consent, and now issues of consent at the centre of the debate on campus rape culture come into play. The lady of the troubadour song never consents, for she does not speak at all, but the notion of consent is still significant because, if the songs are read closely, the troubadour often glosses over the issue of consent. As E. Jane Burns succinctly summarizes: "Simply put, the lover professes publicly to serve the lady and carry out her wishes *all the while presuming* that his entreating and/or valor will bring both amorous gratification and social renown to himself."[22] The feudal contract is based upon a service agreement, but the troubadour makes several presuppositions when he argues the lady owes him her affection.

One way of exposing these presuppositions is to ask students to restate a troubadour's claims, and then to work backwards to undercover the premises upon

---

20 Paul Zumthor, *Essai de poétique médiévale* (1972; repr., Paris: Editions du seuil, 2000), 229, original emphasis. "The poets known then as *trouvères* gave us the first 'lyric' poetry to dawn over the horizon of the French language: a verbal mode that refers entirely and exclusively to an 'I' who, although endowed with only a grammatical existence, anchors nevertheless the discursive program and its modalities" (my translation).
21 See especially the objections raised in Sarah Kay's discussion in *Subjectivity in Troubadour Poetry* (Cambridge: Cambridge University Press, 1990), 5–16.
22 Burns, "Courtly Love: Who Needs It?" 33.

which the claim rests. When a troubadour asserts that the lady should reward him for his service, I ask my students to tell me what premise underlines that assertion. Someone might suggest that we have to assume that he is, in fact, doing service. Or someone might offer further qualifications: he has to be doing satisfactory service. Since singing and praising his lady publicly constitutes, at least in part, his service, and because we are hearing the song, we may conclude he is performing service on her behalf. As listeners, we might even judge that he is doing satisfactory service, if it is a good song. But then we peel back another layer: if he is doing service, what must have occurred before that service began? The lady and the poet must have entered into a service pact in which the lady has accepted the man as her loyal vassal. Do we have any evidence of that consent on the part of the lady? Yes, perhaps she gave her consent, but the entire universe of the *canso* rests upon a presupposition that, translated into modern parlance, might be, "She wanted it." Once again, when these logical jumps are exposed and broken down for students, it can lead to productive discussion of consent, especially affirmative consent.

Presuppositions can be uncovered through closer linguistic and rhetorical analysis as well. Through certain tenses, modals, and impersonal, sentential formulas, troubadours employ a rhetorical sleight of hand to support the logical scaffolding examined above. I alert my students to beware of modals like "should" ("deu" in Old Occitan) used to prescribe the lady's behaviour. In "Can l'erba fresch' e.lh folha par" (PC 70.39),[23] Bernart de Ventadorn states:

> Be *deuri'* om domna blasmar,
> can trop vai son amic tarzan,
> que lonja paraula d'amar
> es grans enois e par d'enjan.
>
> (49–52, emphasis added)[24]

Not only does the troubadour talk about how ladies should be blamed, he attributes this idea to the proverbial "one": *one*, i.e., *we*, should fault ladies who resist advances. I try to show my students as well that the troubadour preemptively shifts blame for long harangues about loving onto her: if his suit sounds insincere, it is because the lady has let it go on too long. Upon whose authority does he pronounce this statement? The inability to answer such questions should put students on alert to uncover what other social attitudes are attributable to no one in particular.

Troubadours may manipulate the service paradigm in other ways that preempt a woman's refusal. In "En cest sonet coind'e ieri" (PC 29.10), Arnaut Daniel claims

---

23 In keeping with prevailing scholarly norms, trobadour and trobairitz (or women troubadours) songs are identifed by their Pillet-Carstens (P.-C.) number from A. Pillet and H. Carstens, *Bibliographie des Troubadours* (Halle: Niemeyer, 1933).

24 "One truly *should* blame a lady when she puts off her lover too long, for prolonged speech about love is a great annoyance and looks like deception."

that he is indeed serving his lady, in keeping with the terms of the feudal political metaphor. He claims that his reward has not yet been proffered:

> Ges pel maltraich q'ieu soferi
> de ben amar no.m destoli,
> si tot me ten en desert,
> c'aissi.m fatz los motz en rima.
> Pieitz trac aman c'om que laura,
> c'anc plus non amet un ou
> cel de Moncli N'Audierna.
>
> (36–43)[25]

Arnaut manipulates his service into a self-fulfilling prophecy: if I sing and she fails to respond, that is all well and good, because it allows me to compose more songs. No matter how the lady responds, the troubadour will keep singing, keep serving, and keep claiming his reward. So her refusal to go along means only that she wants him to continue. In other words, no means yes.

Students might suggest since we have no way to verify the singer's claims, we ought to take the troubadour at his word. But by adding voices of the women troubadours or trobairitz, we get some idea of how noble women might have thought about *fin'amors* and women's place in it. True, some songs praise the male lover, but more often, the lady complains of the man's treachery and betrayal in her own *cansos*. The Comtessa de Dia laments:

> A chantar m'er de so q'ieu no volria,
> tant me rancur de lui cui sui amia,
> car eu l'am mais que nuilla ren que sia;
> vas lui no.m val merces ni cortesia
> ni ma beltatz ni mos pretz ni mos sens,
> c'atressi.m sui enganada e trahia
> com degr'esser s'ieu fos desavinens.
>
> (1–8)[26]

Similarly, Na Castelloza complains:

> Amics, s'ie.us trobes avinen,
> humil e franc e de bona merce,

---

25 "In spite of the pain I endure, I don't stray from loving well; even if she keeps me in solitude, for thus I compose words and set them to rhyme. I suffer more in loving than one who plows because the one from Monclin didn't love Lady Audierna even a bit (lit. even an egg) more than I do her."

26 PC 46.1. "I must sing of what I'd rather not, I'm so angry about him whose friend I am, for I love him more than anything; mercy and courtliness don't help me with him, nor does my beauty, or my rank, or my mind; for I am every bit as betrayed and wronged as I'd deserve to be if I were ugly." I take all citations and translations of trobairitz song from Matilda Bruckner, Laurie Shepard. and Sarah White, *Songs of the Women Troubadours* (New York: Garland, 1995).

be.us amera, quand era m'en sove
q'us trob va mi mal e fellon e tric.

(1–4)[27]

An analysis of presuppositions in these texts turns up a very different result from a similar study of troubadour songs. The Comtessa lists all of the traits that a lover praised in her, in return for which she accepted his advances, and now she is spurned as if the suitor believed the exact opposite of what he had proclaimed. Na Castelloza contends that *if she had found* her lover kind, she would have loved him, but obviously, she found the opposite. After this oblique assertion in the subjunctive mood—thereby insinuating that she would have liked to have found him kind, etc.—she confirms her experience with a declaration in the indicative: "I find you evil, harsh and false to me."[28] Juxtaposing these texts to the open-ended declarations of troubadours not only shows that the troubadour takes his lady's consent for granted, but also exposes the shaky foundation upon which he establishes his suit.

Trobairitz make their suspicions further known also in *tensos* or debate poems. In those poetic exchanges, especially those between lovers, women challenge traditional male discourse, and men find themselves unable to respond adequately. In "Bona dona d'una re qu.us deman" (PC 87.1; 75.1), for example, Betran debates an anonymous lady about when a man should reveal his true feelings. In the end, the lady calls out the ludic, even artificial, nature of their sexual politics:

Amics Bertran, ben es iocs cumunals
q'eu am celui qu'es mos amics corals,
e l'amics voill que sia, sabez cals?
fis e ficels, vertadiers e no fals
ni trop parliers ni ianglos ni gabaire
mas de bon prez a son poder sivals
c'aissi cove fors e dinz son repaire.

(36–42)[29]

The lady refers to their dealings, almost dismissively, as a game before utilizing words long associated with troubadour descriptions of themselves as they pursue the lady: "fis e ficels, vertadiers e no fals" (Perfect and faithful, truthful and undeceiving). The lady turns the male-authored discourse of seduction into an

---

27 PC 109.1. "Friend, if I had found you kind, humble, frank and merciful, I'd love you well; but now I recall that I find you evil, harsh and false to me."
28 For a short but compelling study of female- vs. male-voiced rhetoric in troubadour and trobairitz poetry, see Joan Ferrante, "Notes toward the Study of a Female Rhetoric in the Trobairitz," in *The Voice of the Trobairitz: Perspectives on the Women Troubadours*, ed. William D. Paden (Philadelphia: University of Pennsylvania Press, 1989).
29 "Friend Bertran, this is a game we share for I love the one who is my heartfelt lover, and do you know how I want that friend to be? Perfect and faithful, truthful and undeceiving, not too talkative, or indiscreet, or boastful, but very worthy at least as far as he can be, because it's fitting at his home or away from it."

expression of her own desires. She may engage in the game, but at a deeper level, the lady is not buying what the man is selling.[30]

Of course, consent, sex, and subsequent betrayal do not constitute rape. However, the *canso*, for all of its talk about what women should do in public with implied threats to a woman's reputation by blaming her for leading men on, may very well be characterized as coercive texts. The *canso* is not a rape text the same way that the *pastorela* is: it is more insidious, but ultimately more productive in terms of raising awareness of rape culture. The *canso* does not describe a rape, but it could be interpreted as walking right up to the line and subliminally urging men to cross it. Rape culture accepts that rape happens; it tolerates a certain amount of sexual violence. We need to expose the mechanics of a misplaced tolerance that would through rarified language normalize regressive attitudes towards gender roles and sexual violence. If our students are incapable of understanding how knowledge and power are connected and how cultural artefacts like poetry and song are not only products of culture but also producers of culture, attitudes will not change and the cycle of violence will continue. It is not a matter of "judging" medieval attitudes towards women and sex, but of understanding them, and then taking the tools needed to arrive at that comprehension and encouraging the students to use them to better analyze their own cultural situation.

Works Cited

Andersen-Wyman, Kathleen. *Andreas Capellanus on Love? Desire, Seduction, and Subversion in a Twelfth-Century Latin Text.* New York: Palgrave Macmillan, 2007.

Andreas Capellanus. *The Art of Courtly Love by Andreas Capellanus.* Introduction, translation, and notes by John Jay Parry. New York: Columbia University Press, 1990.

Angyal, Chloe. "Romantic Comedies Teach Women That Stalking Is a Compliment." *The Huffington Post*, January 28, 2016. www.huffingtonpost.com/entry/romantic-comedies-teach-women-that-stalking-is-a-compliment_us_56a8fa1fe4b0f7179928a17d (accessed February 19, 2016).

Binkley, Collin, Jill Riepenhoff, Mike Wagner, and Sara Gregory. "Reports on College Crime Are Deceptively Inaccurate." *The Columbus Dispatch*, August 30, 2014. www.dispatch.com/content/stories/local/2014/09/30/campus-insecurity.html (accessed February 20, 2015).

Bloch, Howard. *Medieval Misogyny and the Invention of Western Romantic Love.* Chicago: University of Chicago Press, 1991.

---

30 I further elaborate the idea that troubadour rhetoric that goes unchallenged in the *canso* is, in fact, called into question in *tensos* (debate poems) between men and women. The man, unable to buttress his own arguments, must back down. See Daniel E. O'Sullivan, "The Man Backing Down from the Lady in Trobairitz *Tensos*," in *Founding Feminisms in Medieval Studies: Essays in Honor of E. Jane Burns*, eds. Laine E. Doggett and Daniel E. O'Sullivan (Woodbridge: Brewer, 2016).

Bruckner, Matilda, Laurie Shepard, and Sarah White. *Songs of the Women Troubadours*. New York: Garland, 1995.

Burns, E. Jane. "Courtly Love: Who Needs It? Recent Feminist Work in the Medieval French Tradition." *Signs: Journal of Women in Culture and Society* 27 (2001): 23–57.

Carter, Cynthia. "The Transformative Power of Cultural Criticism: bell hooks' Radical Media Analysis." In *Radical Mass Media Criticism: A Cultural Genealogy*, edited by David Berry and John Theobald, 212–33. Montreal: Black Rose Press, 2006.

Center Against Rape and Domestic Violence. "About Sexual Assault." http://cardv.org/aboutsexualassault.php (accessed February 20, 2015).

Cropp, Glynnis. *Le Vocabulaire courtois des troubadours de l'époque classique.* Geneva: Droz, 1975.

Erdely, Sabrina Rubin. "A Rape on Campus: A Brutal Assault and Struggle for Justice at UVA." *Rolling Stone*, November 19, 2014. www.rollingstone.com/culture/features/a-rape-on-campus-20141119 (accessed February 20, 2015).

Evans, Ruth, ed. *A Cultural History of Sexuality*. Vol. 2. Oxford: Berg, 2010.

Ferrante, Joan. "Notes toward the Study of a Female Rhetoric in the Trobairitz." In *The Voice of the Trobairitz: Perspectives on the Women Troubadours*, edited by William D. Paden, 63–72. Philadelphia: University of Pennsylvania Press, 1989.

Garcia, Justin R., Chris Reiber, Sean G. Massey, and Ann M. Merriwether. "Sexual Hookup Culture: A Review." *Review of General Psychology* 16 (2012): 161–76. www.apa.org/monitor/2013/02/sexual-hookup-culture.pdf (accessed February 20, 2015).

Gaunt, Simon. *Gender and Genre in Medieval French Literature*. Cambridge: Cambridge University Press, 1995.

Gravdal, Kathryn. *Ravishing Maidens: Writing Rape in Medieval French Literature and Law*. Philadelphia: University of Pennsylvania Press, 1991.

Haidu, Peter. "A Perfume of Reality: Desublimating the Courtly." In *Shaping Courtliness in Medieval France: Essays in Honor of Matilda Tomaryn Bruckner*, edited by Daniel E. O'Sullivan and Laurie Shepard, 25–45. Cambridge: Brewer, 2013.

Helwick, Christine. "Affirmative Consent, the New Standard." *Inside Higher Ed*, October 23, 2014. www.insidehighered.com/views/2014/10/23/campuses-must-wrestle-affirmative-consent-standard-sexual-assault-essay (accessed February 20, 2015).

hooks, bell. *Outlaw Culture: Resisting Representations*. New York, Routledge, 1994.

Jensen, Frede. *Troubadours Lyrics: A Bilingual Anthology.* New York: Peter Lang, 1998.

Kay, Sarah. *Subjectivity in Troubadour Poetry.* Cambridge: Cambridge University Press, 1990.

Kingkade, Tyler. "Colleges Are Reporting More Sexual Assaults, and That's a Great Sign." *Huffington Post*, October 12, 2014. www.huffingtonpost.com/2014/10/12/college-sexual-assault-numbers-clery-reports_n_5967412.html (accessed February 20, 2015).

Lazar, Moshé. *Amour courtois et fin'amors dans la littérature du XIIe siècle.* Paris: Librairie C. Klincksieck, 1964.

———. "*Fin'amor.*" In *A Handbook of the Troubadours*, edited by F. R. P. Akehurst and Judith Davis, 61–100. Berkeley: University of California Press, 1995.

National Coalition for Men, "False Accusations." http://ncfm.org/2009/01/issues/false-accusations (accessed February 20, 2015).

National Institute of Justice. "Measuring Frequency." www.nij.gov/topics/crime/rape-sexual-violence/campus/Pages/measuring.aspx (accessed February 20, 2015).

O'Sullivan, Daniel E. "The Man Backing Down from the Lady in Trobairitz *Tensos.*" In *Founding Feminisms in Medieval Studies: Essays in Honor of E. Jane Burns*, edited by Laine E. Doggett and Daniel E. O'Sullivan, 45–60. Woodbridge: Brewer, 2016.

O'Sullivan, Daniel E., and Laurie Shepard, eds. *Shaping Courtliness in Medieval France: Essays in Honor of Matilda Tomaryn Bruckner.* Cambridge: Brewer, 2013.

Paterson, Linda. "*Fin'amor* and the Development of the Courtly *Canso.*" In *The Troubadours: An Introduction*, edited by Simon Gaunt and Sarah Kay, 28–46. Cambridge: Cambridge University Press, 1999.

Pillet, Alfred, and Henry Carstens. *Bibliographie des Troubadours.* Halle: Niemeyer, 1933.

Schultz, James. *Courtly Love, the Love of Courtliness, and the History of Sexuality.* Chicago: University of Chicago Press, 2006.

Shear, Michael D., and Elena Schneider. "Obama Unveils Push for Young People to Do More against Campus Assaults." *The New York Times*, September 19, 2014. www.nytimes.com/2014/09/20/us/politics/obama-campaign-college-sexual-assaults.html?_r=0 (accessed February 20, 2015).

Smith, Geri L. *The Medieval French Pastourelle Tradition: Poetic Motivations and Generic Transformations.* Gainesville: University of Florida, 2009.

Spanke, Hans. *G. Raynauds Bibliographie des altfranzösischen Liedes, neu bearbeitet und ergänst.* Leiden: Brill, 1955.

Vines, Amy N. "Invisible Woman: Rape as a Chivalric Necessity in Medieval Romance." In *Sexual Culture in the Literature of Medieval Britain*, edited by Amanda Hopkins, Robert Rouse, and Cory James Rushton, 133–47. Cambridge: Brewer, 2014.

Wallensköld, Axel, ed. *Les Chansons de Thibaut de Champagne, Roi de Navarre.* Paris: Champion, 1925.

Yoffe, Emily. "The College Rape Overcorrection." www.slate.com/articles/double_x/doublex/2014/12/college_rape_campus_sexual_assault_is_a_serious_problem_but_the_efforts.html (accessed February 20, 2015).

Zumthor, Paul *Essai de poétique médiévale.* 1972. Reprint, Paris: Editions du seuil, 2000.

Chapter 12

THE KNIGHT COERCED: TWO CASES OF RAPED MEN IN CHIVALRIC ROMANCE

DAVID GRUBBS

A major shift has occurred in how higher education understands and confronts rape. This shift is seen most practically in campus life as colleges and universities adopt policies that define rape according to the positive consent ("yes means yes") model: that is, without the explicit assent of both parties, any sex-related activity constitutes sexual assault, and any sexual intercourse constitutes rape. It is natural that this shift should be engaged in departments of languages and literature, often a haven for ignored voices, and so enter medieval literature classrooms. Not that talk of rape has even been alien in that environment: Geoffrey Chaucer's "The Wife of Bath's Tale" famously hinges on a rape's aftermath, while Chaucer himself, like Thomas Malory, was accused of complicity in an act of *raptus*. However, as the campus conversation on rape shifts to new channels, so too the medieval literature classroom may enrich its own conversation about rape with the positive consent model's insights. This essay will apply those insights to the cases of two raped men in chivalric romances: Sir Launcelot of Malory's *Morte d'Arthur* and Sir Perion of the Spanish *Amadis de Gaula*.

Medieval Literature in the Gen Eds: A Pedagogical Note

One issue must be raised before we proceed: in order for the positive consent model to enrich our classroom conversations about rape in medieval literature, those conversations need to be happening. And whether they're happening often hinges on the courses and students in question. The approach this essay takes is shaped by the teaching setting in which I labour, and the methods I've found that make conversations of this kind possible in these conditions.

   I teach at a small private liberal arts college.[1] Our students are all undergraduates, most of whom are athletes, and many the first in their families to pursue secondary

---

1 The author is currently working at a different institution than this essay describes. Special thanks to the English majors of Central Christian College of Kansas for their part in discussions that helped inform this essay.

education. Our English majors number (from year to year) a dozen or less. As a result, the bulk of my teaching load is in the general education courses of the English department—composition and sophomore-level writing-intensive litera- ture courses. In these writing-intensive literature courses, most students are not English majors, and have no previous literature course work beyond high school (and that usually minimal).

Sophisticated conversations about literature are challenging under these circumstances. Indeed, medieval literature itself is daunting to most unprepared sophomores. To bring to bear the complexities of gender, sexuality, and social power dynamics that are involved in a discussion of rape, then transpose that discussion to an unfamiliar literary, historical, and cultural context—well, perhaps we'd better save this conversation for the upper-division English majors!

But fruitful and complex discussions *can* be brought into a classroom like this: major construction can be done with hand tools, if they're the right tools. In order to equip my students for conversations like this, I aim to select those right tools: approach- able texts, a clear critical perspective, and some readily applied literary approaches to reading the texts. This essay is, essentially, an exercise in this method.

In the following sections, we will examine the critical perspective for this project— the positive consent model of rape—then apply that critical perspective through two literary approaches: a close reading of the text alone, and a reading supported by cultural context research. That leaves one final comment to be made: a note about the editions used of Malory's *Le Morte d'Arthur* and the Spanish *Amadis de Gaula*. The *Morte* used with students was a modernized language edition based on Caxton's printed version; it was accessible for students, but still suitable for a close reading as a medieval text.[2] In this essay, Vinaver's edition has been cited instead, without change to the substance of the close reading.[3] The *Amadis* translation used with students is Robert Southey's nineteenth-century rendering: it is archaic but readable, and close enough to the Spanish text to support close reading.[4] This English translation is cited in this essay, with the Spanish text provided in the footnotes, because the English text was the basis of the discussion developed in this essay.[5]

Seeing through Gray: Positive Consent as Interpretive Aid

The positive consent model's strength is the clarity it brings to those cases that traditional "no means no" approaches to rape regard as ambiguous or "gray." "Gray"

---

2 Thomas Malory, *Le Morte d'Arthur* (New York: Modern Library, 1999).
3 Thomas Malory, *The Works of Sir Thomas Malory*, ed. Eugène Vinaver (Oxford: Clarendon Press, 1967).
4 Garci Rodríguez de Montalvo, *Amadis of Gaul*, vol. 1, trans. Robert Southey (London: John Russell Smith, 1872). Southey (incorrectly) considers *Amadis* the work of Vasco Lobeira. My citations preserve the correct attribution to Garci Rodríguez de Monalvo in order to prevent confusion.
5 Garci Rodríguez de Montalvo, *Amadis de Gaula: Historia de este Invencible Caballero*, vol. 2 (Barcelona: Juan Oliveres, Impresor, 1848).

rape" is the term often used to designate those instances of intercourse that are, from one participant's perspective, unwanted and therefore traumatic, yet are not violent assaults or, from the other participant's perspective, in the face of obvious resistance or refusal.[6] Criminal codes often implement an older understanding of rape that assumes women will resist unwanted sexual advances with verbal refusal ("no means no") and, in the event of violent assault, violent resistance. An unwanted sexual encounter that does not result in bodily injury (an indication of violence, and, by inference, resistance) or was not preceded by an obvious refusal (preferably one attested by witnesses or the accused's confession) would be, in this "no means no" view, not a clear instance of rape at all. By focusing on obvious assent—"yes means yes"—the positive consent model reorients our understanding of rape around the will, around the agency of persons and their freedom to choose or refuse bodily contact. In so doing, the "grayness" of "gray rape" dissolves: an unclear case of an assaulted body becomes a clear case of a coerced will. The positive consent model also shifts our focus from physical force to social or psychological force: the "soft" means by which one person may manipulate, circumvent, or impose upon the will of another. In this way, the positive consent model serves to bring to light instances of sexual coercion which a rape-as-physical-assault model misses or dismisses.

In this essay, the positive consent model will be used to shed light on one particular "gray" category of rape in medieval literature: that of men coerced into intercourse with women, specifically Sir Launcelot of Malory's *Morte d'Arthur* and Sir Perion of the Spanish *Amadis de Gaula*. In traditional models of rape, the notion of a raped man, especially by a woman, is nigh unthinkable. This blind spot is due, argues Julia Serano, to the prevalence of a "predator/prey mindset" regarding sexuality that governs the American culture's thinking about rape:

> I call this phenomenon the predator/prey mindset, and within it, men can only be viewed as sexual aggressors and women as sexual objects ... [T]he predator/prey mindset essentially ensures that men cannot be viewed as legitimate sexual objects, nor can women be viewed as legitimate sexual aggressors. This has the effect of rendering invisible instances of man-on-man and woman-on-woman sexual harassment and abuse, and it makes the idea of woman-on-man rape utterly inconceivable.[7]

In other words, the rape-as-assault model is just one manifestation of this predator/prey mindset: men conquer in intercourse, while women, willingly or unwillingly, surrender. From this perspective, that sex with a woman could ever be forced upon an unwilling man is unimaginable.

---

6 Lisa Jervis cites Laura Sessions Step as the popularizer of this term. Jervis, "An Old Enemy in a New Outfit: How Date Rape Became Gray Rape and Why It Matters," in *Yes Means Yes! Visions of Female Sexual Power and a World without Rape*, eds. Jaclyn Friedman and Jessica Valenti (Berkeley: Seal Press, 2008). Kindle e-book.

7 Julia Serano, "Why Nice Guys Finish Last," in Friedman and Valenti, *Yes Means Yes!*

Such a scenario was also unimaginable in the context of medieval jurisprudence. According to Corrine Saunders, "the crime of *raptus* was understood as one against women, and related to other gendered issues of marriage, virginity, and consent," and the laws declared that "only women could bring a legal appeal of *raptus*," while "for men there was no legal counterpart to the process of appeal of rape open to women." While "men as well as women could be abducted or sexually violated, ... any such crime would have been considered assault rather than ravishment in legal terms." The unimaginableness of a raped man is not restricted to legal writing: according to Saunders, "literature rarely engages with the issue of sexual violence against men."[8]

As was noted above, a great advantage of the positive consent model of rape is the light it sheds on the "gray" cases, whether those are cases under adjudication or potential cases still preventable through education. This clarifying power is what makes the positive consent model a useful tool when discussing "gray" cases of coerced men in medieval literature. Narratives shape moral imagination, certainly, but moral imagination also shapes one's understanding of a narrative: the traditional model's inability to read the "gray" cases as stories of rape is, in this sense, a case of limited moral imagination impeding narrative understanding. Conversely, the positive consent model expands our moral imagination by focusing on agency and mechanisms of coercion, freeing us to see through the gendered tropes of the predator/prey mentality, and to call a sexual violation of personal agency, whatever its accidental features, a *rape*. Thus, though the traditional model prevailed in medieval legal discourse, applying the positive consent model to medieval texts isn't necessarily an anachronistic imposition. As we will see, this approach to the cases of Launcelot and Perion highlights an emphasis on agency and coercion already present in the texts, explicitly and implicitly. In so doing, it helps readers better navigate the complexities of choice, force, and culpability at play in each episode.

In these brief case studies, we will consider the roles of agency and coercion through two distinct literary approaches. We will examine Launcelot's case through a close reading, attentive to ways the voices in the story, both of the narrator and the characters, speak of agency and moral culpability. Perion's case, more laconic by far than Launcelot's, we will consider in light of mechanisms of coercion implicitly at work in the scene, which a consideration of cultural context will make evident. With moral imaginations shaped by the positive consent model, we can apply these familiar methods of reading both fruitfully and ethically to these cases of raped men.

The Rape of Sir Launcelot (*Morte d'Arthur*)

One of the strengths of close reading is its ability to hear the voices in a story that might otherwise be suppressed by the concerns of the central narrative. In an epic story large in scope and scale, a single voice can be lost in the grand din, but a close reading may recover it. Malory's *Morte d'Arthur* is such a large and grand sequence

---

8 Saunders, *Rape and Ravishment in the Literature of Medieval England* (Cambridge: Brewer, 2001), 20.

of tales, full of sweeping and highly coloured action; still, Malory has made space for isolated voices, if one has ears to hear. Such voices are included in the extended episode we will consider in this section: Elayne of Corbyn's sexual entrapment of Launcelot and its aftermath.[9] In particular, the voices in this episode contend over principles of agency and moral right and culpability. Who has the freedom to act and to choose? Who has the moral right to make a determinative choice? Whose choices and actions deserve moral censure? As we will see, though Launcelot's voice in this episode is disregarded, even for a time silenced, he has the last word: that whatever else may have happened, he was raped.

Launcelot's Rape: Man vs. Narrative

At the beginning of these events, we easily see how Launcelot's voice could be ignored. The episode begins by announcing its enormous consequences for King Arthur and his Round Table: "Speke we of Sir Launcelot du Laake and of Sir Galahad, Sir Launcelottis sonne, how he was begotyn and in what maner." An oracular hermit arrives at Arthur's court to explain the import of Sir Galahad's conception and birth: "this same yere he shall be bygotyn that shall sytte in that Syege Perelous, and he shall wynne the Sankgreal."[10] Clearly great events are in the offing, culminating in that sacrament of chivalry, the quest of the Holy Grail. Onto this grand stage, Launcelot walks in ignorance, not knowing that his story is (in a sense) already written in prophecy.

Launcelot's part in this tale begins with his rescue of Elayne from the tower of Corbyn, where "she boyleth in scaldynge watir," a magical torment from Morgan le Fay.[11] Under the terms of Morgan's curse, only Launcelot, "the beste knyght of the worlde," can rescue Elayne.[12] Even first-time readers can discern the early stirrings of a romantic entanglement, as Launcelot, "the beste knyght of the worlde," first sees Elayne, "the fayryst lady … that ever he sawe." Elayne's beauty is emphasized twice more in this same five-sentence episode: she is "the fayryst lady of that contrey," and, when Launcelot saw her clothed, he again "thought she was the fayryst lady that ever he saw."[13] The stage seems set for a generic courtly love plot, for in chivalric romance no better pair can be imagined than the "beste knyght of the worlde" and the "fayryst lady of the contrey."

Launcelot is not a generic knight, however. He has, at this point in the *Morte*, many episodes of narrative experience under his belt, and the first things we learn of Launcelot in the *Morte* have not changed: his puissance and his love for Queen

---

9 These episodes are in books 11 and 12 of Caxton's edition. Vinaver's edition places these episodes in section 14 of "The Book of Sir Tristram de Lyones." Spelling variants of names abound in the Arthurian material: I have used Malory's most consistent spellings.

10 Thomas Malory, *The Works of Sir Thomas Malory*, ed. Eugène Vinaver (Oxford: Clarendon Press, 1967), vol. 2, 791.

11 Ibid.

12 Ibid, 792.

13 Ibid.

Gwenyver.[14] So, yes, "sir Launcelot thought [Elayne] was the fayryst lady that ever he saw," but then the narrator adds, "but yf it were quene Gwenyver."[15] Launcelot is still Launcelot; that he has wandered into the ideal scenario for a chivalric love story is immaterial, because he remains Gwenyver's loyal lover. Malory's touch here is subtle as he hints at the forces in play: on one hand, narrative inevitability, manifest as foreshadowing, prophecy, and the coalescing of powerful generic tropes; on the other hand, the will of a single character, Launcelot.

Launcelot becomes further entangled in narrative inevitability in his second adventure in Corbyn. Having rescued the damsel in distress, he is asked to fight a dragon sealed in a local tomb. The stakes of this combat are engraved in gold on the tomb: "HERE SHALL COM A LYBARDE[16] OF KYNGES BLOOD AND HE SHALL SLE THIS SERPENTE. AND THIS LYBARDE SHALL ENGENDIR A LYON IN THIS FORAYNE CONTREY WHYCHE LYON SHALL PASSE ALL OTHER KNYGHTES."[17] In the face of this prophecy, Launcelot opens the tomb and kills the dragon. Whether Launcelot comprehends the tomb's prophecy, the narrator does not inform us. Still, with the dragon dispatched, we expect that the "engendering" mentioned will follow shortly.

King Pelles, Elayne's father, is certainly clear on the prophecy's implications, even if Launcelot isn't. After learning Launcelot's name, King Pelles feasts the knight royally, displaying before him the Holy Grail (more foreshadowing). In this welcome, Pelles has a hidden agenda:

> And fayne wolde kynge Pelles have found the meane that sir Launcelot sholde have ley by his doughter, fayre Eleyne, and for this entente: the kynge knew well that sir Launcelot shulde gete a pusyll[18] uppon his doughtir. Whyche shulde be called sir Galahad, the good knyght by whom all the forayne cuntrey shulde be brought oute of daunger; and by hym the Holy Grayle sholde be encheved.[19]

Probably "the kynge knew well" that Launcelot was destined to father Galahad because of the prophecy on the dragon's tomb. And yet there is a complication, one known already to readers, and now revealed to Pelles: "Than cam furth … Dame Brusen, and she seyde unto the kynge, 'Sir, wyte you well Sir Launcelot lovyth no lady in the worlde but all only quene Gwenyver.' "[20] Here the conflict between narrative inevitability and Launcelot's will enters the awareness of the characters, in the form of a prophecy in peril.

The decision of King Pelles and the actions of Dame Brusen at this point are somewhat paradoxical. Thus far, the force of destiny has prevailed: Elayne *was*

---

14 Ibid., vol. 1, 253. "Sir Launcelot de Lake … passed all other knyghtes … Wherefore quene Gwenyvere had hym in grete favoure aboven all other knyghtis, and in certain he loved the quene agayne aboven all other ladyes dayes of his lyff."
15 Ibid., vol. 2, 792.
16 Leopard.
17 Malory, *Works*, vol. 2, 793.
18 Child.
19 Malory, *Works*, vol. 2, 794.
20 Ibid.

rescued by "the beste knyghte of the worlde," and the dragon *was* slain. Moreover, Pelles thinks of future prophesied events as certain: "Sir Launcelot *shulde* gete a pusyll," and so forth. Pelles's "shulde" echoes the hermit's "shall" from the beginning of the episode. Yet, Pelles "fayne wolde ... have found the meane" to get Launcelot and Elayne into bed: he seems determined not to let destiny run its course, but instead wants to seize the reins himself and bring the prophecy safely to its proper destination. Likewise, Dame Brusen brings up Launcelot's love for Gwenyver only to counter it. Brusen has a plan, and does not hesitate to take on the role of *diabolus ex machine*: "Sir, wyte you well Sir Launcelot lovyth no lady in the worlde but all only quene Gwenyver. And therefore worche ye be my counceyle, and I shall make hym to lye with youre doughter, and he shall not wyte but that he lyeth by quene Gwenyver."[21] When faced with this conflict between prophecy and Launcelot's will, Pelles and Brusen choose to bypass Launcelot's will: that is, they choose to plot rape.

Of course, that what follows is rape should not simply rest on assertion. By common medieval legal definitions, what Pelles and Brusen plot is not *raptus*: Launcelot is not abducted, eliminating *raptus* in one sense, and he would not have been permitted to bring a suit of *raptus* (sexual assault) before the magistrate, because he is a man. What happens to Launcelot is, to apply the modern term, a "gray rape." Here is where the positive consent model comes into play, guiding us to pay attention to the matter of agency and coercion. As already stated, Brusen's plan is a circumvention of Launcelot's agency, not overt coercive force: Launcelot "shall not wyte but that he lyeth by quene Gwenyver"; his assent will be gotten, but under false pretenses.

Brusen's means to circumvent Launcelot's agency are two: simple trickery and something like inebriation. First, Brusen sends Launcelot a counterfeit summons from Gwenyver, accompanied, as a token of authenticity, by a ring "as she [Gwenyver] was wonte for the moste parte to were." Launcelot's response is enthusiastic: "whan sir Launcelot saw that tokyn, wyte you well he was never so fayne."[22] This is clear language of agency: Launcelot's desire is engaged, and he assents to this invitation readily. Once he arrives at the site of his promised tryst with Gwenyver, a castle near Corbyn, he is led to a bedroom, and there given a drink: "And than dame Brusen brought sir Launcelot a kuppe full of wyne, and anone as he had drunken that wyne he was so asoted and madde that he myght make no delay but wythoute ony let he wente to bedde. And so he wente[23] that mayden Elayne had bene quene Gwenyver."[24] The effects of this drink are, in some ways, similar to inebriation: Launcelot's rational faculties are impaired (he is "asoted and madde"), as well as his senses (implied by "wente/weened"). One difference from ordinary inebriation (since alcohol usually affects the body as a depressant) is the urgency this drink apparently lends to Launcelot's libido: "he myght make no delay but wythoute ony let

---

21 Ibid.
22 Ibid.
23 Believed ("weened").
24 Malory, *Works*, vol. 2, 795.

he wente to bedde." Whatever is in this cup, be it the work of pharmacy or sorcery, Launcelot is not in his right mind: he is, according to current college sexual assault codes, not capable of giving authentic consent. Thus, though the narrator informs us of Launcelot's assent—"wyte you well that sir Launcelot was glad"[25]—his agency is compromised through deception and drugs.

Launcelot's Reaction: Placing Blame

The aftermath of this sexual entrapment, this rape, is telling: if we yet fear that the positive consent model leads us to an anachronistic imposition on the text, studying Launcelot's reaction will help confirm the reading thus far. The deed done, Launcelot and Elayne sleep until morning, till Launcelot rises at dawn to open the window: "And anone as he had unshutte the wyndow the enchauntemente was paste. Then he knew hymselff that he had done amysse. 'Alas!' he seyde, "that I have lyved so long, for now am I shamed."[26] With light comes both revelation and the sting of conscience, for Launcelot's first thought is self-condemnation ("he had done amysse"). Given the context, we may infer that this guilt stems not from shame at the sexual act itself, but from discovering that he has not been with Gwenyver. However, his mind turns swiftly from guilt to rage: "And anone he gate his swerde in his honde and seyde, 'Thou traytoures! What art thou that I have layne bye all this nyght? Thou shalt dye ryght here of myne hands!' "[27] His violent words are shocking—indeed, Launcelot himself is later appalled at the memory of threatening a woman. However, it also underscores the depth of feeling evoked by this sexual deception: her act is a betrayal ("traytoures"), in his mind worthy of death. What's more, we see Launcelot's sense of utter vulnerability, along with a suggestion of fear that his companion may be other than human: "what art thou that I have layne bye all this nyght?" In a moment, Launcelot will regain his sang froid; now he is stripped of composure, feeling only shame, anger, terror, and profound injury.

Alarmed by Launcelot's threats, Elayne makes her defences. Her first is to invoke her pregnancy, along with the necessity of prophecy: "Sle me nat, for I have in my wombe bygetyn of the that shall be the moste nobyleste knyght fo the worlde."[28] Launcelot is not swayed, indeed hardly seems to hear her: "A, false traytoures! Why haste thou betrayed me?" Later in the scene, Elayne makes an even more overt appeal to prophecy—"I have obeyde me unto the prophesye that my fadir tolde me"—but again Launcelot seems not to hear or understand.[29] He spares and forgives her, in part because of who she is, but more because he does not hold her ultimately responsible for his deception: " 'So God helpe me,' seyde sir Launcelot, 'I may nat wyte [thys to] you; but her that made this enchauntemente upon me and

---

25 Ibid.
26 Ibid.
27 Ibid.
28 Ibid., 796.
29 Ibid.

betwene you and me, and I may fynde her, that same lady dame Brusen shall lose her hede for her wycchecrauftys, for there was never knyght disceyved as I am this nyght."[30] Saying no more, Launcelot takes his leave of Elayne. More scenes intervene, including Galahad's birth and visions of the Grail, but of these matters Launcelot has no comment. When rumours of Galahad's paternity reach Queen Gwenyver, she "was wrothe, and she gaff many rebukes to sir Launcelot."[31] His response to this chastisement is to tell the only version of the story he ever tells, "how he was made to lye by [Elayne], 'in the lyknes of you, my lady the quene.'"[32] Though Launcelot has forgiven Elayne, his sense of injury lingers as he remembers how, deceived, his loyal ardour for Gwenyver had been suborned to compel him into sex with another woman.

This event is tragic enough; its tragedy is compounded because it has a sequel. Though now there is no prophecy to fulfil, Elayne aims to bed Launcelot because "out of mesure she loved hym."[33] There is little need to examine this second event in detail, for the two entrapments are mirrors: again Brusen contrives to get Launcelot into bed with Elayne; again Launcelot believes the woman with him is Gwenyver; again a night of (seemingly) consensual passion ends with the shock of revelation, this time as Gwenyver herself intervenes to break up the tryst.[34] On this occasion, Launcelot does not so readily resume his courtly manners; instead, faced with a second deception and Gwenyver's scorn at his apparent second betrayal, Launcelot goes mad:

> And whan sir Launcelot awooke oute of hys swoghe, he lepte oute at a bay-wyndow into a gardyne, and there wyth thornys he was all to-cracched of his vysage and hys body, and so he ranne furth he knew nat whothir, and was as wylde [woode][35] as ever was man. And so he ran two yere, and never man had grace to know hym.[36]

We should note the irony that Launcelot's madness is blamed, by most characters, on Gwenyver's anger at Launcelot. Elayne first makes this accusation: "Madame, ye ar gretly to blame for sir Launcelot, for now have ye lost hym, for I saw and harde by his countenaunce that he ys madde for ever."[37] Indeed, when Launcelot's cousin Bors suggests to Elayne that "betwyxt you bothe [Elayne and Gwenyver] ye have destroyed a good knyght," she retorts, "As for me … I seyde nevir nother dede thynge that shulde in ony wyse dysplease hym." Bors does not correct her, nor does anyone else; to everyone but Launcelot, she is the beautiful Elayne, daughter of the Grail King, mother of the Grail Knight, an agent of destiny and the woman who (by any

---

30 Ibid.
31 Ibid., 802.
32 Ibid.
33 Ibid., 803.
34 Ibid., 803–6.
35 Violently insane.
36 Malory, *Works*, vol. 2, 806.
37 Ibid, 806. Later in the same conversation, she repeats the claim: "I dare undirtake he ys marred for ever, and that had you made."

narrative justice) should really be Launcelot's partner.[38] In the excitement of the search for lost Launcelot, Elayne's role in the affair is all but forgotten.

Launcelot gets the last word on the matter, however. He does not stay mad forever; after many adventures, he finds his way back to the kingdom of Pelles, where he is restored to sanity through the power of the Holy Grail.[39] His initial response is (again) shame, but afterward he insists on speaking with Elayne: "Fayre lady Elayne, for youre sake I have had muche care and angwyshe, hit nedyth nat to reherse hit, ye know how ... And all was for the cause that ye and dame Brusen made me for to lye be you magry [maugre] myne head."[40] Here the statement is blunt. In Launcelot's mind, his madness and misfortunes all stem from one event: when Elayne and Brusen "made me for to lye by you [maugre] mine head." The compulsion in the act is not only implied ("made"), but plainly stated with the phrase "[maugre] mine head": in other words, "against my will." What matters most to Launcelot is not the fallout of the event, the deleterious results to his health and his status. He is equally unconcerned by matters of prophecy and destiny, and the role his paternity of Galahad would play in the coming quest of the Grail. What matters is that he was coerced, his agency compromised, his assent gotten by manipulation: he was raped. This time Elayne does not try evasion: "That ys trouthe, seyde dame Elayne."[41]

The Rape of Sir Perion (*Amadis de Gaula*)

The second case we will examine is that of Sir Perion in the fourteenth-century Spanish romance *Amadis de Gaula*. Enormously influential in Spain, English readers are most likely to know *Amadis de Gaula* as one of the favourite books of Cervantes's Don Quixote. Unfettered by the strictures of Arthur's Matter of Britain or Charlemagne's Matter of France, *Amadis* is lively, inventive, and expansive, yet still firmly located in the fictional world of chivalry it shares with Chretien, Malory, and the great *chansons de geste*. One feature *Amadis* shares with its literary siblings is an interest in romantic encounters, not only between well-established characters, but also between a knightly protagonist and an unknown, often nameless, maiden. Amadis, the titular character, resists the blandishments of these random maidens; his brother Galaor tends to be more accepting. However, one encounter between Amadis and Galaor's father, Perion, and a nameless maiden ends not in amiable dalliance but in extorted sex—and the victim is Perion.

---

38 Ibid. Elayne makes the case to Gwenyver for her right to Launcelot: "And yf ye were nat, I myght have getyn the love of my lorde sir Launcelot; and a grete cause I have to love hym, for he hadde my maydynhode and by hym I have borne a fayre sonne whose [name] ys sir Galahad. And he shall be in hys time the beste knyght of the worlde." Launcelot's loyalty to Gwenyver is what denies her the storybook romance she thinks she deserves.

39 Ibid., 824.

40 Ibid., 825.

41 Ibid.

Perion's Rape: Short, then Silent

The episode is brief and easily missed. Unlike Elayne's two entrapments of Launcelot, both described in some detail and followed with details of their repercussions, the encounter between Perion and the nameless maiden takes no more than a page. This event occurs in Perion's younger days as a knight errant; it is told in *Amadis de Gaula* as the history of another character, Perion's son Florestan, whose existence was previously unknown to Perion and his other sons. Perion, "a young man and of a good heart," roams "two years in Germany" seeking adventure; during that time, he happens to be lodged for the night with "the Count of Selandia."[42] On this night, his sleep is interrupted: "Ere long he felt a damsel embracing him, and her mouth joined to his."[43] Perion's response is not receptive—"waking thereat, [he] draw[s] back"—at which the woman takes offence: "she cried out, How is this, sir? would you rather be alone in the bed?" Perion notes that she is beautiful—"the fairest woman that ever he saw"—but needs more information before deciding his next move: "tell me, quoth he, who you are?"

> She answered, one that loves you, and gives you her love.—First tell me your name?—Why do you distress me with the question?—I must know.—I am the Count's daughter.[44]

Perion's response is censure and refusal: "It becomes not a woman of your rank to commit this folly: I tell you I will not do this wrong to your father." The damsel is

---

42 Montalvo, *Amadis of Gaul*, 229. Spanish text for this paragraph, Montalvo, *Amadis de Gaula*, 11–12:

> Sabed que siendo el rey Perion mancebo buscando las aventuras con su esforzado y valiente corazon por muchas tierras extrañas, vivió en Alemania dos años, donde hizo tantas cosas en armas, que como por maravilla entre todos los Alemanes contadas eran. Pues tornándose ya á su tierra con mucha gloria y fama, avino la de albergar un dia en casa del conde de Salandia, que fue con el muy alegre por que asi como el rey Perion holgaba de seguir el ejercicio de las armas, y con ellas mucho loor y prez habia alcanzado ... [F]ue el rey Perion llamado á una cámara, donde en un rico lecho se acostó, y como del camino cansado anduviese, adormecióse luego, y no tardó mucho que se halló abrazado de una doncella muy hermosa y junta la su boca con la dél; como acordó quisose tirar á fuera; mas ella le tuvo y dijo: ¿Qué es esto, señor? ¿No holgaréis mejor conmigo en este lecho que no solo? El Rey la cató á la lumbre que en la cámara habia, y vió que era la mas hermosa mujer de cuantas viera, y dijole: ¿Decidme quién sois? Quien quiera que yo sea, dijo ella, os amo grandemente, y quiero darosmi amor. Eso no puede ser si antes no me lo decís: ¡Ay! dijo ella, cuanto me pesa de esa pregunta, porque no me tengais por mas mala de lo que parezco, pero Dios sabe que no es en mi de al hacer. Todavia conviene, dijo él, que lo sepa, ó no haré nada. Antes os lo diré dijo ella: Sabed que soy hija de este conde. El Rey la dijo: Mujer de tan gran guisa eomo vos no comience hacer semejante locura, y agora os digo que no haré cosa en que vuestro padre tan gran enojo haya. Ella le dijo: ¡Ay mal hayan cuantos os loan de bondad, pues sois el peor hombre del mundo, y mas desmesurado! ¿Qué bondad en vos puede haber, desechando doncella tan hermosa y de tan alta guisa? Haré, dijo el rey Perion, aquello que vuestra honra y mia sea, mas no lo que tan contrario á ella es.

43 Ibid.
44 Ibid.

scornful of his scruples, calling him "the worst man in the world" and "most dis-courteous" for refusing the love of "a fair lady of such lineage." Perion remains firm, insisting his rebuff is out of concern for "your honour and my own."[45] Unlike Launcelot, Perion has opportunity to say "no," and he does so emphatically.

The problem is that this nameless damsel will not accept refusal. After hearing Perion's objections, the woman takes drastic measures to secure his compli-ance: "Then, quoth she, I will do that which shall grieve my father more, than if you consent to my will! And she leapt up and took King Perion's sword ... and unsheathed it, and placed the point against her heart:—Will not my father grieve more for my death?"[46] Faced with denial, the nameless damsel threatens suicide with Perion's own sword. This gambit has its desired effect: "he was greatly astonished, and he sprang from the bed, crying, hold! I will perform your will! and he snatched the sword from her, and that night she became pregnant."[47] The episode's conclusion is terse: "On the morrow Perion departed, and never saw her more."[48] Again, Perion's experience is unlike Launcelot's, for once the act is finished, he never makes any further comment about it. We never know what Perion thinks of this event, neither at this point in the story or nor even much later, when he actually meets Florestan, the child conceived this night, for the first time as an adult.[49] Perion's last spoken words in this scene are poignant—"Hold! I will perform your will!" ("Estad que yo haré lo que quereis")—but they are his last words on the subject, ever. Not only that, but this event is never described, even mentioned, again by any other character or even the narrator.

Illuminating Contexts, Interpretive Frameworks

It is clear, then, that with Perion's case we cannot readily follow the same pro-cedure that works so well with Malory's handling of Launcelot's rape, reading closely and listening to the competing voices. Instead, we will turn to another basic technique: drawing upon research to provide illuminating contexts, interpretive frameworks to help make sense of our laconic text. In applying these contexts to our

---

45 Ibid.

46 Ibid., 229–30. Spanish text for this paragraph, Montalvo, *Amadis de Gaula*, 12:

> No, dijo ella, pues yo haré que mi padre tenga mayor enojo de vos que si mi ruego hiciésedes. Entonces se levantó, y fue á tomar la espada del Rey, que cabe su escudo estaba, y aquella fue la que pusieron despues á Amadis en el arca cuando lo echaron en el mar, como se os ha en el comienzo de este libro contado, y tiróla de la vaina y puso la punta della en derecho del corazon y dijo: Agora sé lo que mas le pesará á mi padre de mi muerte que de lo al. Cuando el Rey esto vió, maravillóse, y dió un gran salto del lecho contra ella, diciendo: Estad que yo haré lo que quereis, y sacando la espada de la mano la abrazó amorosamente, y cumplió con ella á su voluntad aquella noche, donde quedó preñada, sin que el Rey mas la viese, porque en siendo venido el dia se partió del conde continuando su camino.

47 Ibid., 230.

48 Ibid.

49 Ibid., vol. 2, 203.

reading, we will focus our attention particularly on the unnamed damsel's actions and Perion's response, with the goal of understanding why her action is so effectively coercive. Briefly, we will consider three contexts: first, the modern context of discourse about abusive relationships; second, the medieval medical context of the pathology of lovesickness; and third, the chivalric romance context of the rights of the lovesick.

For modern readers, like my own college students, their initial reaction will probably be aligned with Perion's own visceral horror ("greatly astonished"). The situation is shocking enough in itself: the swift turn from unwanted seduction to threatened suicide would be powerfully disturbing to anyone, especially mere moments after waking. However, among my students, this shock was followed by a kind of resentment. The unspoken assumption of the damsel's suicide threat—that Perion is, in some sense, culpable for her action—was perceived by student readers as an unfair imposition of moral responsibility. Also, actions of self-violence are often, today, perceived as "cries for help" (a sympathetic assessment) or "just trying to get attention" (a more cynical assessment). As a result, my students saw the damsel's threat as blatantly manipulative and an attempt to gain control over Perion.

In such an interpretation, my students were in line with current discourse about abusive relationships, especially within the realm of social work and law enforcement. It is typical for lists of "abuser behaviours" in these contexts to include threats of self-violence, including suicide: according to the *Handbook of Domestic Intervention Strategies*, "threats of suicide" are one "factor" indicating the presence of "emotional abuse and intimidation" in a relationship.[50] Indeed, "threats of suicide by abuser" are considered by social workers as an important indicator during "crisis assessment" to "determine if client is in immediate danger."[51] Pancney and Jylland cite as an example of this abusive tactic a situation quite like Perion's: "Threats of suicide also have been used as a form of coercion and blackmail." Perhaps the most common example would be the lover who is using coercive tactics to continue a relationship: "If you leave me, my life is not worth living; I'll kill myself."[52] In light of this modern interpretive framework, a reader might be inclined to regard Perion as the dupe of an obvious ploy; my students regarded him with sympathy, but faulted him for not "seeing through" the damsel's power play and calling her bluff.

From this modern perspective, then, it is clear that the damsel's suicide threat is a means of coercion, but it is less clear why it is so effective. For that, we must

---

50 Evan Stark, "Preparing for Expert Testimony in Domestic Violence Cases," in *Handbook of Domestic Violence Intervention Strategies: Policies, Programs, and Legal Remedies*, ed. Albert R. Roberts (New York: Oxford University Press, 2002), 236.

51 Diane L. Green and Brandy Macaluso, "The Social Worker in a Domestic Violence Shelter," in *Social Workers' Desk Reference*, 2nd ed., ed. Albert R. Roberts (New York: Oxford University Press, 2009), 101.

52 Ronald J. Pancner and Carl W. Jylland, "Depressive Disorders," in *Psychopathology and Psychotherapy: From DSM-IV Diagnosis to Treatment*, 2nd ed., eds. Len Sperry and Jon Carlson (New York: Routledge, 1996), 142.

turn to another context to serve as an interpretive framework: medieval medicine's pathology of lovesickness. Lovesickness (*amor heroes*) was reckoned by medieval physicians to be a "mental disease," traditionally "associated with melancholy and mania."[53] While for theologians mental diseases "pose fundamental questions about the relation of soul and body," this was not a problem for physicians, since "in Galenic medicine the operations of the soul are a function of the body's humoral composition."[54] The cause of lovesickness was "the sight of a beautiful form" which caused "the soul to go mad with desire":

> [T]he mind "overestimates" the value of the perceived object and hence desires it excessively. This overestimation, however, can only take place if the material composition of the brain is corrupt, that is, the imagination must be excessively cold and dry so that the overestimated image adheres abnormally and excites the concupiscible power [sexual desire].[55]

Lovesickness could infect both men and women. While medieval medical treatises on lovesickness typically assumed a male patient in their discussion of cases, immoderate erotic desire was considered a feminine weakness: Wack notes that "ancient and medieval culture saw excessive love as characteristic of women," as witnessed by Isidore of Seville's comment that "love beyond all measure among the ancients was called womanly love [*femineus amor*]."[56] Many cures for lovesickness were suggested, but most authorities believed the best way "to restore proper humoral balance" was "therapeutic intercourse."[57] Indeed, the "most efficacious among the somatic remedies is intercourse with the desired person."[58] While religious authorities might protest, "therapeutic intercourse seems to have posed no ethical dilemma to most of the doctors who wrote on lovesickness": if lovesickness was a bodily malady, it was liable to a bodily cure, and physicians could not so readily dismiss such an effective remedy on the ground of moral scruples.[59]

The ethical calculus of the treatment of lovesickness was governed by two major considerations: the life-threatening danger of lovesickness, and the impaired agency of the lovesick. Lovesickness brought with it more than mere unhappiness, because the "dynamic interaction of body and mind increases the lover's bodily suffering while the disturbed balance of his physical complexion further unbalances him psychologically"; as a result, the patient "may lapse into a melancholy passion."[60] This love-induced depression was considered a real threat: "[Lovesickness] is a truly serious and devastating condition that endangers the sanity and even the very life of

---

53 Mary Frances Wack, *Lovesickness in the Middle Ages: The Viaticum and Its Commentaries* (Philadelphia: University of Pennsylvania Press, 1990), 6.
54 Ibid., 7, 8.
55 Mary Frances Wack, "Lovesickness in Troilus," *Pacific Coast Philology* 19 (1984): 56.
56 Wack, *Lovesickness in the Middle Ages*, 13.
57 Ibid., 41.
58 Wack, "Lovesickness in Troilus," 56.
59 Wack, *Lovesickness in the Middle Ages*, 41.
60 Ibid., 40.

the afflicted party, since the melancholy desperation and madness of lovesickness lead to suicidal thoughts and actions."[61] Medical intervention in lovesickness was, therefore, a matter of life and death. The urgency of the situation was heightened by the patient's impaired agency. While lovesickness might lead to desires and actions outside the accepted bounds, the condition was itself a disease, not a choice:

> The theory of material causality, that is, the humoral theory of health and disease upon which medieval medicine rested, was implicitly deterministic because the patient could not always control the balance of humors affecting his health. The body was a complex combination of elements subject to alteration by physical causes outside the patient's will … The etiology of *amor hereos* … assigns contributing roles to chance and to the material composition of the body, but ignores free will both practically and theoretically.[62]

In other words, the patient does not choose his condition, and so "the patient is not held 'guilty' or 'responsible' for his illness."[63] With the patient's life at risk, due not least to his (or her) impaired faculties of choice and reason, the ordinary ethical considerations that governed sexual intercourse were suspended.[64]

This medieval medical perspective on lovesickness is probably, to a large degree, what lies behind chivalric romance's insistence on the rights of the lovesick. This theme is especially important in *Amadis*: a major plot arc of Book 2 concerns a dissension between the lovers Amadis and Oriana that results in Amadis's languishment in lovesick exile. However, a more helpful example for this discussion may be drawn from Malory: Elayne of Astolot's unrequited love for Launcelot and her resulting death.[65] From the moment of Elayne's introduction into the story, we know that her love has doomed her. Launcelot encounters Elayne while lodged by her father, the baron of Astolot. As usual, he made an impression:

> So thys olde barown had a doughtir that was called that tyme the Fayr Maydyn off Astolot, and ever she behyld sir Launcelot wondirfully. (And, as the book sayth, she keste such a love unto Sir Launcelot that she cowde never withdraw hir loove, wherefore she dyed. And her name was Elayne le Blanke [the Fair].)[66]

---

61 Teresa Scott Soufas, *Melancholy and the Secular Mind in Spanish Golden Age Literature* (Columbia: University of Missouri Press, 1990), 69.
62 Wack, "Lovesickness in Troilus," 57.
63 Ibid., 56.
64 Ibid., 59. Wack cites Chaucer's Troilus as an example of this principle: "Because Troilus suffers from a malady that he didn't choose (that is, medically speaking), because this malady is life-threatening, and because its optimal cure happens to be intercourse, both Troilus and Pandarus are willing to elude the moral complexities of the situation by an appeal to medical necessity which carries with it no clearcut assessment of the morality of the cure."
65 These episodes are in Book 18 of Caxton's edition. Vinaver's edition places these episodes in section 2 of "The Book of Sir Launcelot and Queen Guinevere."
66 Malory, *Works*, vol. 2, 1067–68.

In this first reference to Elayne, we already see the signs of lovesickness: the infection through vision ("she beheld wondirfully"), the immoderate passion ("she cowde never withdraw hir loove"), and the destructive end ("wherefore she dyed"). After Launcelot has worn her token in a joust (and so incurred the wrath of Gwenyver), Elayne attempts to secure Launcelot's love for herself by appealing directly to his pity: "Now, fayre knyght and curtayse knyght ... have mercy uppon me, and suffer me nat to dye for youre love."[67] When Launcelot refuses such a relationship, whether married or not, Elayne's response is resignation: "Alas! Than ... I must dye for youre love."[68] And so she does: she "made such sorow day and nyght that she never slepte, ete, nother dranke," till at the end of ten days, she dies.[69]

That Elayne's actions cause her death is clear in the text; that she is reckoned responsible for those actions is not. She considers her death a *fait accompli*, and her father seems to agree, telling Launcelot, "I cannat se but that my doughtir woll dye for youre sake."[70] In Elayne's deathbed confession, she speaks of her death as the inevitable result of irresistible passion: "I loved thys noble knyght, sir Launcelot, oute of mesure. And of myselff ... I had no myght to withstonde the fervent love, wherefore I have my deth."[71] Indeed, her final wish is to have her body transported to Camelot (via boat) along with a letter that accuses Launcelot of her death:

> Moste noble knyght, my lorde sir Launcelot, now hath dethe made us two at debate for youre love. And I was youre lover, that men called the Fayre Mayden of Astolate. Therefore unto all ladyes I make my mone, yet for my soule ye pray and bury me at the leste, and offir ye my masse-peny: thys ys my laste requeste.[72]

Her letter places her in the position of one presenting a suit of complaint before a court: she and Launcelot are in contention ("at debate") to settle recompense for her injury ("dethe") which he caused ("for youre love," i.e., "due to love for you"); the court is "all ladyes," and the recompense sought is her funeral rites (prayer, burial, and a special Mass). Though Launcelot resists the accusation—"God knowyth I was never causar of her deth by my wyllynge"—even Gwenyver faults him for preventing Elayne's death: "Ye myght have shewed hir some bownté and jantilnes whych myght have preserved her lyff."[73] Even though Launcelot's defence that "I love nat to be constrayned to love" is accepted by king and queen as technically valid, still Arthur insists that "hit woll be youre [Launcelot's] worshyp that ye oversé that she be entered worshypfully."[74] Launcelot, his defence notwithstanding, still finds his reputation (his "worshyp") in jeopardy: though he has a right to his scruples, Launcelot's

---

67 Ibid., 1089.
68 Ibid.
69 Ibid., 1092.
70 Ibid., 1090.
71 Ibid., 1093–94.
72 Ibid., 1096.
73 Ibid., 1097.
74 Ibid, 826.

coterie seems to feel he should not have been so unbending, that he is not so "jantil" as he ought to be. This is the closest the *Morte* ever comes to assigning responsibility for Elayne's death: it is, at least somewhat, Launcelot's fault, because he made her (love)sick, and then withheld the cure.

Context Applied: Understanding Perion's Silence

When considered within these three illuminating contexts, we can see more clearly why the unnamed damsel's threats of suicide are so effectively coercive. Perhaps more crucially, we can better understand both Perion's ready acquiescence and our own bafflement in response. In light of current thinking about abusive relationships, modern readers readily recognize the damsel's threat as a form of manipulation, but may be puzzled by Perion's apparent inability to "see through" her attempt at coercion. Where we expect to find outrage—where we would *feel* outrage—there is none expressed, only resigned acceptance.

This is where medieval ideas about lovesickness, described medically and then dramatized in chivalric romance, become helpful. Within these contexts, the situation (according to medieval eyes) becomes clearer: the unnamed damsel is obviously lovesick, as evidenced by her readiness to seek death in the face of rejection, like Elayne of Astolot. Indeed, her case seems to surpass Elayne's in its severity: Elayne maintained enough composure to seek Launcelot's love diplomatically, and sought death by nonviolent means; the unnamed maiden pursues direct seduction almost immediately, and her means of suicide is equally precipitate. This difference of manifestation is anticipated in medieval diagnoses of lovesickness: as Wack observes, lovesickness is "associated with melancholy and mania," so we might call Elayne's lovesickness melancholic and the damsel's manic.[75] More importantly, the damsel, like Elayne, is not fully in control of her behaviour: her reason is unbalanced, her agency compromised by excessive passion, so that she cannot be held responsible for her actions.

Having made this diagnosis, we are prepared to appreciate Perion's side of the story. He is, as a knight in *Amadis*, as alert to the realities of love in chivalric romance as any knight in Malory. He would, when presented with the signs of lovesickness, understand them; moreover, as a knight in this chivalric romance world, he would feel keenly the sensitive position in which he is placed. As Launcelot is held (though in a mitigated sense) responsible for the slow death of Elayne of Astolot, so Perion could hardly avoid blame for this damsel's sudden suicide. He is the only one who knows of the situation, he is the only one who can intervene—and there is, all the doctors agree, only one best cure for so serious a case of lovesickness. Compelled by a concern for honour and duty, Perion rescues the unnamed damsel from her insane self-destructiveness by means of therapeutic intercourse. Thus his acquiescence, but also his silence, for why would he speak? From this perspective, the matter is

---

75 Wack, *Lovesickness in the Middle Ages*, 6.

shameful, and best hushed up: Perion was forced to do, albeit reluctantly, what was distasteful but necessary. Where a modern reader sees coercion, Perion sees a difficult but *right* choice.

Concluding Thoughts

As these case studies have shown, the positive consent model's emphasis on agency and coercion permits us to see into the complexities of otherwise ambiguous cases. We have also seen that basic literary techniques—close reading and focused contextual reading—can apply this critical perspective in ways accessible to beginning students of medieval literature without giving short shrift to the literary, cultural, and ethical nuances. Launcelot's case, on one level, is the clearer of the two: he is blatantly tricked. However, this imposition is defended by Pelles and Elayne with a series of nesting justifications: first, prophecy; then, Elayne's orders from Pelles; finally, Elayne's own sexual rights. Each of these points has, within the world of the *Morte*, a degree of legitimacy. Nonetheless, Launcelot steadfastly insists on his injured status, even in the face of the *Morte*'s implacable narrative impetus toward Galahad and the quest of the Grail. Perion's case, on the other hand, helps illustrate the degree to which mechanisms of coercion can be submerged invisibly within a culture's world view. Perion's victimization, readily apparent to us in the twenty-first century, seems not so obvious to him. When we consider his case in light of medieval views of lovesickness, both medical and literary, we see that the unnamed damsel's extortion of sex via suicide threat is more than just manipulation. From the point of view of Perion's world, the unnamed damsel is no more responsible for her actions than a madman, and she, as one threatened by deadly illness, has a right to any life-saving intervention. This interpretation suggests that Perion would have regarded himself as a rescuer, not a victim: a case of heroism from his perspective, a case of codependence with an abuser from ours. In other words, while the positive consent model helps us clearly hear Lancelot's insistent "No," it also helps us appreciate the subjective and social complexities behind Perion's reluctant "Yes."

Works Cited

Green, Diane L., and Brandy Macaluso. "The Social Worker in a Domestic Violence Shelter." In *Social Workers' Desk Reference*, 2nd ed., edited by Albert R. Roberts, 95–102. New York: Oxford University Press, 2009.

Jervis, Lisa. "An Old Enemy in a New Outfit: How Date Rape Became Gray Rape and Why It Matters." In *Yes Means Yes! Visions of Female Sexual Power and a World without Rape*, edited by Jaclyn Friedman and Jessica Valenti. Berkeley: Seal Press, 2008. Kindle e-book.

Malory, Thomas. *Le Morte d'Arthur*. New York: Modern Library, 1999.

———. *The Works of Sir Thomas Malory*, edited by Eugène Vinaver. Oxford: Clarendon Press, 1967.

Montalvo, Garci Rodríguez de. *Amadis of Gaul.* Vol. 1. Translated by Robert Southey. London: John Russell Smith, 1872.

———. *Amadis de Gaula: Historia de este Invencible Caballero.* Vol. 2. Barcelona: Juan Oliveres, Impresor, 1848.

Pancner, Ronald J., and Carl W. Jylland, "Depressive Disorders." In *Psychopathology and Psychotherapy: From DSM-IV Diagnosis to Treatment*, 2nd ed., edited by Len Sperry and Jon Carlson, 115–57. New York: Routledge, 1996.

Saunders, Corinne. *Rape and Ravishment in the Literature of Medieval England.* Cambridge: Brewer, 2001.

Serano, Julia. "Why Nice Guys Finish Last." In *Yes Means Yes! Visions of Female Sexual Power and a World without Rape*, edited Jaclyn Friedman and Jessica Valenti. Berkeley: Seal Press, 2008. Kindle e-book.

Soufas, Teresa Scott. *Melancholy and the Secular Mind in Spanish Golden Age Literature.* Columbia: University of Missouri Press, 1990.

Stark, Evan. "Preparing for Expert Testimony in Domestic Violence Cases." In *Handbook of Domestic Violence Intervention Strategies: Policies, Programs, and Legal Remedies*, edited by Albert R. Roberts, 216–52. New York: Oxford University Press, 2002.

Wack, Mary Frances. *Lovesickness in the Middle Ages: The Viaticum and Its Commentaries.* Philadelphia: University of Pennsylvania Press, 1990.

———. "Lovesickness in Troilus." *Pacific Coast Philology* 19 (November 1984): 55–61.

Chapter 13

TEACHING RAPE TO THE HE-MAN WOMAN HATERS CLUB: CHRÉTIEN DE TROYES AT A MILITARY SCHOOL

ALAN BARAGONA

Medieval literature professors have probably always been uneasy about their authors' sometimes ambivalent attitude towards rape and often uncomfortable addressing it in the classroom. But frequently, context and current events conspire to make medieval literature an especially vivid and useful distant mirror of the present. At a time when the country has reached a crisis point of rape awareness both in the military and in schools, the treatment of rape in medieval literature becomes, not a problem for teachers, but a nearly perfect vehicle for addressing the issue with students at a military college.

At the end of 2014, the U.S. Education Department's Office of Civil Rights had cases pending at ninety-two colleges and universities for possible violations of the law in regards to the way they handle alleged sexual harassment and sexual assaults.[1] It was the culmination of a year in which the issue was frequently in the news. Barely two years before, in January 2012, the documentary film *The Invisible War*, about the frequency of rape in the U.S. military and how military authorities dealt with it, was released. By the middle of that year, the Department of Defense began to change policies on how rapes were investigated,[2] and by 2013, there were Senate hearings.[3] Besides the government and media attention they have drawn in back-to-back years, colleges and the military have much in common when it comes to the traumatic aftermath of rape, and in most respects, the military is a more intensified mirror image of college.

---

1 Juliet Eilperin, "Harvard to Adjust Policies on Sex Assault, Harassment," *The Washington Post*, December 31, 2014, A3.

2 Lisa Daniel, "Panetta, Dempsey Announce Initiatives to Stop Sexual Assault," American Forces Press Service, April 16, 2012, accessed January 16, 2015, www.defense.gov/news/newsarticle.aspx?id=67954.

3 Jennifer Steinhauer, "Veterans Testify on Rapes and Scant Hope of Justice," *New York Times*, March 13, 2013, accessed January 16, 2015, www.nytimes.com/2013/03/14/us/politics/veterans-testify-on-rapes-and-scant-hope-of-justice.html?_r=0.

In both cases, the sense of betrayal is strong. At college, if you are raped by a schoolmate, you have been violated by someone with whom you have developed an institutional bond. It is abstract and artificial, and it may not be very strong depending on the individual, but some part of every college milieu, from the freshman year on, is devoted to uniting the students in "school spirit," a sense of loyalty to the place. Part of that bond is a tacit expectation of trust and safety among peers. If the rapist is not a student but a staff member, the betrayal can be even greater. People have entrusted their children to school officials. For those who still consider faculty and staff to be *in loco parentis*, an assault by one of them is abuse by a parental figure.

In the military, the betrayal can be even more deeply felt. Training is meant to build a bond that is neither artificial nor abstract, because it is a practical necessity for unit cohesion, essential to the military mission, and vital to individuals' survival. "Band of Brothers" (and now of Brothers and Sisters) is not just a cliché. When a comrade you depend on for your safety harms you in the deepest possible way, the betrayal rises to the level of a kind of treason, and the psychological scar is deeper. When the rapist is a superior officer, it can undermine everything you believe about the society you have entered, often full of high ideals. A commanding officer is even more of a surrogate parent than a college staff member, a patriarchal or matriarchal leader whose role it is first to protect you and then to train you to protect yourself. Rape by a superior officer thus can lead to a sense of personal failure, as well as betrayal.

Both in colleges and in the military, the institutional response can be complicated by the very nature of the institutions. Colleges have no real authority to judge a crime, no way to provide the accused with due process in a trial. One of the universities being examined by the Department of Education's OCR "changed the burden of proof in determining whether a sexual assault or incident of harassment has taken place to a 'preponderance of evidence,' which is the standard the Education Department recommends."[4] Predictably, its law school faculty objected, saying the new policies "lack the most basic elements of fairness and due process."[5] Since it was the law school itself that "had been under scrutiny for four years,"[6] one might suspect this was a case of circling the wagons, but the principle of "innocent until proven guilty" is not easy to dismiss.

Unlike a school, the military does have a legally binding judicial system and means to try alleged malefactors for crimes. However, it also has the organizational hurdle of a hierarchy and a bureaucracy which may not be likely to hold authority figures to account. Chain of command is ingrained in the military system and culture for practical reasons, but this obviously can work against justice when the alleged rapist might actually be the victim's commanding officer or "brother officer." When the chiefs of staff of every military branch balk at taking authority in a rape case out

---

4 Eilperin, "Harvard to Adjust Policies," A3.
5 Ibid.
6 Ibid.

of the hands of lower officers,[7] it is part of their ingrained faith in the idea of chain of command, but it tends to look rigid and self-serving.

This is especially true because, even though women have played an increasingly important role in the American military for years, attitudes rooted in thousands of years of all-male warrior cultures quite naturally still permeate the concept of the soldier. Much, though not all, of the problem of rape in colleges lies in fraternities, small, closed, and close-knit male societies. Within the university system, social fraternities are a sub-culture. But the concept of fraternity is foundational to the entire military system, and the down side of the "Band of Brothers" can sometimes be that sisters are not really, fully accepted into the band.

Now imagine an institution that naturally combines and compounds all these qualities, for good and ill. Obviously, it is the military school. If the real military contains all the college's problems with rape in a more concentrated form, a military school concentrates them even further by having a kind of dual personality. Everything is doubled. Moreover, since military schools, except for the federal academies, remained all-male for years after the U.S. military itself began to integrate women, the issue of misogyny tends to be even more vexing than in either college fraternities or branches of service. At the same time, thanks to the very nature of a military college, discussing rape in medieval literature does not have to be a daunting prospect of awkward moments in class. Cadets tend to have a natural affinity for the romance of the Middle Ages. Often, it was their exposure in childhood to stories of knights that first planted the notion of idealized military service. That connection is reinforced at schools like the Virginia Military Institute where even the architecture is "carpenter Gothic," with machicolation that makes buildings look like castles. Consequently, a class in medieval literature is a natural opportunity to open the eyes of the young adults, both male and female, who may need it most.

I came to the Virginia Military Institute (VMI) in 1986, three years before the rejection of a woman's application led to a discrimination suit against the school and ten years before a Supreme Court decision forced VMI to admit women for the first time since its founding in 1839. Even in my first year there, however, the school was already feeling social pressure to go co-ed, and I found myself discussing the issue frequently with cadets in class and out. At the same time, I was learning about the deeply traditional culture of the school. All cadets lived in a single barracks. Fraternities had not been allowed since 1885 so the student body would be as cohesive as possible, but that meant the Corps itself was a fraternity. Because of the nature of barracks, one of the most common adjectives used to describe life at VMI was "Spartan," but the more I learned about most (but not all) cadets' attitudes towards women and co-education, the more I thought "monastic" would be more appropriate. It was apt not only because barracks life was ascetic and because

---

7 Craig Whitlock, "Military Chiefs Balk at Sexual-Assault Bill," *The Washington Post*, June 4, 2013, accessed January 16, 2015, www.washingtonpost.com/world/national-security/military-chiefs-balk-at-sex-assault-bill/2013/06/04/cd061cc4-cd1c-11e2-ac03-178510c9cc0a_story.html.

VMI's architecture is Carpenter Gothic; it was apt because cadets were like medieval clerics who chose celibacy and then had to convince themselves it was the right choice. Cadets naturally gravitated towards anti-feminism and for much the same reason as twelfth-century monks: the easiest way to justify a choice to give something up is to denigrate it, like Aesop's fox and the grapes.

A case in point, the matter of women and honour. The most important principle at VMI is its Honour Code, and when the lawsuit to admit women began, some cadets in my classes actually argued co-education would undermine this essential and sacrosanct code because "women have no honour." It was easy enough to point out that many of them had sisters and all of them had mothers, and they probably thought their mothers, at least, were not dishonourable.[8] There were occasionally sputtering attempts to walk their argument part way back, but the fact they would make that remark at all, secure in the knowledge they would not be shunned by their classmates, is a measure of how commonplace misogynist attitudes could be in the school at the time.

This is not quite the same as saying misogyny was necessarily deep-seated, however. The shallowness with which they held that particular, and particularly absurd, belief is demonstrated by how little thought they had actually given it and how easy it was to uproot. In addition, there was the curious circumstance that the misogyny among these young men, unlike your average bigotry, could be somewhat ambivalent, even nuanced. Perhaps a better way to put it is that it was diluted by their upbringing in the twentieth century. Every cadet was only partly insulated by the walls and traditions of VMI which nurtured attitudes from the 1840s. The best example of this is the pseudo-tradition of the He-Man Woman Haters Club.

In 1982, about when the calls for co-education, which eventually led to the lawsuit and the great culture shift, were getting loud, a single cadet added to the list of his organizations under his First Class (senior) yearbook picture "He-Man Woman Haters Club." It is unclear whether there really was an informal club by that name in barracks (certainly no such club existed officially), whether it was a running gag among cadets in general, or whether this was the cadet's personal joke. In any case, the joke spread. In 1983, it appeared under three First Classmen's portraits. In 1986, it reached a high of eight. Thereafter, it tapered off, disappearing from 1991 to 1993, and making its last appearance under two pictures in 1995, the year before the Supreme Court's decision. Cadets from that time suggest it was never really even an informal organization but was a satirical retort to the accusation that cadets who wanted VMI to remain all-male were misogynists, which they denied. On the one hand, then, it was an in-your-face parody of outsiders' perceptions of VMI.

At the same time, there was a certain amount of self-deprecatory humour in the gag. Certain people younger than I, who thought there might really be such a club, were appalled, but anyone of a certain age would know it was a reference to the He-Man Woman Haters Club in the Little Rascals movies. As such, it was an acknowledgement

---

8 Of course, this is merely a step towards teaching male students to empathize with women as human beings, not just as mothers and sisters.

that woman-hating was a matter of immaturity. Any cadets who really did harbour such feelings were like little boys in their barracks clubhouse with a "No Gurls Allowed" sign on the door, cases of arrested development. It is entirely possible the joke was both a denial that cadets were necessarily woman haters and a tacit admission that there was at least some truth in the stereotype, a trace of misogyny in the Corps. In 1988, a satirical story in *The VMI Cadet* newspaper, written by a cadet calling himself "Flash Gordon," was titled "Malicious Macho Males Make More Mayhem." It opened with the lines "The He-Man Woman Haters Club, a society rooted in the ideals of male self suf-ficiency [sic] and superiority, or an organization composed of insecure men incapable of sustaining [sic] a meaningful relationship with a warm, caring young lady? The question boggles the mind."[9] It goes on to say the club had always been associated with the rugby team, which may or may not have been true, but would be no surprise. Yet, even as it seems to be making fun of the idea of such an Animal House social club at VMI, the article itself ridicules the "bims" (bimbos) who follow the rugby team and who supposedly cause the "acts of outrageousness" by the males, "believed to have been provoked by stupidity on the part of several unwitting females attending VMI Rugby Football Club celebrations."[10] The cadet writer, while making fun of the "outrageous" macho mayhem or perhaps of people's perception that this is how cadets behave, cannot help but indulge in a little he-man woman-hating humour himself.

Much of all this half-serious misogyny was simply a pose, a performance, reinforced, if not actually brought on, by the natural machismo of the all-male military environment. However, the impression could have significant, serious consequences for cadets and alumni. One of my former students visited me soon after graduating and told a story of how he introduced himself to the commanding officer of his squad, a female captain, who learned he was a VMI grad and said, "Oh, a woman hater." He had the good sense only to cringe rather than to defend himself. It may also have affected alumni's personal lives. The national divorce rate peaked in the 1980s,[11] the time when all of this was brewing at VMI, and there is strong evi-dence that the divorce rate was then and continues to be higher in the military than among civilians,[12] not because of war but because of the general stresses of military life.[13] When I first came to VMI, there was anecdotal evidence that the divorce rate

---

9 Flash Gordon, "Malicious Macho Males Make More Mayhem," *The VMI Cadet*, September 16, 1988, 6, accessed January 16, 2015, http://digitalcollections.vmi.edu/cdm/compoundobject/collection/p15821coll8/id/18853/rec/1.

10 Gordon, "Malicious Macho Males," 6.

11 "Marriages and Divorces, 1900–2009," InfoPlease Databases, Pearson Education, Inc., accessed January 16, 2015, www.infoplease.com/ipa/A0005044.html.

12 Jennifer Hickes Lundquist, "A Comparison of Civilian and Enlisted Divorce Rates During the Early All Volunteer Force Era," *University of Massachusetts Journal of Political and Military Sociology*, 35 (2007): 199–217, accessed January 16, 2015, www.redorbit.com/news/health/1274867/a_comparison_of_civilian_and_enlisted_divorce_rates_during_the/#GvStbEjFLKZFfviP.99.

13 D. Lester, "The Effect of War on Marriage, Divorce and Birth Rates," *The Journal of Divorce and Marriage* 19 (1993): 229–31, accessed January 16, 2015, www.ncbi.nlm.nih.gov/pubmed/12179705.

among VMI alumni was even higher than the rate in the military generally. Whether that is true or not, the hardening of cadets' views against admission of women to VMI may very well have influenced their personal lives. For example, once in my Arthurian Legend class, during a discussion of Malory's treatment of Guenivere's infidelity, a cadet who interpreted Malory as anti-feminist asserted, "Malory really got women right." This young man was engaged to be married. It is difficult not to imagine how this attitude affected his relationship to his fiancée.

In fact, in my experience, the prevalence of anti-feminism in medieval literature can bring out misogyny in students when it exists, especially in an all-male environment which makes boys feel comfortable making cracks against females, even more so when that environment is besieged by the threat of a monstrous regiment of women demanding admission. And only when misogyny comes out in the open can it be effectively addressed. The presence of the most extreme expression of misogyny, rape, in medieval stories and, in the case of Chaucer and Malory, as an issue in the lives of the authors, makes a medieval literature course an ideal venue for educating young men about rape and how to think intelligently and maturely about it. This is especially so at a military school, not only because of the vexed history of gender relations I have been recounting, but because cadets see themselves as the inheritors of the legacy of chivalry.

At VMI, this sense could be quite literal. When I first came to VMI, there was another code besides the Honour Code which all cadets were required to memorize and follow. It was then called "The Code of the Gentleman." The Honour Code, like its single penalty for violating it, expulsion, was and still is simple and straightforward: "A cadet will not lie, cheat, steal, nor tolerate those who do." The Code of the Gentleman, by contrast, was long and complicated, 327words, with 13 "thou shalt nots" and 2 "thou shalts." Importantly, it opens by connecting gentlemanly behavior to honour and by evoking medieval chivalry: "Without a strict observance of the fundamental Code of Honor, no man, no matter how 'polished,' can be considered a gentleman. The honor of a gentleman demands the inviolability of his word, and the incorruptibility of his principles. He is the descendant of the knight, the crusader, he is the defender of the defenseless and the champion of justice—or he is not a gentleman."[14] The phrase "defender of the defenseless" will remind any medieval literature professor of the Lady of the Lake's lessons on chivalry for Lancelot in *The Vulgate Cycle Lancelot*[15] and also of the oaths King Arthur makes his knights swear on the occasion of his wedding in Malory.[16]

The list of admonitions has several things to say about the knightly gentleman's treatment of women. "A Gentleman … **Does not** speak more than casually about his wife or girl friend. **Does not** go to a lady's house if he is affected by alcohol …

---

14 Taylor McClure, "Chivalry and the VMI Code of the Gentleman: An Investigation into the Origins of the Code in Arthurian Literature," unpublished paper, July 2005, 49.

15 Norris Lacy, ed., *The Lancelot-Grail Reader* (New York: Garland, 2000), 97.

16 Sir Thomas Malory, *The Morte Darthur: The Winchester Manuscript*, Oxford World Classics, ed. Helen Cooper (Oxford: Oxford University Press, 1998), 57. (For the purposes of this essay, I am citing the textbook I use in my Arthurian Legend course.)

Does not hail a lady from a club window. A Gentleman **never** discusses the merits or demerits of a lady ... **Does not** slap strangers on the back nor so much as lay a finger on a lady."[17] The prohibitions against any kind of offence against a lady, especially anything that might be conceived as uninvited physical intimacy, is consistent with the more explicit code in Malory for knights "always to do ladies, damosels, and gentlewomen and widows succor; strengthen them in their rights, and never to enforce them, upon pain of death" (Malory 57). Here it is mainly women who are the defenceless in need of defenders (traditionally gentlemanly sexism), and rape is expressly forbidden.

The Code of the Gentleman was included in *The Bullet*, popularly known as "the Rat Bible," a booklet full of rules and traditions that all Rats (freshmen) were required to be familiar with and follow. It would be wrong, however, to assert that the Code of the Gentleman was ever as important to cadets as the Honour Code. The vast majority of cadets have always lived as strictly as possible according to the Honour Code. For many, however, the chief manifestation of the Code of the Gentleman was that cadets were required to tip their covers (hats) to women. Moreover, despite the archaic language, the impression of many cadets themselves that the Code of the Gentleman was a tradition of long standing, possibly going back to the founding of the school in 1839, was wrong. It appears not to have been written before 1981, the first year it was published in *The Bullet*. It was copied almost word for word from the 1937 edition of Emily Post's *Etiquette in Society, in Business, in Politics, and at Home*, which was available in VMI's library at the time.[18] It is reasonable to assume it is no accident that it was composed as the pressure to go co-ed was mounting and the year before the first appearance in print of the He-Man Woman Haters Club.

No medieval works are more relevant to VMI's version of chivalry and of antifeminism in those days than the romances of Chrétien de Troyes. In fact, I know about the origins of VMI's Code of the Gentleman because a cadet became curious about its connection to Chrétien's treatment of chivalry after studying it in my Arthurian Legend course and did a summer research project with me. Chrétien, of course, is writing at the beginning of the codification of chivalry, and cadets can immediately and perhaps more deeply than civilian students appreciate his focus on the challenges of balancing three different codes, the code of war, the code of love, and the code of religion. Studying *Yvain, or The Knight with the Lion* begins the cadets' examination of the problem the knight faces of reconciling his public obligation to be a warrior with his private duty as a husband. Having proved himself by defeating the Knight of the Fountain and falling in love with and marrying his widow, the Lady of Landuc, Yvain is celebrated by King Arthur's knights. However, Gawain, Arthur's champion, warns Yvain not to rest on his laurels as a domesticated married man but to continue to fight and gain honour. Thus the chivalric code of love is in tension with the chivalric code of war. Although it means temporarily losing her protector, the Lady of Landuc agrees to let Yvain leave as long as he returns in

---

17 McClure, "Chivalry and the VMI Code," 49.
18 Ibid., 50–53.

one year. Yvain gets caught up in the glory of tournaments and forgets his promise, which leads to his rejection by his wife and a fall into a Tristan-like love madness. The rest of the story follows Yvain's attempt to restore the balance between those two tines of the three-pronged code of chivalry.[19]

Cadets are uniquely positioned to understand this tightrope walk. Not only did VMI cadets have the Honour Code and the Code of the Gentleman to follow, they had other loyalties which they took extremely seriously but which, as in Chrétien, could be at odds with each other. The Honour Code's requirement to turn in a cheating Brother Rat is only one of the more obvious examples. Cadets are still required to salute the statue of Stonewall Jackson as they exit the front gate of barracks. However, cadets do not necessarily take this as merely empty protocol. I once taught a cadet from New York who was a "prior service" Marine enlistee. He had, in fact, been on the runway to fly to Beirut when the Marine barracks were bombed there in 1983. He confided to me that he was troubled by the requirement. He considered Jackson and Lee traitors to their country. He was so uncomfortable saluting the statue that he asked for advice from his father, a New York police officer and a veteran. His father told him, when enemy officers meet, they salute each other, not out of respect but as a military courtesy, and he should do the same for Jackson. This is typical of the degree to which VMI cadets think hard about their traditions and how keenly they can feel it when their traditions conflict.[20]

Similarly, as we have seen, the Code of the Gentleman begins by connecting gentlemanliness to honour and then defining it partly in terms of how a gentleman treats a lady, but cadets' ambivalent feelings towards women, especially in a time when the school's all-male status was being challenged, were in direct conflict with the respect they were required to show them. Medieval knights faced the same problem. Even as the controversy at VMI was coming to a boil, Georges Duby was writing of chivalry that the centrepiece of the system of values is male honour, but male honour depends on women.[21] *Fraternitas* and *amicitia* on the one hand, *amor* and *Mariolatry* on the other, in this respect the military culture in modern America is not entirely different from the warrior culture of twelfth-century France. Male cadets are at exactly the age when boys wrestle with their masculine identity, and studying medieval chivalry, especially through Chrétien's romances, can crystallize their thinking.

---

19 Chrétien de Troyes, *Yvain, or The Knight with the Lion*, trans. Ruth Harwood Cline (Athens, GA: University of Georgia Press, 1984), *passim*.

20 There is also the fact that cadets are training to be officers in the United States military at a school whose legacy is tied to defending states' rights in the Civil War. In the mid-1830s, the school's founder, J. T. L. Preston, wrote that cadets are "ready in every time of deepest peril to vindicate [their native state's] honor or defend her rights" (William Couper, *One Hundred Years at V.M.I.* [Richmond: Garrett and Massie, 1939], 15–20). Those words became prophetic when war pitted their state against their national government. They still resonate at VMI, because its earliest claim to military fame is that it is the only Corps of cadets to have actually fought in battle under their own flag. Cadets are required to memorize the quotation.

21 Georges Duby, *The Knight, the Lady, and the Priest: The Making of Modern Marriage in Medieval France*, trans. Barbara Bray (New York: Pantheon Books, 1983), 220.

Lancelot, or The Knight of the Cart is the perfect follow-up to *Lion*. It takes the next step in the theme of gender relations, from duty towards your beloved to the problem of violence against women. The central story is about the *raptus* of Guinevere, not precisely a kidnapping, as in Malory, but a carrying off as a prize. Meleagant, a knight from the Land of Gorre, comes to Arthur's court to say he is holding a group of Arthur's people captive. When Arthur fails to do anything about it, Meleagant challenges any knight of Arthur's choosing to fight for possession of the queen. Kay extracts a rash promise from Arthur to name him the champion, but Meleagant defeats him, and carries Guinevere off, with Lancelot in pursuit.[22] Guinevere is not actually sexually assaulted by Meleagant, but only because she is "carefully confined" (l. 3362) in Gorre by his father, King Bademagu.

This is an opportunity to discuss the medieval distinction between *raptus* as kidnapping and *raptus in carne* as physical sexual rape. The root meaning of *raptus* as theft can lead to a discussion of how the word came to be limited to sexual assault. First, there are the Celtic *aitheda*, stories of women kidnapped to the Otherworld,[23] but undoubtedly more important to Chrétien are the litany of kidnappings and ravishing of women from classical mythology, which he certainly knew. K. Sarah-Jane Murray, among others, has clearly established the range of Chrétien's classical allusions, especially in the *Cart*,[24] so to some extent, behind the taking of Guinevere by Meleagant lie the rape of the Sabine Women, Philomela, and Lucrece by men, and of Persephone, Leda, Europa, and Danaë by gods. Between lecture and discussion, students realize quickly that the meaning of *raptus* shifted easily from carrying off any person to stealing what medieval men certainly considered women's most precious possession, their "virtue" and therefore their "honour."

This flows naturally into thinking about the medieval concept of the difference between a knight's honour and woman's honour. One can raise the economic reading of a woman's virginity/virtue/honour as her main commodity in the marriage market or focus on Christian doctrine at face value (which are not mutually exclusive). Cadets, however, are mainly intrigued by the gendered notion that honour is somehow naturally different for a woman than a man. In her short essay for the 1992 *Approaches to Teaching the Arthurian Tradition*, "Women in Arthurian Literature," Maureen Fries writes that male "[h]eroes are knowers; heroines are 'what can be known' (Campbell 116), the lures that lead the hero to self-realization, their greatest virtue their beauty and marriage the target for which that beauty is aimed."[25] Guinevere is a heroine because she is "the prime female instrument

---

22 Chrétien de Troyes, *Lancelot, or The Knight of the Cart*, trans. Ruth Harwood Cline (Athens, GA: University of Georgia Press, 1990).
23 Jean Frappier, *Chrétien de Troyes: The Man and His Work*, trans. Raymond J. Cormier (Athens: Ohio University Press, 1982), 101–3.
24 K. Sarah-Jane Murray, *From Plato to Lancelot: A Preface to Chrétien de Troyes* (Ithaca: Syracuse University Press, 2008), 218–35.
25 Maureen Fries, "Women in Arthurian Literature," in *Approaches to Teaching the Arthurian Tradition*, eds. Maureen Fries and Jeanie Watson (New York: The Modern Language Association of America, 1992), 155. Quoting Joseph Campbell, *The Hero with a Thousand Faces*, 2nd ed. (Princeton: Princeton University Press, 1968).

around which male action will continue to turn."[26] In Chrétien's *Cart*, she is "carried off and imprisoned, fought for and defended, freed and returned home and fought for again, not at her own will but at the will of and/or the agreement between the males of the poem. Heroines are predicated by passive verbs; to heroes belong the active ones."[27] Cadets, both male and female, understand why, in a medieval warrior culture dominated by men, it would seem natural for a heroine's honour to be defined differently than a man's, as something to be defended, mainly by the male. It is one major way men defined their roles in the code of love component of chivalry.

The one depiction of violent sexual assault in the *Cart* is a fake one. As Lancelot pursues Meleagant, he takes shelter for the night with a lady identified as "the Amorous Hostess." She turns out to be both an obstacle to his rescue of Guinevere and a test of his devotion. The Amorous Hostess stages an attempted rape by two knights and four axemen in order, Dido-like, to distract Lancelot from his quest to rescue Guinevere and to keep him for herself (ll. 931ff.). Significantly, she says of the rapist in the Old French, "il me honira ... a force" (ll. 1073, 1077)[28] "he will dishonour me by force," echoed three hundred years later by Malory's phrase "never to enforce them" (Malory 57). Such use of sexual force is depicted as unacceptable. However, typically, Chrétien injects moral complexity into what should be a straightforward circumstance. Lancelot feels genuinely torn between his duty to stop the violence in front of him and his double duty to rescue Guinevere as his queen and his love.

> The knight stood still before the door.
> "Oh, God, what can I do?" he swore,
> "the reason that has brought me here
> Is no less than Queen Guinevere.
> ...
> I'll be disgraced if I remain."
>
> (ll. 1095–98, 1105)

In class discussion we consider whether Chrétien is presenting this as a real dilemma, in which the knight must weigh preventing the rape of a woman he does not know against his other obligations, or as a sign that Lancelot's judgment is skewed by his passion for Guinevere. (Significantly, it is the first time in the text Guinevere is named,[29] showing how large she brooks in his mind at this moment.) Most cadets assume the latter, and, of course, Lancelot does decide in favour of risking his queen to save the Hostess, only to find he has been manipulated—not for the last time.

The Amorous Hostess also provides the most curious aspect of the treatment of rape in *The Knight of the Cart* and potentially the most fruitful in the classroom,

---

26 Fries, "Women in Arthurian Literature," 155.
27 Ibid., 155–56.
28 Chrétien de Troyes, *Le Chevalier de la Charrete, Les Romans de Chrétien de Troyes III*, ed. Mario Rocques (Paris: Librairie Honoré Champion, 1978), 33. (Though cadets read the English translations of Cline, I make frequent comparisons in class to the Old French editions of Rocques.)
29 Chrétien, *Lancelot*, 217.

the Custom of Gorre. She explains to Lancelot that in Gorre no knight would be so dishonourable as to rape a woman travelling alone, but if she has a protector, she is fair game and can be won with the defeat of her companion (ll. 1302–16). Meleagant invokes this tradition when Bademagu prevents him from raping her: "My son considers it unjust, / because he led her off with him" (ll. 3364–5). Critics have widely noted that this custom has a bearing, not only on Meleagant's "winning" of Guinevere from her inept defender, Kay, but also on Lancelot's sexual liaison with the queen once he has, in turn, defeated Meleagant the first time.[30] The custom has also occasioned the observation that, in Chrétien's fantasy, women are safer without a knight protector and is consistent with John Frederic Benton's contention that "Courtesy was created by men for their own satisfaction, and it emphasized a woman's role as an object, sexual or otherwise … When men ignored chivalry, women were better off."[31] The notion seems ludicrous that a man who feels it is honourable to force a woman to his will if he can take her from another knight would somehow be prevented by honour from taking advantage of a woman alone. The whole premise appears to mark Gorre as a surreal otherworld.

In *Perceval, or The Story of the Grail* Chrétien is far more psychologically realistic when the Proud Knight assumes Perceval has forced the Lady in the Tent to give him more than a kiss, because she must have wanted it and, he says, only a fool would not rape her when he had the chance.

> "… he who would kiss and do no more,
> when there is nobody to spy,
> is wrong to let the chance slip by.
> …
> No doubt, though she defends herself,
> as everyone has always known,
> she wants to lose this fight alone
> and wants to win all other matches.
> Although she grabs his throat, and scratches,
> and bites, and struggles, and delays,
> she hopes to lose, for all she says.
> …
> … she wishes to be roughly wooed,
> and then she feels no gratitude."
>
> (ll. 3860–62, 3866–72, 3875–76)

Students recognize this blame-the-victim attitude as still current today. In addition, knowing Perceval's nature, as well as what he did and did not do, they realize the

---

30 See Matilda Tomaryn Bruckner, "*Le Chevalier de la Charette,*" in *The Romances of Chrétien de Troyes: A Symposium,* ed. Douglas Kelly (Lexington: French Forum, 1985), 132–81; and Donald Maddox, *The Arthurian Romances of Chrétien de Troyes: Once and Future Fictions* (Cambridge: Cambridge University Press, 1991).

31 John Frederic Benton, "Clio and Venus: An Historical View of Medieval Love," in *The Meaning of Courtly Love,* ed. F. X. Newman (Albany: SUNY Press, 1968), 35.

Proud Knight is seeing Perceval through the lens of himself. We should not therefore dismiss the possibility that the custom is Chrétien's wry commentary on knightly sexual entitlement, almost a forerunner of Margaret Atwood's short story "Rape Fantasies," in which the main character's rape fantasy is not sex with a stranger but the fond hope that a rapist might have mercy on her.[32]

Another view students should consider, though, is that Chrétien's point is comparable to the modern assertion that rape is not about sex but about power. In Chrétien's scenario, it is not even about power over women but about power over other men. Students can see the custom as an extension of a convention usually presented as perfectly reasonable and fairytale romantic, the winning of a lady (sometimes one whom the knight has never met) in a tournament. Sex becomes merely a by-product of competition. Competition is something VMI cadets, especially in the all-male days, understood well. In addition to the males' natural, testosterone-fuelled competitiveness, cadets are required to take part in intramural sports as part of their physical training. Layered on top of all that is the competition to go beyond the requirements in military training and to achieve rank in the Corps. All of this is recognizable in knightly behaviour.

Even before the dilemma of the staged rape in *Knight of the Cart* and the paradox of travelling under the Custom of Gorre, Lancelot faces his first, and more important, dilemma that bears on his honour, the choice of whether to ride in the cart, the episode that gives the tale its name. While in hot pursuit of Meleagant and Guinevere, Lancelot rides two horses to death and is left without a steed. He comes upon a rude dwarf driving a cart and faces the choice of walking (and further delaying the rescue) or riding. However, Chrétien invents a custom that knights ride in carts only when they have committed a crime. They are exposed to public shame as if in a pillory, as well as losing all their property and rank (ll. 33539). Chrétien has combined the French tumbril with the English "shaming cart,"[33] creating a genuine dilemma for Lancelot's honour.

Again we have a conflict between the codes of the warrior and of love, which cadets will recognize as analogous to Yvain's, but more severe. Yvain can diminish his honour staying home with his wife, or he can gain more honour by going off to tournaments and risk alienating his love. Lancelot faces the loss of what honour he has, at least giving a very public impression of having lost his honour, or letting down his love when she is in real danger. The code of the warrior, which demands not only that he defend the defenceless but that he achieve honour in combat and hold on to it at all costs, clashes with the code of love, which puts the needs of the beloved above your own. Cadets, whose Honour Code is founded on the strictest honesty rather than glory in battle, are nevertheless willing to take as a given that a twelfth-century knight might hold his personal honour as a warrior as highly as

---

32 Margaret Atwood, "Rape Fantasies," in *The Norton Anthology of Literature by Women*, eds. Sandra Gilbert and Susan Gubar (New York: Norton, 1985), 2303–7.
33 David J. Shirt, "Chrétien de Troyes et une coutume anglaise," *Romania* 94 (1973): 178–95, cited by Cline in *Lancelot*, 215.

they hold their integrity as trustworthy persons. They can appreciate that Chrétien presents Lancelot's impulse to protect his reputation as a matter of Reason in debate with Love. Cline's translation says "as Love and Reason part" (l. 365), but it is worth pointing out that the Old French says it is Reason which parts ways with Love ("Reisons, qui d'Amors se part," l. 365).[34] Reason, in this case concern for his honour, makes Lancelot hesitate. It is "only two steps of delay," but that small hesitation is "to his mischance" (ll. 360b–61). The consequence for him is anger and rejection from Guinevere when he arrives to save her (in fairytale fashion, Chrétien does not explain how she knows about the two steps) and manipulation by her later to test his devotion.

What complicates both of Lancelot's moments of truth (the cart and the staged rape) is the circumstance that Guinevere, a victim of *raptus*, is also, as pointed out earlier, at risk of *raptus in carne*. Common sense would tell Lancelot this before it is confirmed by King Bademagu (ll. 3362–3). In the case of the Amorous Hostess, Lancelot is arguably facing an unquestionable dilemma, having to choose which rape to prevent. In the case of the cart, however, it is a choice between Guinevere's safety and his reputation.

The awareness that Guinevere is being threatened with rape can have a profound effect on students' opinion of Guinevere's scornful treatment of Lancelot for hesitating even two steps to get on the cart, or so she says eventually. Even before the moment when she turns her back on him, cadets recognize that Lancelot may be listening to Pride as much as to Reason in the debate with Love. However, they are not at first inclined to see it as a Deadly Sin. Their study of *The Knight with the Lion* has already taught them one of the balancing acts of the medieval knight is between the sin of Pride and what a medieval audience would consider a laudable, necessary concern for building his reputation. Moreover, in the case of Lancelot, the lapse is only momentary, after all, and he accepts the blow to his reputation for the sake of Guinevere's welfare, then undergoes enormous hardships to rescue her. Thus, when she rejects him for hesitating even for a second, most cadets react by shaking their heads at her ingratitude. I should add this did not change when women joined the Arthurian class. By that time, in fact, the females may have felt more willing to rip Guinevere than the males were in a co-educational classroom. Civilian male and female students I have taught elsewhere have been equally disdainful of Guinevere for her behaviour, and I assure my students this was likely the reaction of most of Chrétien's audience, as well. When Lancelot acknowledges she is right to condemn him, the majority of students, male and female, cadets and civilians, judge that he is henpecked (they use a different word) in typical anti-feminist fashion that turns the "natural" power structure of gender upside down. In this respect, students, especially cadets, tend to be Robertsonian, interpreting medieval depictions of male–female relationships rather unromantically through the lens of Christian moral order.[35]

---

34 Chrétien de Troyes, *Le Chevalier*, ed. Rocques, 12.
35 D. W. Robertson, Jr., "The Concept of Courtly Love as an Impediment to the Understanding of Medieval Texts," in *The Meaning of Courtly Love*, ed. F. X. Newman (Albany: SUNY Press, 1968), 1–18.

That reaction invariably leads to one of the most interesting class discussions in the course, when I ask students to consider the situation from Guinevere's point of view, especially asking the males to put themselves in her place. Most acknowledge that, to a woman trapped in a cell with only an old man protecting her from his rapist son, the moment of Pride that makes Lancelot hesitate only an instant might understandably be blown out of proportion in her mind. Then I ask them to put themselves back in Lancelot's shoes after he learns why she is angry. I give them an analogy. Would they feel badly if their home burned down and they didn't rush back into the flames to save their dryer? Of course not. Would they feel guilty if they hesitated momentarily to rush back into the flames to save their pet and the pet died? Almost always yes. If they saved the pet? Then, no, because the hesitation was the instinct of self-preservation. Then I ask whether they would feel at least a twinge of guilt if they hesitated before saving their wife or husband? Their child? Most agree they probably would not hesitate at all to save their child but would certainly feel some guilt if their survival instinct almost overcame their parental instinct. Invariably someone says that, as horrible as being raped is, Guinevere is only potentially at risk, which is not as horrifying as surely burning to death. When I agree but ask them whether sacrificing reputation to prevent a rape remotely compares to risking one's life, the argument essentially ends. Even if they still disapprove of Guinevere and Lancelot, they recognize the possibility of a new way of looking at them.

Medieval literature and Chrétien's works in particular were an ideal tool to tap into cadets' psyches, to help them reconsider their preconceptions through the shock of recognition of medieval conventions. When the cadet remarked that Malory got the flaws of women right, all I had to do was point out that Malory usually depicted dwarfs as evil and ask him if he thought Malory got dwarfs right. It was a moment when the lightbulb went on for him. The key is finding a cultural inroad and then showing them how it can branch out. And never to take umbrage at their sexual insensitivity, as if it were a fixed part of their character. Every student is just one draft of a work in progress.

Works Cited

Atwood, Margaret. "Rape Fantasies." In *The Norton Anthology of Literature by Women*, edited by Sandra Gilbert and Susan Gubar, 2299–307. New York: W. W. Norton, 1985.

Benton, John Frederic. "Clio and Venus: An Historical View of Medieval Love." In *The Meaning of Courtly Love*, edited by F. X. Newman, 19–42. Albany: SUNY Press, 1968.

Bruckner, Matilda Tomaryn. "*Le Chevalier de la Charette.*" In *The Romances of Chrétien de Troyes: A Symposium*, edited by Douglas Kelly, 132–81. Lexington: French Forum Publishers, 1985.

Chrétien de Troyes. *Le Chevalier de la Charrete*: *Les Romans de Chrétien de Troyes*. Edited by Mario Rocques. Paris: Librairie Honoré Champion, 1978.

———. *Lancelot, or The Knight of the Cart.* Translated by Ruth Harwood Cline. Athens: University of Georgia Press, 1990.

———. *Perceval, or The Story of the Grail.* Translated by Ruth Harwood Cline. Athens: University of Georgia Press, 1983.

———. *Yvain, or The Knight with the Lion.* Translated by Ruth Harwood Cline. Athens: University of Georgia Press, 1984.

Couper, William. *One Hundred Years at V.M.I.* Richmond: Garrett and Massie, 1939.

Daniel, Lisa. "Panetta, Dempsey Announce Initiatives to Stop Sexual Assault." American Forces Press Service, April 16, 2012. www.defense.gov/news/newsarticle.aspx?id=67954 (accessed January 16, 2015).

Duby, Georges. *The Knight, the Lady, and the Priest: The Making of Modern Marriage in Medieval France.* Translated by Barbara Bray. New York: Pantheon Books, 1983.

Eilperin, Juliet. "Harvard to Adjust Policies on Sex Assault, Harassment." *The Washington Post*, December 31, 2014, A3.

Frappier, Jean. *Chrétien de Troyes: The Man and His Work.* Translated by Raymond J. Cormier. Athens: Ohio University Press, 1982.

Fries, Maureen. "Women in Arthurian Literature." In *Approaches to Teaching the Arthurian Tradition*, edited by Maureen Fries and Jeanie Watson, 155–58. New York: Modern Language Association of America, 1992.

Gordon, Flash. "Malicious Macho Males Make More Mayhem." *The VMI Cadet*, September 16, 1988, 6. http://digitalcollections.vmi.edu/cdm/ compoundobject/collection/p15821coll8/id/18853/rec/1 (accessed January 16, 2015).

Lacy, Norris, ed. *The Lancelot-Grail Reader.* New York: Garland, 2000.

Lester, D. "The Effect of War on Marriage, Divorce and Birth Rates." *The Journal of Divorce and Marriage* 19 (1993): 229–31. www.ncbi.nlm.nih.gov/pubmed/12179705 (accessed January 16, 2015).

Lundquist, Jennifer Hickes. "A Comparison of Civilian and Enlisted Divorce Rates during the Early All Volunteer Force Era." *University of Massachusetts Journal of Political and Military Sociology* 35 (2007): 199–217. www.redorbit.com/news/health/1274867/a_comparison_of_civilian_and_enlisted_divorce_rates_during_the/#GvStbEjFLKZFfviP.99 (accessed January 16, 2015).

Maddox, Donald. *The Arthurian Romances of Chrétien de Troyes: Once and Future Fictions.* Cambridge: Cambridge University Press, 1991.

Malory, Sir Thomas. *The Morte Darthur: The Winchester Manuscript.* Oxford World Classics. Edited by Helen Cooper. Oxford: Oxford University Press, 1998.

McClure, Taylor. "Chivalry and the VMI Code of the Gentleman: An Investigation into the Origins of the Code in Arthurian Literature." Unpublished paper. July 2005.

Murray, K. Sarah-Jane. *From Plato to Lancelot: A Preface to Chrétien de Troyes.* Ithaca: Syracuse University Press, 2008.

Pearson Education, Inc. "Marriages and Divorces, 1900–2009." InfoPlease Databases. www.infoplease.com/ipa/A0005044.html (accessed January 16, 2015).

Robertson, D. W., Jr. "The Concept of Courtly Love as an Impediment to the Understanding of Medieval Texts." In *The Meaning of Courtly Love*, edited by F. X. Newman, 1–18. Albany: SUNY Press, 1968.

Steinhauer, Jennifer. "Veterans Testify on Rapes and Scant Hope of Justice." *New York Times*, March 13, 2013. www.nytimes.com/2013/03/14/us/politics/ veterans-testify-on-rapes-and-scant-hope-of-justice.html?_r=0 (accessed January 16, 2015).

Whitlock, Craig. "Military Chiefs Balk at Sexual-Assault Bill." *The Washington Post*, June 4, 2013. www.washingtonpost.com/world/national-security/military-chiefs-balk-at-sex-assault-bill/2013/06/04/cd061cc4-cd1c-11e2-ac03-178510 c9cc0a_story.html (accessed January 16, 2015).

Chapter 14

RAPE, IDENTITY, AND REDEMPTION: TEACHING "SIR GOWTHER" IN THE COMMUNITY COLLEGE CLASSROOM

WILLIAM H. SMITH

It's tempting to begin this essay with a discussion of the challenges involved in teaching medieval literature at the community college level. The problem, of course, is that any notion of "the community college level" is, by necessity, fragmentary. The defining characteristic of community college students is their diversity—demographically, economically, and intellectually—and that diversity makes it virtually impossible to talk about any single characteristic approach to teaching in the community college environment. My own institution, Weatherford College, attracts mainly "traditional" students, i.e., students aged eighteen to twenty-four who have recently graduated high school. As a result, the average age of our student body is twenty-three, well below the national average age of twenty-nine for community college students.[1] Nevertheless, almost every class I teach contains a few "non-traditional" students, usually older students with families and previous careers. Furthermore, even the traditional students, those who have recently graduated from high school, come from remarkably diverse environments. Weatherford College is approximately 25 miles west of the Dallas–Fort Worth metroplex. Many of our students come from the relatively affluent suburban districts to our east, but many more come from very small, mostly rural school districts to our west. Several of my students each semester compete on our nationally recognized Rodeo team, a fact which I mention simply to point out that my teaching experience may not have much in common with that of an instructor in more urban community colleges or in other parts of the country.

All this is not to say that my approach to teaching literature is not informed by the fact that I teach at a community college, of course. Because my students often come to higher education with very little previous exposure to literature—and, more to the point, because almost none of my students are potential English majors—both

---

[1] "Students at Community Colleges," *Community College Trends and Statistics*, American Association of Community Colleges, www.aacc.nche.edu/AboutCC/Trends/Pages/student satcommunitycolleges.aspx.

my choice of texts and my approach to those texts are likely different in many ways from those of my colleagues at major research universities, for example. As a medievalist, obviously I'm interested in providing my students with a solid introduction to major works from the period, which means that I teach *Beowulf* and *The Canterbury Tales*, but because I know that my students are non-majors and, thus, won't be handicapped by an incomplete coverage of the canon, I have some freedom to choose interesting, less well-known texts for inclusion in my British Literature survey.

Several years ago, I started teaching the Middle English romance "Sir Gowther" in conjunction with the slightly more common "Havelok the Dane" as a way of exposing students to medieval offerings beyond the usual suspects. Both texts work well as examples of the romance genre, and both introduce important and interesting aspects of medieval society. As readers familiar with these texts know, both stories comment on the nature of identity in the medieval world, and that idea usually forms the basis for our discussion of the romances. But students are quick to point out that, although these texts share some part of a common theme, "Sir Gowther" is by far the more memorable of the two pieces, a fact which is due in large part to the presence of disturbing scenes of rape and other sexual violence in the story. Though these scenes do have some potential to disturb some students, the questions they raise about consent, culpability, and redemption make the text a valuable window into both late medieval culture and our own.

Usually dated to the late fourteenth century,[2] "Sir Gowther" tells the story of a brutal man who eventually confronts his true nature and repents of his sins. The text opens with a brief discussion of the way devils in the past would sometimes impregnate women by taking the form of the woman's husband, specifically referencing the birth of Merlin as an example. The author then introduces the characters of the Duke and Duchess of Austria, who had been childless through ten years of marriage, until one day in an orchard the Duchess is taken sexually by a demon in the physical form of her husband. The child conceived as a result of this encounter grows quickly and in monstrous ways—as an infant, he kills nine wetnurses through his violent suckling, for example. As a young adult, Gowther engages in a wide variety of cruel and violent activities, most notably raping an entire community of nuns and then setting fire to the nunnery. After an old earl accuses him of being the offspring of a fiend, Gowther confronts his mother, who tells him the secret of his paternity. The effect of this knowledge upon Gowther is dramatic; he immediately

---

2 "Sir Gowther" appears in two fifteenth-century manuscripts, London, British Library Royal MS 17.B.43 and National Library of Scotland MS Advocates 19.3.1. The two versions differ substantially, with the Royal text omitting some of the more explicitly violent scenes, most notably the scene in which Gowther rapes and kills a convent of nuns, discussed at some length below. The only full critical edition of the romance is found in an unpublished 1963 dissertation, but an eminently usable classroom edition was published in the TEAMS series (Anne Laskaya and Eve Salisbury, eds., *The Middle English Breton Lays* (Kalamazoo: Medieval Institute Publications, 1995), available online at http://d.lib.rochester.edu/teams/publication/laskaya-and-salisbury-middle-english-breton-lays).

rides to Rome to request absolution from the Pope. For penance, the Pope requires that Gowther abstain from speaking and that he eat only food that he has taken from the mouth of a dog. Gowther accepts his penance and travels to a far country, where he takes up residence as a fool for an emperor. The rest of the romance treats Gowther's service to the emperor, who is facing attack by a nearby sultan's army. In each of three successive battles, Gowther prays to God for assistance and receives in return a horse and armour, which he uses to rout the Saracens. The only witness to Gowther's bravery is the emperor's mute daughter. When Gowther is wounded in the last battle, the emperor's daughter swoons and falls out of her tower. On her apparent deathbed, the daughter suddenly awakens and speaks for the first time, instructing Gowther that his penance has been satisfied. Gowther marries the emperor's daughter, eventually becoming emperor himself, but not before he returns to Austria and has built both a Benedictine abbey and a new convent to compensate for his earlier destruction of the nunnery.

Much of the scholarship regarding "Sir Gowther" focuses on questions of generic classification and source identification,[3] issues that are well outside my students' concerns. Our discussion of this text in my literature survey class is, in fact, limited in a variety of ways. Most importantly, my students rarely possess the necessary skills to read the text in its original Middle English verse, so we read a Modern English prose translation freely available online.[4] While the translation is very readable and generally faithful to the text, some important points in the romance and in our discussion of it are inevitably affected by the translator's choices. Because my class is often these students' first real experience with medieval literature, the students are also unaware of much of the context informing "Sir Gowther," such as the author's use of traditional romance motifs and themes.

One of the clearest examples of the influence of the romance tradition occurs early in the text, in the scene in which the demon impregnates Gowther's mother. Several details in that scene play on conventions of medieval romance, from the description of the fiend laying the Duchess down under a tree (the scene of many supernatural seductions in romance literature)[5] to the poet's declaration that the child conceived is actually Merlin's half-brother, since the fiend in question was apparently the same that begat the famous sorcerer. These references are not meaningful to my students; they haven't read any of the other romances that contain such arboreal encounters, and though a few of them may have heard of Merlin, even those aren't very clear on the role he plays in Arthurian stories.

---

3 See, for example, E. M. Bradstock, "*Sir Gowther*: Secular Hagiography or Hagiographical Romance or Neither?," *Journal of the Australasian Universities Language and Literature Association* 59 (1983): 26–47. On the question of sources, particularly the relationship between "Sir Gowther" and the "Robert the Devil" legend, see n. 13 below.

4 "Sir Gowther," in *"Harken to Me": Middle English Romances in Translation*, eds. George W. Tuma and Dinah Hazell, a special edition of *Medieval Forum* (2009), www.sfsu.edu/~medieval/romances/gowther.html.

5 Laskaya and Salisbury cite "Sir Orfeo" and "Sir Degaré" as examples of texts containing this motif.

Of course, students at all levels are often ignorant of cultural contexts and medieval literary conventions. In this case, however, that ignorance makes it much more difficult for students to interpret the conception scene. What are they to make of the demon in disguise? By opening with a reference to other children ("Merlyng and mo"; line 10) conceived in this manner, the text simultaneously condemns and normalizes this arrangement. To further muddy the waters, I introduce the story of King Arthur's conception. Arthur is a character that at least most students have heard of, though few of them know the story, originally from Geoffrey of Monmouth, of his father Uther's magic transformation for the purpose of sleeping with Igraine, the wife of his enemy, Gorlois. If time permits, I sometimes show a clip from John Boorman's 1981 film *Excalibur*,[6] which dramatizes this scene. Students are usually interested in the common theme in these two stories, but they're confused when I ask them whether Uther's actions constitute a rape of Igraine. They know that there's something deeply unethical about Uther's deception of Igraine, but they're hesitant to classify the sexual act as a rape, since Igraine does not appear to be completely unwilling. Geoffrey's version of the story complicates their reactions by portraying Uther and Igraine as a relatively happy couple after Igraine's husband dies in battle, referring at one point to the great love between them.[7] If Uther and Igraine ended up loving each other, some students reason, is it really fair to call their first sexual encounter, fraught though it is with ethical implications, a "rape"?

"Sir Gowther" avoids some of these difficulties by revealing Gowther's true father to be a demon, rather than a lustful king and future husband. In other respects, however, the situation in "Sir Gowther" is actually more complicated than the story of Uther and Igraine. The text implies that the Duchess was desperate to conceive a child. She prays to God and the Virgin Mary that she be able to conceive a child, "On what maner scho ne rogth" ("in what manner, she didn't care"; line 66). Though the text never suggests that the demon who appears in the orchard is, in fact, an answer to the Duchess's prayer, these lines nevertheless lead some students (and even a few scholars) to question whether the wife was a willing participant in the sexual act. In informal response papers, my students have referred to Gowther's mother "being unfaithful" or "resorting to desperate measures by conceiving a child with a 'shaggy fiend.'" One student response put so much of the blame on Gowther's mother that the demonic nature of his father is elided entirely: "His mother was the one who went out and had sex with a random guy who looked like her husband."

It's easy to criticize students for somewhat thoughtless responses, but scholars of "Sir Gowther" seem to grapple with the question of the mother's culpability as well. Many studies of the romance use the term "seduction" rather than "rape" to describe the scene.[8] Jeffrey J. Cohen deals with the question directly, arguing that

---

6 *Excalibur*, directed by John Boorman (1981; Warner Bros., 1983).

7 "Commanserunt deinde partier non minimo amore …," Geoffrey of Monmouth, *The History of the Kings of Britain*, ed. Michael D. Reeve (Woodbridge: Boydell, 2007), VIII.535.

8 See, for example, Francine McGregor, "The Paternal Function in *Sir Gowther*," *Essays in Medieval Studies* 16 (1999): 67–78; Henry Vandelinde, "*Sir Gowther*: Saintly Knight and

"the moment of origin remains indecipherable (was it rape? was it desired? a rape-in-desire? …)."[9] To be sure, many other critics find much less ambiguity in the scene. Corinne Saunders, for example, says that the text "negates any possibility of the woman's collusion through its sharp emphasis on her helplessness and shock at the revelation of her lover's identity."[10] Saunders may be overstating the point, however. Certainly it's true that the mother expresses shock when the demon reveals his identity, but the text does not specify whether that shock is the result of finding out that her lover is not her husband or that he is a devil, specifically, rather than just "a random guy who looked like her husband."

At any rate, I suspect that for at least some of my students, the question of the mother's knowledge may be skirting the real issue. For many students, "rape" remains tied inextricably to violence; if there is no struggle, for these students, there can be no "rape." Luckily, the text offers other, much less ambiguous, examples of rape, and these examples the students have no difficulty understanding as such. There's little question that one of the most memorable scenes in the romance, certainly the scene that cements Gowther as a truly despicable character, occurs when he and his men rape an entire convent full of nuns before burning them and the convent to the ground.[11] The text presents this episode as the ultimate act of Gowther's evil early life, and my students respond to it accordingly. But even here, the text subtly moves the focus away from the fact of the rape and toward the identity of the victims.[12] When Gowther travels to Rome to seek absolution, the Pope accuses him not of rape but of destroying Holy Church ("For thu hast Holy Kyrke destryed"; line 283). My students often echo the Pope's reasoning in their own condemnations of Gowther; when enumerating Gowther's crimes, they focus much more on his violence and the fact that he attacks Christians than on his identity as a rapist.

Because my primary interest in teaching "Sir Gowther" (and in pairing it with "Havelok the Dane") lies in questions of medieval notions of identity, the students' emphasis on Gowther's violent and anti-religious nature, rather than a specific act

---

Knightly Saint," *Neophilologus* 80 (1996): 139–47; Ilan Mitchell-Smith, "Defining Violence in Middle English Romances: 'Sir Gowther' and 'Libeaus Desconus,' " *Fifteenth-Century Studies* 34 (2009): 148–61.

9 Jeffrey J. Cohen, "Gowther among the Dogs: Becoming Human c. 1400," in *Becoming Male in the Middle Ages*, eds. Jeffrey Jerome Cohen and Bonnie Wheeler (New York: Garland, 1997), 219–44.

10 Corinne J. Saunders, *Rape and Ravishment in the Literature of Medieval England* (Rochester: Brewer, 2001), 225.

11 As mentioned earlier, one of the two fifteenth-century manuscripts that contain "Sir Gowther" omits the mention of rape in this scene, leaving Gowther simply to force the nuns back into the nunnery before burning it down.

12 Not surprisingly, the word "rape" does not appear in the Middle English text. In the demon seduction/rape scene, the text states "With hur is wyll he wroghtth" (l. 72), and when Gowther rapes the nuns, he is said to have "leyn hom by" (l. 188). The most direct reference occurs when the poet is discussing Gowther's general reign of terror and says that he would "take wyffus ageyn hur wyll" (l. 197). The Modern English translation that we use in class also generally refers to the rapes in an oblique way, though the translation of line 197 does contain the word "rape" ("Sir Gowther," *Medieval Forum*).

of sexual violence, offers an interesting opportunity to refocus our discussion. In "Havelok," the primary narrative tension is found in the fact that Havelok is the "true" king of Denmark by right of birth. Because his father was king, Havelok *is* the king, even while the usurper Godard occupies the throne. After discussing "Havelok," my students are ready to talk about Gowther's "true" identity. They immediately recognize that the text is presenting Gowther as inheriting an evil nature directly from his fiendish father. At this point, I present the story of "Robert the Devil," which is usually seen as the primary medieval source for "Sir Gowther."[13] In that story, the mother asks the devil for help when she is unable to produce a son. Like Gowther, this child lives an extremely violent early life but repents once he finds out the secret of his nature. Significantly, though, Robert is presented as possessing an evil nature because of his mother's contract with the devil, not because the devil is actually his father. In other words, the author of "Sir Gowther" has altered the details of the story, resulting in a heightened emphasis on the relationship between paternity and identity.

Once students recognize this theme in the story, they often begin to question Gowther's own culpability for his actions. He didn't ask to be the child of a demon, they reason. The text reinforces this notion by showing Gowther to be violent even as an infant: he kills nine wetnurses and tears off his mother's nipple though his suckling (an episode which my students tend to treat as an example of quasi-sexual violence). The fact that his violent nature appears so early in his life demonstrates for some students that Gowther is evil by nature, not by choice. As one student pointed out, "babies are the purest any human can be, having no control of their actions, yet the simple survival and nourishment of baby Gowther involved nine deaths." Other students, of course, resist this notion, citing contemporary controversies about the role of parentage and upbringing in criminal behaviour. They don't like it, in general, when criminal defendants cite a rough childhood as an excuse for bad behaviour in their adult lives, and so they're unwilling to let Gowther off the hook for his clearly wicked actions simply because of the circumstances of his birth.

That doesn't mean that they are ready to write Gowther off as a rapist by nature, however. Since we've raised the issue of "true identity" earlier in the class, students are ready to grapple with the question of what Gowther's "true identity" is. Some students do argue that, because of the circumstances of his birth, Gowther is "truly" evil by nature, but others take the penitential point of the romance more to heart, arguing that Gowther's later virtues outweigh his earlier violence. Many students end up discussing this idea in contradictory ways. In informal response papers, students often suggest that in the second half of the romance, Gowther is required

---

13 The introduction to Laskaya's and Salisbury's edition of "Sir Gowther" discusses the relationship between this text and the "Robert the Devil" legend but also points out the wealth of other source material for the romance. For example, on the relationship between "Sir Gowther" and a twelfth-century Breton *lai*, see Florence Leftwich Ravenel, "*Tydorel* and *Sir Gowther*," *PMLA* 20 (1905): 152–77. A good discussion of the differences between "Sir Gowther" and the "Robert the Devil" legend is found in Andrea Hopkins, *The Sinful Knights: A Study of Middle English Penitential Romance* (Oxford: Clarendon Press, 1990), 145–58.

to "erase" his true identity, implying simultaneously that he is inherently a rapist and that it's possible to void that inherent reality. One memorable student response dealt with the issue in surprisingly subtle ways, asking, "Can it surely be said that he acted only on his parental heritage when he raped and burned the nuns? Isn't it also human to rape and murder?"[14]

The question of Gowther's "true identity" has obvious repercussions on the way students think of his violent behaviour, especially the rapes which he commits. The question we often arrive at is whether we should think of Gowther as a rapist or as the virtuous knight and emperor at the end of the story. This question is similar to one we'll ask a few class meetings later, when discussing "The Wife of Bath's Tale." In that story, the fact of the rape seems little more than a plot device. Chaucer presents the knight as a man who needs to learn a lesson, but so little attention is paid to the circumstances that lead to the knight's eventual marriage to the hag that I often need to remind students that the knight who is rewarded with a beautiful, faithful, and obedient wife at the end of the tale is the same character who began the story as a rapist. In "Sir Gowther," there's very little danger of the students forgetting the main character's crimes. But by and large, my students are ready to forgive Gowther— or at least to treat him as a fundamentally reformed character—at the end of the story. His penance seems so extreme and his behaviour at the emperor's court so virtuous that students (especially students unfamiliar with the concept of assigned penance) generally view Gowther's redemption as complete.[15] Astute students may even notice that Gowther's virtuous actions in the second half of the story mirror somewhat his violent actions in the first half. Whereas the Pope has accused him of "destroying Holy Church" in the first half of the story, his actions in the second half are directed at defending the (presumably Christian) emperor against the Saracens. Furthermore, by saving the emperor's daughter from being taken against her will by the Sultan, Gowther is essentially preventing her from being raped, thus "repaying"—in the logic of the romance—his rape of the nuns earlier in the story. At the end of the story, Gowther completes this process by returning home to Austria and building a new convent in reparation for the one he burned down and by providing for a new, legitimate (and non-demonic) husband for his widowed mother. This backward motion through the terrain of his earlier sins is enough to convince my students that Gowther has, indeed, "erased" his identity as a rapist.

But here we've arrived at a key difference between medieval notions of identity and our own. At this point, I ask students to examine their own attitudes toward

---

14 The text deals implicitly with the question of Gowther's humanity not only in his conception but also in the penance assigned to him by the Pope. By requiring that Gowther procure food directly from dogs and abstain from the characteristically human act of speech, the Pope appears to be highlighting Gowther's earlier inhuman behaviour. See, for example, David Salter, *Holy and Noble Beasts: Encounters with Animals in Medieval Literature* (Cambridge: Brewer, 2001), 71–81.

15 The armour and steed provided by God (presumably) for Gowther to use in the three days of battle are black, red, and white, respectively, a progression which many critics connect to Gowther's spiritual purification. See, for example, Jessie Laidlay Weston, *The Three Days' Tournament: A Study in Romance and Folklore* (London: D. Nutt, 1902).

Gowther's redeemed identity in the context of our societal attitudes toward sex offenders. Do they believe, in an age defined by cultural institutions like the National Sex Offender Registry, that rapists are able, even in the best of cases, not just to be rehabilitated but actually to redeem themselves through a series of virtuous deeds? Would they be okay with a reformed Gowther living in their neighbourhood? It doesn't take long for students to see through these questions, of course. They are quick to remind me that what we're discussing is "just a story," and that they consider Gowther's transformation no more realistic than the shining light of kingship that emanates from the sleeping Havelok's mouth.

In general, my students are reluctant to treat "Sir Gowther" as a story about the consequences of rape in identity formation, and for that I can't really blame them. For all of my attention to the idea, the text doesn't put much emphasis on the scenes of rapes in the story, and as a result, my students don't emphasize it either. I've struggled, in fact, with the best way to teach this story. Should I teach "Sir Gowther" as a social romance dealing primarily with the idea of patrimony? Should I teach it as a penitential romance that argues that even the most despicable person can be saved through confession and public penance? Again, my answer to these questions is informed not so much by who my students are as by who they are not. Since they aren't English majors, for example, it's not particularly important that my students understand how this particular story fits into the genre of medieval romance overall. Even if it were, the pace of an introductory survey class, combined with the fact that my students often bring in virtually no previous knowledge of the medieval world, makes such an approach untenable. My ultimate goal is simply to give them a glimpse into an unfamiliar literature and a culture while also helping them to see that the concerns of this very old and often very strange literature are not completely divorced from problems that exist today, and "Sir Gowther" serves very well in this capacity. While they may not be English majors, and while they may not encounter much in the way of rape awareness campaigns on our largely non-residential campus,[16] they are, nevertheless, college students at a time when the problem of sexual assault on college campuses is clearly part of our cultural consciousness. By thinking about the way this text treats rape as an inheritable evil that can serve as a powerful marker of inhuman identity, while also trivializing it as a sin that can be redeemed through virtuous actions, students are engaging with very old and complex ideas that nevertheless have a clear resonance in their own worlds.

---

16 Unlike many community colleges, Weatherford College actually does have dormitories, but only about 200 of our more than 5,000 students live on campus.

Works Cited

Bradstock, E. M. "*Sir Gowther*: Secular Hagiography or Hagiographical Romance or Neither?" *Journal of the Australasian Universities Language and Literature Association* 59 (1983): 26–47.

Cohen, Jeffrey J. "Gowther among the Dogs: Becoming Human c. 1400." In *Becoming Male in the Middle Ages*, edited by Jeffrey Jerome Cohen and Bonnie Wheeler, 219–44. New York: Garland, 1997.

Excalibur. Directed by John Boorman. 1981; Warner Bros., 1983.

Geoffrey of Monmouth. *The History of the Kings of Britain*. Edited by Michael D. Reeve. Woodbridge: Boydell, 2007.

Hopkins, Andrea. *The Sinful Knights: A Study of Middle English Penitential Romance*. Oxford: Clarendon Press, 1990.

Laskaya, Anne, and Eve Salisbury, eds. *The Middle English Breton Lays*. TEAMS. Kalamazoo: Medieval Institute Publications, 1995. Available online at http://d.lib.rochester.edu/teams/publication/laskaya-and-salisbury-middle-english-breton-lays.

McGregor, Francine. "The Paternal Function in *Sir Gowther*." *Essays in Medieval Studies* 16 (1999): 67–78.

Mitchell-Smith, Ilan. "Defining Violence in Middle English Romances: 'Sir Gowther' and 'Libeaus Desconus.'" *Fifteenth-Century Studies* 34 (2009): 148–61.

Ravenel, Florence Leftwich. "*Tydorel* and *Sir Gowther*." *PMLA* 20 (1905): 152–77.

Salter, David. *Holy and Noble Beasts: Encounters with Animals in Medieval Literature*. Cambridge: Brewer, 2001.

Saunders, Corinne J. *Rape and Ravishment in the Literature of Medieval England*. Rochester: Boydell, 2001.

"Students at Community Colleges." *Community College Trends and Statistics*, American Association of Community Colleges. www.aacc.nche.edu/AboutCC/Trends/Pages/studentsatcommunitycolleges.aspx (accessed March 1, 2016).

Tuma, George W., and Dinah Hazell, eds. "Sir Gowther." In *"Harken to Me": Middle English Romances in Translation*, a special edition of *Medieval Forum*, 2009. www.sfsu.edu/~medieval/romances/gowther.html (accessed January 12, 2016)

Vandelinde, Henry. "*Sir Gowther*: Saintly Knight and Knightly Saint." *Neophilologus* 80 (1996): 139–47.

Weston, Jessie Laidlay. *The Three Days' Tournament: A Study in Romance and Folklore*. London: D. Nutt, 1902.

NOTES ON CONTRIBUTORS

Alan Baragona is Professor Emeritus at Virginia Military Institute, where he taught courses in medieval literature, Shakespeare, sports literature, science fiction, film, and composition. He is two-time recipient of VMI's Distinguished Teaching Award and in 2011 received the Southeast Medieval Association Award for Teaching Excellence. He is the author of *Shakespeare's Prop Room: An Inventory* (with John Leland, McFarland, 2016) and several articles on teaching, including "Everything Old is New Again: Medieval Drama for High School," *The Once and Future Classroom. Consortium for the Teaching of the Middle Ages*, 9 (2011), https://once-and-future-classroom.org/archives/?page_id=705; "The Long and the Short of It: Teaching Chaucer's Verbal Music," in *Interpretation and Performance: Essays for Alan Gaylord* (The Chaucer Studio Press, 2013); and "The Text-Appeal of Medieval Drama for a Texting Generation," *Studies in Medieval and Renaissance Teaching* (2014).

Christina DiGangi received her MMS (Master of Medieval Studies) and PhD in Medieval Studies from the University of Notre Dame. She is Assistant Professor of English at Dawson Community College (Montana University System), and her recent research focuses on feminine figures in John Lydgate's political writing.

Suzanne Edwards holds an MS and PhD from the University of Chicago in Language and Literature. She is Associate Professor of English and a core faculty member of Women, Gender, and Sexuality Studies at Lehigh University, where she teaches courses on medieval literature, gender, and sexuality. She was the recipient of the 2011 Junior Award for Distinguished Teaching. She is the author of *The Afterlives of Rape in Medieval English Literature* (Palgrave, 2016).

David Grubbs is Assistant Professor of English at Houston Baptist University and formerly was instructor of English at Central Christian College of Kansas. His doctoral dissertation (PhD in English, University of Georgia, 2014) reads the Creation Song in *Beowulf* in conversation with patristic and early medieval polemical theology. Introducing undergraduates to the delights of medieval studies is his idea of a good time.

Alison Gulley is Professor of English and affiliate faculty in Gender and Women's Studies at Appalachian State University in Boone, NC, where she teaches courses in medieval literature and History of the English Language. She is the author of *The Displacement of the Body in Ælfric's Lives of the Virgin Martyrs* (Ashgate, 2014), and several articles including "Knockin' on Heaven's Door: Sexual Renunciation, Apocalyptic Anticipation, and Liminality in Ælfric's Lives of the Virgin Spouses," *Journal of English and Germanic Philology* 117 (2018).

Elizabeth Harper is Assistant Professor of English at Mercer University in Macon, Georgia, and previously taught at the University of Central Arkansas. Her publications include "Pearl in the Context of Fourteenth-Century Gift Economies," *The Chaucer Review* 44 (2010) and " 'A Tokene and a Book': Reading Images in Dives and Pauper," *The Yearbook of Langland Studies* 28 (2014).

Emily Houlik-Ritchey holds an MA and PhD in English literature from Indiana University, where she received the Culbertson Teaching Award. She is Assistant Professor at Rice University and was previously a Post-Doctoral Teaching Fellow at University of California, Santa Barbara. Her teaching experience includes medieval literature and genre courses. She has published on Chaucer, Gower, and the Sultan of Babylon. The latter essay won the Essay Prize in theMedieval Literature from *Literature Compass*.

Elizabeth A. Hubble directs the University of Montana-Missoula's Women's, Gender, and Sexuality Studies Program, which offers a major, minor, and graduate certificate. She received her PhD in Medieval French Literature from the University of Michigan–Ann Arbor in 2002, where her dissertation analyzed representations of masculinity and male friendship in medieval French romance. She served as the co-chair of the University of Montana's University Council on Student Assault from 2012 to 2016, and co-authored the mandatory sexual assault prevention tutorial PETSA.

Daniel E. O'Sullivan is Professor of French in the Department of Modern Languages at the University of Mississippi, where he received the Mississippi Humanities Council Teacher of the Year for the University of Mississippi for 2008–2009. He is the author or editor of several books and articles, chiefly on medieval vernacular song as well as the history of chess: *Marian Devotion in Thirteenth-Century French Lyric* (University of Toronto, 2005), *Chess in the Middle Ages and Early Modern Age* (De Gruyter, 2012), *Shaping Courtliness in Medieval France: Essays in Honor of Matilda Tomaryn Bruckner* (with Laurie Shepard, D. S. Brewer, 2013), and *Founding Feminisms in Medieval Studies: Essays in Honor of E. Jane Burns* (with Laine E. Doggett, D. S. Brewer, 2016). He also co-edited the critical text *Les Eschéz d'Amours*, with Gregory Heyworth and Frank Coulson (Leiden: Brill Publishers, 2013), and his critical edition, *Les Chansons de Thibaut de Champagne: Textes et mélodies*, with Christopher Callahan and Marie-Geneviève Grossel (Champion, 2018).

Wendy Perkins earned her MS and PhD in Criminal Justice from the University of Cincinnati. She is Assistant Professor at Marshall University, and she teaches several criminal justice and sociology courses at the undergraduate and graduate level. Dr. Perkins has contributed articles on sexual violence, rape, and victimology to encyclopedias on crime, police science, and juvenile violence, and has authored several guides for criminal justice professionals, for the Indiana Coalition Against Sexual Assault. Since 2007, she has been the Director of Warren County United to End Family Violence. Before entering academia, she was a police officer, violent crime resource specialist, and instructor at the Indiana Law Enforcement Academy, training new and veteran officers in sexual and domestic violence investigation.

Tison Pugh is Professor of English at the University of Central Florida and author of editor of several books in medieval studies, including *Chaucer's (Anti-)Eroticisms and the Queer Middle Ages* (Ohio State University Press, 2014), *An Introduction to Geoffrey Chaucer* (University Press of Florida, 2013; 2014), and, with Angela Jane Weisl, *Medievalisms: Making the Past in the Present* (Routledge, 2012). He is also the recipient of two undergraduate teaching awards at UCF.

William H. Smith is a Professor of English at Weatherford College, where he has taught classes in British Literature, Medieval World Literature, and Science Fiction Literature, among others. His research interests focus on Old English literature, especially the literature of learning and personal devotion, and on the application of statistical textual analysis methods to medieval literature.

Alexandra Sterling-Hellenbrand is Professor of German and Director of Global Studies at Appalachian State University in Boone, North Carolina, where she teaches courses in German language and literature and leads a study abroad class on the Arthurian tradition. Her research focuses on pedagogy, medievalism, and women and gender in Middle High German, with particular interest in the intersections of medieval literature and the visual or musical arts. She is author of *Topographies of Gender in Middle High German Arthurian Romance* (Routledge, 2001) and several articles.

Misty Urban is the author of *Monstrous Women in Middle English Romance* and co-editor of a volume of essays, *Melusine's Footprint: Tracing the Legacy of a Medieval Myth* (Brill, 2017). She has essays published and forthcoming on medieval romance, medieval misogyny, and Shakespeare's queens. She teaches and runs the Writing Center at Muscatine Community College and curates a website devoted to feminism, literature, and women in/and/of books at www.femmeliterate.net.

INDEX

Note: **bold** page references indicate tables; *italics* indicate figures; 'n' indicates footnotes.